THE LIFE

OF

SAM HOUSTON.

SAM HOUSTON.

THE

LIFE

OF

SAM HOUSTON.

(𝔗𝔥𝔢 𝔬𝔫𝔩𝔶 𝔄𝔲𝔱𝔥𝔢𝔫𝔱𝔦𝔠 𝔐𝔢𝔪𝔬𝔦𝔯 𝔬𝔣 𝔥𝔦𝔪 𝔢𝔳𝔢𝔯 𝔭𝔲𝔟𝔩𝔦𝔰𝔥𝔢𝔡.)

"WHOEVER LOVES AND SUPPORTS THAT CONSTITUTION STRICTLY, IS MY FELLOW."

Gen. Houston's Speech on the Compromise Measures.

ILLUSTRATED.

NEW YORK:

J. C. DERBY, 119 NASSAU STREET.

BOSTON : PHILLIPS, SAMPSON & CO.   CINCINNATI : H. W. DERBY.

1855.

W. H. TINSON,
STEREOTYPER,
24 Beekman Street.

PUDNEY & RUSSELL,
PRINTERS,
79 John Street.

CONTENTS.

CONTENTS.

CONTENTS.

CONTENTS.

LIFE OF SAM HOUSTON.

SECTION FIRST.

A REPUBLIC IN THE FORESTS.

I.

THERE are moments in our lives on which fortune suspends our future history ; and when we meet the crisis like men, she takes care of the future for us. Once past the hour of trial, there are no more hardships to undergo, no more dangers to encounter. The gates, which guard the way to glory, are swung wide open to the advancing hero, and he treads the path of light and triumph, as the Roman conqueror marched up to the temple of Jupiter, through the streets of the Eternal City.

II.

So, too, there are days in the lives of Nations, when fortune suspends the enduring glory of a people upon a single hour— when they are called to decide what their future history shall be—whether their banners shall float over new empires, extending their liberty, laws, and civilization over oppressed and benighted millions, crushing old structures of despotism, breaking the arm of the tyrant, and melting away the rotten fabrics of hoary superstitions, to emancipate whole peoples—*or*, whether the wheels of their national greatness shall stand still, and the solemn prolamation go forth, that they have reached the furthest limits of their civilization—that the race of their daring young men is suddenly arrested—that there shall be no new field for untrodden adventure and lofty achievement—that the world, and even despotism itself, may roll *its* wheels of conquest up to their frontier borders, and enlarge the empire of tyranny and superstition at its will, for *they* have done *their* work. They have extended the bright circle of their freedom and power, till they can extend it no longer. No bold woodsman may pass their limits, and plunge off into the wilds, to cut out for himself and his children a home in *God's* own forests, for his government will never protect the squatter adventurer, albeit the James River settler, and uncompromising Puritan, were nothing more.

III.

And if so be that one after another of these forest heroes has led the way through the green woods beyond the Sabine, and they can, at least, show the traveller the smoke of ten thousand new cottages, wreathing up into the clear blue sky of New Estramadura ; and if so be this new race of Puritans, Cavaliers, Huguenots and outlaws, all fraternally mingled, have built up the beautiful fabric of a new, free commonwealth, for all the world to come for a home ; and done it withal, while they were protecting their wives and little children from savages, made remorseless by Puritan *fire-water*, and from the enervated, perfidious Mexicans—why, even after these hunter-legislators, these squatter-founders of States, have done all the hard work, this old Republic, whose wheels can roll no further, will not even accept what no other nation ever had to offer—the free gift of a mighty domain, declared independent, as New York and Virginia were eighty years ago, although the offering be made without money and without price

IV.

Yes, these trial days come to nations, as they come to men. One of those Rubicon-hours came on the cold bleak Rock of Plymouth, where a little band of liberty-loving men landed, under the cover of a keen northern blast, to begin the great business for which Anglo-Saxons crossed the Atlantic, of founding free commmonwealths. Virginia, too, had *her* hour, and her cavaliers went through Indian-haunted woods, as Marshal Ney's cavalry charged through the Black Forest.

At last, after much debate, and more stupid misconception, the New Republic came, and laid on our Federal Altars her young shield. It was riddled with rifle bullets, and battered by the *tranchant* strokes of the tomahawk. You need not have looked very close to have seen, too, the ghostly image of Mexican treachery, filling up the interstices. What an offering was this ! A young hero-people, a new Rome, coming out of the forests, walking in light, and clothed in strength,— advancing in manliness up to our altars.

V.

When the future historian shall tell his readers that the Young Republic was driven away from our capitol, and her shield hurled back in her face—they will not believe it. That the Representatives of America debated, hesitated, laughed Texas to scorn—will, to the next generation, seem a malignant invention of the historian. But it was so—and the last resource of Republicanism was resorted to. The Texan banner was flung to the breeze, and the people of this country were asked to settle the question. And over the hills of New England, the rallying cry rang, where the young American Eagle first unfurled his wings—and far up the valley of the Mississippi, and down to the Florida coast—and back came the glorious shout of a grateful welcome, and Texas came into the Union.

VI.

It was a proud day when her senators took their seats. Greatest of the Texans, came that wondrous man, who stood by the side of the Young Republic, leaning on his rifle, and rocked her infancy in those far-off wilds. Yes, there he stood, on the threshold of the Senate Chamber, bringing in his arms—not like the triumphant generals of Rome—the fine gold or precious stones of distant barbaric princes, lashed to his victorious car—but a new and a vast empire. There stood the tall, erect form of the care-worn chieftain—his locks turned prematurely grey by the hardships of a revolutionary frontier life. His wounds were upon him ; he had bled freely in the service of two Republics. Let us inquire something of his history.

SECTION SECOND.

ANCESTRY AND YOUTH.

I.

GEN. SAM HOUSTON was born the 2d of March, 1793, in Rockbridge county, Virginia, seven miles east of Lexington, at a place known as Timber Ridge Church. The day of his birth he was, many years afterwards, to celebrate as the anniversary of the birth of a new republic—for it was on his natal day that Texas declared herself free and independent.

II.

His ancestors, on his father's and mother's side, are traced back to the Highlands of Scotland. They are there found fighting for "God and liberty," by the side of John Knox. During those times of trouble, they emigrated with that numerous throng of brave men and women, who were driven away from their Highland homes to seek a refuge in the north of Ireland. Here they remained till the siege of Derry, in which they were engaged, when they emigrated to Pennsylvania. For more than a century these families seemed to have kept together in all their wanderings, and at last a union was formed between them, by the marriage of his parents, who had been sometime settled in Virginia, when the birth of the subject of this book took place.

III.

His father was a man of moderate fortune ; indeed, he seems to have possessed the means only of a comfortable subsistence. He was known only for one passion, and this was for a military life. He had borne his part in the Revolution, and was successively the Inspector of Gen. Bowyer's and Gen. Moore's Brigades. The latter post he held till his death, which took place in 1807, while he was on a tour of inspection among the Alleghany Mountains. He was a man of powerful frame, fine bearing, and indomitable courage. These qualities his son inherited, and they were the only legacy he had to leave him.

IV.

His mother was an extraordinary woman. She was distinguished by a full, rather tall, and matronly form, a fine carriage, and an impressive and dignified countenance. She was gifted with intellectual and moral qualities, which elevated her, in a still more striking manner, above most of her sex. Her life shone with purity and benevolence, and yet she was nerved with a stern fortitude, which never gave way in the midst of the wild scenes that chequered the history of the frontier settler. Her beneficence was universal, and her name was called with gratitude by the poor and the suffering. Many years afterwards, her son returned from his distant exile, to weep by her bedside when she came to die.

V.

Such were the parents of this man. Those who know his history, will not be astonished to find that they were of that noble race, which first subdued the wilderness of Virginia, the forests of Tennessee, and the ferocity of their savage inhabitants. It is a matter of some interest to inquire, what were the means of education offered to this Virginia boy. We have learned from all quarters, that he never could be got into a schoolhouse, till he was eight years old, nor can we learn that he ever accomplished much, in a literary way, after he did enter. Virginia, which has never become very famous for her district schools, had still less to boast of forty years ago. The State made little or no provision, by law, for the education of its citizens, and each neighborhood was obliged to take care of its rising population. Long before this period, Washington College, had been removed to Lexington, and a "Field school" was kept in the ruined old edifice, once occupied by that institution. This school seems, from all accounts (and we have taken some pains to inform ourselves about this matter), to have been of doubtful utility. Houston is said to have learned to read and write, and to have gained some imperfect ideas of ciphering. Late in the fall and the winter, were the only seasons he was allowed to improve even the dubious advantages of such a school. The rest of the year he was kept to hard work. If he worked very well, he was sometimes permitted to run home from the fields, to be in time to retain his place in spelling. But it is doubtful if he ever went to such a school more than six months in all, till the death of his father, which took place when he was thirteen years old. This event changed at once the fortunes of the family. They had been maintained in comfortable circumstances, chiefly through the exertions of the father, and now they were to seek for other reliances.

VI.

Mrs. Houston was left with the heavy burden of a numerous

family. She had six sons and three daughters. But she was not a woman to succumb to misfortune, and she immediately sold out her homestead, and prepared to cross the Alleghany Mountains, and find a new home on the fertile banks of the Tennessee River. Those of our readers who live in a crowded population, surrounded by all that embellishes civilized life, may be struck with the heroism of a Virginia woman who, fifty years ago, took up her journey through those unpeopled regions ; and yet few of them can have any adequate conception of the hardships such a heroine had to encounter. We hope the day may come when our young authors will stop writing and dreaming about European castles, with their crazy knights and lady-loves, and hunting through the mummy-haunted halls of the pyramids, and set themselves to work to glean the unwritten legends of heroism and adventure, which the old men would tell them, who are now smoking their pipes around the roof-trees of Kentucky and Tennessee—a race which is too rapidly fading away : to return no more.

VII.

There is room for the imagination to play around the toilsome path of this widow and her children, as she pushed her adventurous way to her forest home. Some facts, too, of wild interest, are in our possession—but we shall hurry on with our story, for, if we mistake not, our readers will find romance enough in this history, to satisfy the wildest fancy. Fired still with the same heroic spirit which first led them to try the woods, our daring little party stopped not till they reached the limits of the emigration of those days. They halted eight miles from the Tennessee River, which was then the boundary between white men and the Cherokee Indians.

VIII.

Young Houston was now set to work with the rest of the family, in breaking up the virgin soil, and providing the means of subsistence. There seems to have been very little fancy in his occupations, for some time; he became better acquainted than ever with what is called hard work,—a term which has a similar signification in all languages and countries.

There was an Academy established in that part of East Tennessee, about this time, and he went to it for a while, just after Hon. Mr. Jarnagin, who long represented his State in the United States Senate, had left it. He had got possession, in some way, of two or three books, which had a great power over his imagination. No boy ever reads well, till he feels a thirst for intelligence: and no surer indication is needed that this period has come, than to see the mind directed towards those gigantic heroes who rise like spectres from the ruins of Greece and Rome, towering high and clear above the darkness and gloom of the Middle Ages. He had, among other works, Pope's Iliad, which he read so constantly, we have been assured on the most reliable authority, he could repeat it almost entire from beginning to end. His imagination was now fully awakened, and his emulation began to be stirred. Reading translations from Latin and Greek, soon kindled his desire to study those primal languages, and so decided did this propensity become, that on being refused, when he asked the master's permission, he turned on his heel, and declared solemnly that he would never recite another lesson of any other kind while he lived— and from what we have been able to learn of his history, we think it very probable that he kept his word! But he had gathered more from the classic world through Pope's Iliad, than many a ghostly book-worm, who has read Euripides or Æschylus among the solemn ruins of the Portico itself. He had caught the "wonted fire" that still "lives in the ashes" of their heroes, and his future life was to furnish the materials of an epic more strange than many a man's, whose name has become immortal.

IX.

His elder brothers seem to have crossed his wishes occasionally, and by a sort of fraternal tyranny quite common, exercised over him some severe restraints. At last they compelled him to go into a merchant's store, and stand behind the counter. This kind of life he had little relish for, and he suddenly disappeared. A great search was made for him, but he was nowhere to be found for several weeks. At last intelligence reached the family, that Sam had crossed the Tennessee river, and gone to live among the Indians, where, from all accounts, he seemed to be living much more to his liking. They found him, and began to question him on his motives for this novel proceeding. Sam was now, although so very young, nearly six feet high, and standing straight as an Indian, coolly replied that "he preferred measuring deer tracks, to tape—that he liked the wild liberty of the Red men, better than the tyranny of his own brothers, and if he could not study Latin in the Academy, he could, at least, read a translation from the Greek in the woods, and read it in peace. So they could go home as soon as they liked."

X.

His family, however, thinking this a freak from which he would soon recover when he got tired of the Indians, gave themselves no great uneasiness about him. But week after week passed away, and Sam did not make his appearance. At last his clothes were worn out, and he returned to be refitted.

He was kindly received by his mother, and, for awhile, his brothers treated him with due propriety. But the first act of tyranny they showed, drove him to the woods again, where he passed entire months with his Indian mates, chasing the deer through the forest with a fleetness little short of their own— engaging in all those gay sports of the happy Indian boys, and wandering along the banks of the streams by the side of some Indian maiden, sheltered by the deep woods, conversing in that universal language which finds its sure way to the heart. From a strange source we have learned much of his Indian history, during these three or four years, and, in the absence of facts, it would be no difficult matter to fancy what must have been his occupations. It was the moulding period of life, when the heart, just charmed into the fevered hopes and dreams of youth, looks wistfully around on all things for light and beauty— "when every idea of gratification fires the blood and flashes on the fancy—when the heart is vacant to every fresh form of delight, and has no rival engagements to withdraw it from the importunities of a new desire." The poets of Europe, in fancy-ing such scenes, have borrowed their sweetest images from the wild idolatry of the Indian maiden. Houston has since seen nearly all there is in life to live for, and yet he has been heard to say that, as he looks back over the waste of life, there's much that is sweet to remember in this sojourn he made among the untutored children of the forest.

XI.

And yet, this running wild among the Indians, sleeping on the ground, chasing wild game, living in the forests, and read-ing Homer's Iliad withal, seemed a pretty strange busi-ness, and people used to say that Sam Houston would either be a great Indian chief, or die in a mad-house, or be governor of the State—for it was very certain that some dreadful thing would overtake him !

Well, it may have been doubtful, and it was for a long time, what all this would end in. But the mystery has cleared away, somewhat, since the battle of San Jacinto. Certain it is that his early life among the Indians was, as the event proved, a necessary portion of that wonderful training that fitted him for his strange destiny. There he was initiated into the profound mysteries of the red man's character, and a taste was formed for forest life, which made him, many years after, abandon once more the habitations of civilized men, with their coldness, their treachery, and their vices, and pass years among the children of the Great Spirit, till he finally led the way to the achievement of the independence of a great domain, and the consolidation of a powerful Commonwealth.

XII.

Guided by a wisdom all His own, the Ruler of Nations led him by an unknown path, and his wild history reminds us of the story of Romulus, who was nurtured by the beasts of the forest, till he planted the foundations of a mighty Empire. With the history of the Father of Rome, the pens of poets have played—and it would seem, after all, to have been but a prophesy in fable, whose fulfilment the world has waited for till our days. Certain it is, too, that no man whose history we know, has lived on this continent, who has had so complete a knowledge of the Indian character—none who could sway so powerful a control over the savage mind. During his entire administration of the government of Texas, not an Indian tribe violated a treaty with the Republic ; and it is nearly as safe to say, that during the administration of others, not a tribe was known to make or regard one.

XIII.

During the latter part of June, 1846, Gen. Morehead arrived at Washington with forty wild Indians from Texas, belonging to more than a dozen tribes. We saw their meeting with Gen. Houston. One and all ran to him and clasped him in their brawny arms, and hugged him like bears, to their naked breasts, and called him Father ; beneath the copper skin and thick paint the blood rushed, and their faces changed, and the lip of many a warrior trembled, although the Indian may not weep. These wild men knew him, and revered him as one who was too directly descended from the Great Spirit to be approached with familiarity, and yet they loved him so well they could not help it. These were the men "he had been," in the fine language of Acquiquask, whose words we quote, "too subtle for, on the war path —too powerful in battle, too magnanimous in victory, too wise in council, and too true in faith." They had flung away their arms in Texas, and with the Comanche chief who headed their *file*, they had come to Washington to see their Father. I said these iron warriors shed no tears, when they met their old friend —but white men who stood by, will tell us what they did. We were there, and we have witnessed few scenes in which mingled more of what is called the moral sublime. In the gigantic form of Houston, on whose ample brow the beneficent love of a father was struggling with the sternness of the patriarch warrior, we saw civilization awing the savage at his feet. We needed no interpreter to tell us that this impressive supremacy was gained in the forest.

XIV.

But we have lost the thread of our story. This wild life among the Indians lasted till his eighteenth year. He had, during his visits once or twice a year to his family, to be refitted

2

in his dress, purchased many little articles of taste or utility to use among the Indians. In this manner he had incurred a debt which he was bound in honor to pay. To meet this engagement, he had no other resource left but to abandon his " dusky companions," and teach the children of pale-faces. As may naturally be supposed, it was no easy matter for him to get a school, and on the first start, the enterprise moved very slowly. But as the idea of abandoning anything on which he had once fixed his purpose, was no part of his character, he persevered, and in a short time he had more scholars to turn away, than he had at first to begin with. He was also paid what was considered an exorbitant price. Formerly, no master had hinted above $6 per annum. Houston, who probably thought that one who had been graduated at an Indian university, ought to hold his lore at a dearer rate, raised the price to $8—one-third to be paid in corn, delivered at the mill, at $33\frac{1}{3}$ cents per bushel—one-third in cash, and one-third in domestic cotton cloth, of variegated colors, in which our Indian professor was dressed. He also wore his hair behind, in a snug queue, and is said to have been very much in love with it, probably from an idea that it added somewhat to the adornment of his person—in which, too, he was probably mistaken.

XV.

When he had made money enough to pay his debts, he shut up his school, and went back to his old master, to study. He put Euclid into his hands. He carried that ugly, unromantic book back and forth to and from the school a few days, without trying to solve even so much as the first problem, and then came to the very sensible conclusion, that he would never try to be a scholar ! This was in 1813. But fortunately an event now took place which was to decide his fate.

XVI.

The bugle had sounded, and for the second time, America was summoned to measure her strength with the Mistress of the Seas. A recruiting party of the United States Army came to Maryville, with music, a banner, and some well-dressed sergeants. Of course, young Houston enlisted—anybody could have guessed as much. His friends said he was ruined—that he must by no means join the army as a common soldier. He then made his first speech, as far as we can learn:—"And what have your craven souls to say about *the ranks* ?—Go to, with your stuff ; I would much sooner honor the ranks, than disgrace an appointment. You don't know me now, but you shall hear of me."

His old friends and acquaintances, considering him hopelessly disgraced, cut his acquaintance at once. His mother gave her consent as she stood in the door of her cottage, and handed her boy the musket:—"There, my son, take this musket," she said, "and never disgrace it: for remember, I had rather all my sons should fill one honorable grave, than that one of them should turn his back to save his life. Go, and remember, too, that while the door of my cottage is open to brave men, it is eternally shut against cowards."

XVII.

He marched off. He was soon promoted to a sergeant. In a short time he became the best drill in the regiment;—soon after he was marched to Fort Hampton, at the head of the Musele Shoals, in Alabama, where he was promoted to an ensign. Returned to Knoxville—assisted in drilling and organizing the Eastern Battalion of the 39th Regiment of Infantry; and from thence marched to the Ten Islands, where he remained encamped for some time. The line of march was then

taken up for Fort Williams. The Regiment descended the
Coosa, and marched for To-ho-pe-ka, or the Horse-Shoe,
where some events took place, deserving a more minute
relation.

SECTION THIRD.

THE SOLDIER.

I.

Most of our readers are doubtless familiar with the history of the great battle of the Horse-Shoe. An undecisive struggle had for a long time been carried on with the Creek Indians, who had avoided the hazards of open warfare, hoping at last, by forest ambuscades, and stealthy eruptions, to weary out a foe they did not dare to meet in a general engagement. But this kind of warfare was soon to be brought to an end. They had a foe to contend with, who out-matched them in subtlety, and all the daring impetuosity of his nature was bent upon their destruction.

II.

General Jackson's army, encamped at Fort Williams, now amounted to more than two thousand men, and his spies were scattered far and wide through the forests. Retreating from village to village and point to point, the enemy had gathered all their effective force on a bend of the Tallapoosa, where a thousand warriors—the chivalry of the Creek Nation—following the guidings of their Prophets, had taken their last stand, resolved to risk all, upon a single struggle. This bend, which they called To-ho-pe-ka or the Horse-Shoe, is accurately described by its name. It is a peninsula of about one hundred acres of land, opening on the north, where it was protected by a massive breastwork—reaching down to the river on both sides—composed of three tiers of heavy pine logs, with two rows of skillfully arranged port-holes.

III.

On the morning of the 27th of March, Gen. Jackson reached the Horse-Shoe, and immediately prepared for action. In a few hours, by a masterly arrangement of his forces, he had completely invested the Peninsula. Gen. Coffee had, early in the morning, crossed the river at a ford two miles below, with a body of mounted men, and nearly all the force of friendly Indians, serving under Gen. Jackson; and at ten o'clock he had drawn up his lines on the south of the bend, cutting off all eseape from three sides of the Peninsula. In the meantime, the General had advanced towards the north side of the bend, with the main army, and drawing up his lines, he ordered the two pieces of artillery to play upon the Indian breastworks. The first gun was fired at about half-past ten o'clock, and a brisk fire maintained till nearly one, apparently without much effect, —the small cannon shot playing almost harmlessly against massive timbers. No opportunity had yet been given to the main army to show their valor ; but a rattle of musketry mingling with the sharp crack of a hundred rifles, was heard, and a heavy column of smoke came rolling up from the southern part of the Peninsula.

IV.

The Cherokees, under General Coffee, had discovered a line of canoes, half concealed by the bushes, on the opposite shore, and, in a few minutes, they swam the stream, and brought them across. Richard Brown, their gallant chief, leaped into a

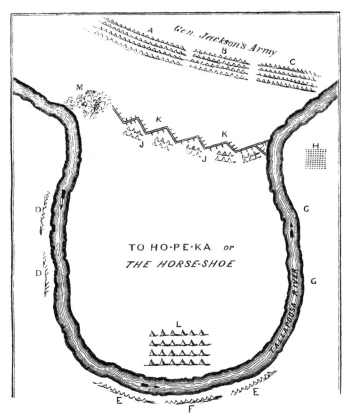

A Branches' Reg't.
B. 39th Regiment.
C. Militia.
DD. Russell's Spies..
EE. Coffee's command.
F & G. Friendly Indian's.

H Women and children.
JJ. Creek Warriors
KK. Breast Work.
L. Cabins.
M. Covered Ravine.

canoe, followed by his brave Cherokees, and with Captain Russell's companies of spies, crossed the river. They first set fire to the cluster of wigwams near the shore, and, as the smoke rose over them, advanced upon the rear of a thousand warriors who were sheltered from the artillery on the north.

V.

When General Jackson's troops heard the firing and saw the smoke, they knew that their companies had crossed the river, and they were impatient to storm the breastworks. But the General held them steady in their lines, till he had sent an interpreter to remove all the women and children in the Peninsula, amounting to several hundreds, to a safe place beyond the river. The moment this was effected, he gave an order to storm the breastworks. The order was received with a shout, and the 39th Regiment, under Colonel Williams, and General Doherty's brigade of East Tennesseans, rushed up with loud cries to the onset, where a short but bloody struggle followed at the port-holes, bayonet to bayonet, and muzzle to muzzle. Major Montgomery was the first man to spring upon the breastworks, but a ball in the head hurled him back. About the same instant, on the extreme right of the 31st Regiment, Ensign Houston scaled the breastworks, calling to his brave fellows to follow him as he leaped down among the Indians—cutting his way.

VI.

While he was scaling the works, or soon after he reached the ground, a barbed arrow struck deep into his thigh. He kept his ground for a moment, till his lieutenant and men were by his side, and the warriors had begun to recoil under their desperate onset. He then called to his lieutenant to extract the arrow, after he had tried in vain to do it himself. The officer made two unsuccessful attempts, and failed. "Try again," said Houston—the sword with which he was still keeping command raised over his head—"and, if you fail this time, I will smite you to the earth." With a desperate effort he drew forth the arrow, tearing the flesh as it came. A stream of blood rushed from the place, and Houston crossed the breastworks to have his wounds. dressed. The surgeon bound it up and staunched the blood. Gen. Jackson, who came up to see who had been wounded, recognizing his young ensign, ordered him firmly not to return. Under any other circumstances, Houston would have obeyed any order from the brave man who stood over him, but now he begged the general to allow him to return to his men. The general ordered him most peremptorily not to cross the outworks again. But, Houston was determined to die in that battle, or win the fame of a hero. He remembered how the finger of scorn had been pointed at him as he fell into the ranks of the recruiting party that marched through the village ; and rushing once more to the breastworks, he was in a few seconds at the head of his men.

VII.

The action had now become general, and more than two thousand men were struggling hand to hand. Arrows, and spears, and balls were flying ; swords and tomahawks were gleaming in the sun ; and the whole Peninsula rang with the yell of the savage, and the groans of the dying.

The thousand warriors who had gathered there that day, were chosen men. A brother of Tecumseh had, some months before, visited all the villages of the Creek Nation, and stirred up their passions for blood and revenge, proclaiming to their prophets that the voice of the Great Spirit had called

"WITH A DESPERATE EFFORT HE DREW FORTH THE ARROW, TEARING THE FLESH
AS IT CAME."

page 32.

him to go on the mission, and that the flower of their people should assemble to give battle to the pale faces, and the day would be crowned with the final destruction of their foes. There was in this strange mission, enough of mystery to inflame all the superstition and malignity of the nation; and, following their prophets, they had at last met the pale faces on the day that would give victory to their people. The day of the battle had come, and warriors by hundreds were falling; but they were firm in the belief of their prophets, who still proclaimed that they should win the day. The Great Spirit, they said, would sweep their enemies away with a storm of wrath, and his signal should be a cloud from Heaven. And it is proper to add, that when the struggle was decided, and the commander-in-chief was issuing an order to stop the carnage, and had sent an interpreter to tell the foe their lives should be spared if they would surrender, a cloud suddenly overspread the sky. The superstitious warriors, believing it the signal of their promised redemption, fired upon the interpreter after his message was delivered, and again the action began.

VIII.

But the eagerly-watched signal ended in a quiet April shower, and no deliverance came to the brave, but devoted people. Not a warrior offered to surrender, even while the sword was at his breast. Hundreds had already fallen, and were weltering in their gore—multitudes of others had been shot or drowned, in attempting to swim the river—the ground of the peninsula was covered only with the dead and dying, and the battle was supposed to be over. To the last moment, the old prophets stood firm, and gazed up towards the sky; around them warriors clustered, feeling to the very last moment

2*

that relief would come. Hope expired only with the expiring groan of the last prophet, and the warrior who gasped at his side.

IX.

But the victory was still incomplete—the work of slaughter was not yet done. A large party of Indians had secreted themselves in a part of the breastworks, constructed over a ravine in the form of the roof of a house, with narrow port-holes, from which a murderous fire could be kept up, whenever the assailants should show themselves. Here the last remnant of the Creek warriors of the Peninsula was gathered, and, as the artillery could not be brought to bear upon the place, they could be dislodged only by a bold charge, which would probably cost the lives of the brave men who made it.

X.

An offer of life, if they would surrender, had been rejected with scorn by these brave, desperate savages, which sealed their fate. Gen. Jackson now called for a body of men to make the charge. As there was no order given, the lines stood still, and not an officer volunteered to lead the forlorn-hope. Supposing some captain would lead forward his company, Houston would wait no longer. Calling on his platoon to follow him, he dashed down the precipitous descent, towards the covered ravine. But, his men hesitated. With a desperation which belongs only to such occasions, he seized a musket from one of his men, and, leading the way, ordered the rest to follow him. There was but one way of attack that could prevail—it was to charge through the port-holes, although they were bristling with rifles and arrows, and it had to be done by a rapid, simultaneous plunge. As he was stopping to rally his men, and had levelled his musket, within five yards of the port-holes, he received two rifle-balls in his right shoulder, and his arm fell shattered to his side. Totally disabled, he turned and called once more to his men, and implored them to make the charge. But they did not advance. Houston stood in his blood till he saw it would do no good to stand any longer, and then went beyond the range of the bullets, and sank down exhausted to the earth. The Indians were at last dislodged from the covered ravine, by its being set on fire. The sun was going down, and it set over the ruin of the Creek Nation. Where, but a few hours before, a thousand brave savages had scowled on death and their assailants, there was nothing to be seen but volumes of dense smoke, rising heavily over the corpses of painted warriors, and the burning ruins of their forti-fications.

XI.

After the perils of this hard-fought engagement, in which he had displayed a heroism that excited the admiration of the entire army, and received wounds which are this day unhealed, he was taken from the field of the dead and wounded, and committed to the hands of the surgeon. One ball was extracted, but no attempt was made to extract the other, for the surgeon said it was unnecessary to torture him, since he could not survive till the next morning. He spent the night as soldiers do, who war in the wilderness, and carry provisions in their knapsacks for a week's march. Comforts were out of the question for any; but Houston received less attention than the others, for everybody looked on him as a dying man, and what could be done for any, they felt should be done for those who were likely to live. It was the darkest night of his life, and it closed in upon the most brilliant day he had yet seen. We can fancy to ourselves what must have been the feelings of the young soldier, as he lay on the

damp earth, through the hours of that dreary night, racked
with the keen torture of his many wounds, and deserted in what
he supposed to be his dying hour.

XII.

But God, whose mysterious Providence guides its chosen
instruments by a way they know not, had yet other work for
him to do—he was yet to pass through many scenes of excitement and heroism; and, at last, to lead a brave band of pioneers
triumphantly through all their struggles and sufferings to the
peaceful enjoyment of a free commonwealth. The military
prowess and heroism Houston displayed throughout that bloody
day, secured for him the lasting regard of Gen. Jackson, whose
sympathies followed him through all his fortunes. More than
thirty years after, when the venerable old chief was trembling
on the verge of life, looking out with undimmed cheerfulness
from the dark inn of mortality upon the summer path of light
that opened before him, he sent for Gen. Houston to hurry to
his bed-side to see him die.

XIII.

On the following day, Houston was started on a litter, with
the other wounded, for Fort Williams, some sixty or seventy
miles distant. Here he remained, suspended between life and
death, for a long time, neglected and exposed, the other regular
officers of the regiment having all been removed to Fort Jackson, or the Hickory Ground. He was taken care of, a part of
the time, by Gen. Johnson, father of the Post-master General
of that name, and by Col. Cheatham—and by them at last
brought back to the Ten Islands, and from thence by Gen.
Dougherty, who commanded the Brigade from East Tennessee,

through the Cherokee Nation, to his mother's house in Blount County, where he arrived in the latter part of May, nearly two months after the battle of the Horse-Shoe.

XIV.

This long journey was made in a litter, borne by horses, while he was not only helpless, but suffering the extremest agony. His diet was of the coarsest description, and most of the time he was not only deprived of medical aid, but even of those simple remedies which would, at least, have alleviated his sufferings. His toilsome way was through the forests, where he was obliged to encamp out, and often without shelter. No one around him had any expectation he would ever recover. At last, when he reached the house of his mother, he was so worn to a skeleton, that she declared she never would have known him to be her son but for his eyes, which still retained something of their wonted expression.

XV.

Under the hospitable roof of that cottage, whose " door was always open to brave men," he languished a short time, and when he had recovered a little strength went to Maryville to be near medical aid. Here his health gradually declined, and in quest of a more skillful surgeon, he was removed to Knoxville, sixteen miles to the eastward. The physician to whom he applied, found him in so low a state that he was unwilling to take charge of him, for he declared that he could live only a few days. But at the end of this period, finding he had not only survived, but begun to improve a little, the doctor offered his services, and Houston was slowly recovering.

When he had become strong enough to ride a horse, he set

out by short journeys for Washington.   He reached the seat of
Government soon after the burning of the Capitol.   In common
with every true friend of his country, his blood boiled when he
saw the ruin that *heroic* people had worked, and he experienced
one of the keenest pangs of his life, in the thought that his right
arm should be disabled at such a moment, and while the foe was
still prowling through the country.   Winter was now advancing,
and with his wounds still festering, he journeyed on to Lexington, Virginia, where he remained till early spring.

Having, as he supposed, sufficiently recovered to be able to
do his duty as a soldier in some situation, he prepared to cross
the mountains.   When he reached Knoxville, on his way to
report himself ready for duty, he heard the glorious news of the
battle of New Orleans.   His furlough had been unlimited.

XVI.

After peace was proclaimed, he was stationed at the canton-
ment of his regiment, near Knoxville, and when the army was
reduced, he was retained in the service as a lieutenant, and
attached to the 1st Regt. of infantry, and stationed at New
Orleans.

In the fall, he had embarked on the Cumberland, in a small
skiff, in company with two young men, one of whom afterwards
became distinguished as Gov. White, of Louisiana.   He was
then a beardless boy, just leaving college.   They passed down
the Cumberland, entered the Ohio, and at last found their way
to the Mississippi, over whose mighty waters they floated
through that vast solitude, which was then unbroken by the
noise of civilized life.   Our voyager had with him a few of those
volumes which have been the companions of so many great and
good men : a Bible, given to him by his mother, Pope's translation of the Iliad, the same book he had kept by him during his

wild life among the Indians—Shakspere, Akenside, and a few of those standard works of fiction, which, like Robinson Crusoe, Pilgrim's Progress, and the Vicar of Wakefield, have become a part of the history of every man who knows how to read. It is not difficult to imagine the effect such works must have produced upon the heated imagination of a young American soldier, voyaging through those impressive solitudes.

After many days their skiff turned a bend in the Mississippi, above Natchez, and far down the river they saw a vessel coming up the stream without sails, sending up a heavy column of smoke. Instead of being a vessel on fire, as they at first supposed, it turned out to be the first steamboat that ever went up the Mississippi river.

At Natchez they exchanged their skiff for the steamboat, and in eight days they reached New Orleans, where Houston reported for duty.

He now had his wounds operated on once more, and the operation nearly cost him his life. The rifle ball, after shattering most completely his right arm just below its juncture with the shoulder, had passed round and lodged near the shoulder-blade. Nothing but an iron constitution had enabled him to endure the enormous suffering he had gone through, and the operation just performed had well-nigh robbed him of his last strength. His lungs were supposed, moreover, to be irreparably injured ; but that indomitable resolution which has borne him triumphantly through all the struggles of his stormy life, never gave way.

XVII.

After a winter of extreme suffering, he sailed in April for New York, where he passed several weeks, with a slight improvement in health. Returning to Tennessee by the way of Washington, after visiting his friends, he reported to the Adjutant-General of the Southern Division, at Nashville, and was detailed on duty in the Adjutant's office, and stationed at Nashville from the 1st of January, 1817. He was attached to the office till the following November, when he was detailed on extra duty as a sub-Indian agent among the Cherokees, to carry out the treaty just ratified with that nation. His feeble health rendered it peculiarly hazardous to encounter the exposures of such an agency, but Gen. Jackson considered it necessary to the public service that he should at least make the attempt, for he could procure the services of no one in whom he could repose such entire confidence. Accordingly, Lieut. Houston, yielding to the importunities of his commander, who, knowing he was unfit for public service, offered him a furlough if he should decline the agency, entered upon his new duties with ardor, and discharged them with marked ability. During that same winter he conducted a delegation of Indians to Washington. When he arrived at the seat of Government, he found that attempts had been made to injure him with the Government, for having prevented African negroes from being smuggled into the Western States from Florida, which was then a province of Spain. These reports had been circulated by the friends of the smugglers, who were then in Congress.

XVIII.

He vindicated himself before the President and the Secretary of War, and showed that in all he had done, he had only endeavored to secure respect for the laws of the country. He was still to show, too, most conclusively, that while he had been occupied laboriously in his new and difficult mission, which he had, as was confessed on all hands, discharged with singular ability, he had been suffering without respite from his painful wounds received in the service of his country. It was the opinion of General Jackson, and all who understood Houston's position and services, at the time, that he was not only entitled to a full and ample exculpation from all blame (which was indeed accorded him), but had a right to expect that his magnanimous sacrifices for the State should have met with a warmer recognition. But he considered himself slighted at the time, and he resigned his first lieutenancy in the army,—at a period, too, when his health rendered it exceedingly doubtful how he was to gain a livelihood. But he acted on the principle he has so often illustrated, that no man should be an almoner upon the bounty of a State who cannot bring to its service talents and acquisitions which would procure higher emoluments in private life. He returned with the Delegation to the agency on Hi-Wassee, and then resigned his commission as sub-agent, and went to Nashville to read law.

SECTION FOURTH.

THE CIVILIAN.

I.

HOUSTON was now in his twenty-fifth year. He had played a heroic part in the national struggle just past—he had become familiar with the hardships the frontier soldier has to encounter —he had seen the treachery and the coldness of artificial life— and he had passed years among the simple-hearted but stern children of the Great Spirit.

With a mind enriched by experience and observation, and a lofty aspiration for enduring fame, he abandoned the life of the soldier, to pursue the calmer path of the civilian. In his wanderings in search of health, his pay in the army had been inadequate to his necessities, and he found himself burdened down by a load of debt. Before he began the study of the law, he sold the last piece of property he possessed, and appropriated the last farthing of the avails to the discharge of his debts ; but a residuum of several hundred still remained unpaid—the balance, however, was soon discharged.

II.

He entered the office of Hon. James Trimble, who told him that eighteen months of hard study would be necessary, before he could be admitted to the bar. He began his studies in June,

1818. He read a few of the standard works prescribed in a course of law studies, and read them thoroughly. He grasped the great principles of the science, and they were fixed in his mind for ever. There is a class of men who are made up, like composite architecture, of the details of beauty stolen from primitive orders; such men constitute the *secondary formations* of society; but the intellectual world, like the frame of nature, reposes upon nobler and more massive strata.

III.

Those men who borrow their lights from others, never lead the human race through great *crises*—they who depend on the strength they gather from books or men, are never equal to lofty achievements. The minds which electrify the world, generate their own fire; such men seldom shine in details—they have no time to attend to them, and they never feel the loss of these secondary lights. The bold mariner, who ventures at once upon the open sea, and regulates his course by a few towering headlands and solitary lights that gleam from afar, can give little information to the coaster about the tiny bays that indent the shore, or the color of the pebbles that glitter on the beach. But he has marked on his chart the dangerous reefs, and the great currents of the ocean, and he is at home with his noble vessel wherever the sun, the moon, and the stars shine.

So it is with those who explore the fields of science. Some men cultivate such studies only to amass details, to use on appropriate occasions, while others enter them only to gather general principles which have a universal application; and, in approaching these two classes, we discover as grand a difference as we do between one of those islands of the Pacific Seas, newly formed by the countless animalculæ of the ocean, and the bold brow of the everlasting mountain.

We have used these illustrations only to convey more perfectly an idea of Houston's character. His teacher had prescribed eighteen months' study : in *one-third of the time* he was
recommended to apply for license, and he was admitted with
éclat. A few months' study had enabled him to pass a searching examination with great honor to himself and his new profession. He immediately purchased a small library on credit, and
established himself in Lebanon, thirty miles east of Nashville,
and began the practice of law. Soon after, he was appointed
Adjutant-General of the State, with the rank of Colonel. In the
meantime he followed up his studies, and the practice of his profession, with earnestness, and so rapidly did he rise at the bar,
that he was, in October of the same year, elected District Attorney of the Davidson District, which made it desirable he should
take up his residence at Nashville.

He was obliged to come in collision with all the talent of one
of the ablest bars of Western America. Every step he trod was
new to him, but he was almost universally successful in prosecu-
tions ; and his seniors who rallied him upon his *recent* advancement, and his *rawness* in the practice, never repeated their
jokes. They discovered, to their mortification, that neither
many books, nor much dull plodding could enable them to measure weapons with a man so gifted in rare good sense and pene-
trating genius.

IV.

We have taken considerable pains to render ourselves familiar
with the various steps of Houston's advancement, till he reached
the highest honors of the State. But we shall be obliged to
pass rapidly over this portion of his history, in order to leave
space to speak more minutely of his subsequent achievements.
The labors of the District Attorney were unceasing, but the fees
were so inconsiderable he resigned his post at the end of twelve

months, and resumed the regular practice of his profession, in which he rose to great and sudden distinction.

V.

In 1821 he was elected Major-General by the field-officers of the division which comprised two thirds of the State. In 1823, he was recommended to offer his name as a candidate for Congress. In the various official stations he had filled, he had won so much respect, and at the bar he had displayed such rare ability, that he was elected to Congress without opposition. His course in the National Legislature was warmly approved by his constituents, and he was returned the second time by an almost unanimous vote.

His course in Congress won for him the universal respect and confidence of the people of Tennessee, and in 1827 he was elected Governor of that State by a majority of over 12,000. His personal popularity was unlimited, and his accession to office found him without an opponent in the Legislature.

VI.

In January, 1829, he married a young lady of respectable family, and of gentle character. Owing to circumstances, about which far more has been conjectured than known by the world, the union seems to have been as unhappy as it was short. In less than three months a separation took place, which filled society with the deepest excitement. Various reports flew through the State, all of them unfounded, and some of them begotten by the sheerest malignity, which divided the people of the State into two hostile parties, and inflamed popular feeling to the last point of excitement. As usual on such occasions, those who were most busy in the affair, were the very ones who

knew least about the merits of the case, and had the least right
to interfere. But unfortunately for the peace of society, there
is everywhere a class of impertinent busy-bodies, who make it
their special business to superintend and pry into the domestic
affairs of their neighbors; and as curiosity must be gratified at
any expense to private character, and such persons always like
to believe the worst, the secrets of no family are exempt from
their malignant intrusions. These are the disturbers of the
peace of society whom the law seldom punishes, although they
perpetrate more crimes than highwaymen and assassins—
burglars of the domestic tranquillity of families—robbers of
others' good name—assassins of the characters of the innocent.

VII.

Thinking, most probably, that they were doing her a kindness,
the friends of the lady loaded the name of Houston with odium.
He was charged with every species of crime man ever committed.
The very ignorance of the community about the affair, by
increasing the mystery which hung over it, only made it seem
the more terrible. In the meantime, Houston did not offer a
single denial of a single calumny—would neither vindicate himself before the public, nor allow his friends to do it for him. He
sat quietly, and let the storm of popular fury rage on. From
that day he has, even among his confidential friends, maintained
unbroken silence, and whenever he speaks of the lady, he speaks
of her with great kindness. Not a word has ever fallen from
his lips that cast a shade upon her character, nor did he ever
allow an unkind breath against her in his presence. Whatever
may have been the truth of the matter, or whatever his friends
may have known or conjectured, he had but one reply for them:
—"This is a painful, but it is a private affair. I do not recognize the right of the public to interfere in it, and I shall treat

the public just as though it had never happened. And remember that, whatever may be said by the lady or her friends, it is no part of the conduct of a gallant or a generous man to take up arms against a woman. If my character cannot stand the shock, let me lose it. The storm will soon sweep by, and time will be my vindicator."

VIII.

He had been elected to every office he had held in the State by acclamation, and he determined instantly to resign his office as Governor, and forego all his brilliant prospects of distinction, and exile himself from the habitations of civilized men—a resolution more likely to have been begotten by philosophy than by crime.

We have no apology to offer for this singular event. If Houston acted culpably, it could not be expected he would become his own accuser. If he were the injured party, and chose to bear in silence his wrong and the odium that fell on him, he certainly betrayed no meanness of spirit, for he never asked the sympathy of the world. But notwithstanding his unbroken silence about the affair, and the sacrifice of all his hopes, he was denounced by the journals of the day, and hunted down with untiring malignity by those who had the meanness to pursue a generous man in misfortune. After his determination to leave the country was known, they threatened him with personal violence. But in this he bearded and defied them.

IX.

But his friends did not desert him while the sun of his fortune was passing this deep eclipse. They gathered around him, and the streets of Nashville would have flowed with blood, if

Houston's enemies had touched a hair of his head. But such ruffians never execute their vows, when they have brave men to deal with, and Houston resigned his office, and taking leave of his friends, he quietly left the city of Nashville. He now turned his back upon the haunts of white men, and there was no refuge left for him but the forests. There he had a *home*, of which the reader has yet heard nothing ; it was far away from civilized life.

While he was roving in his youth among the Cherokees, he had found a friend in their chief, who adopted him as his son, and gave him a corner in his wigwam. In the meantime, the chief with his tribe had removed from the Hi-Wassee country to Arkansas, and become king of the Cherokees, resident there. During their long separation, which had now lasted more than eleven years, they had never ceased to interchange tokens of their kind recollections. When, therefore, he embarked on the Cumberland, he thought of his adopted father, and he turned his face to his wigwam-home, knowing that he would be greeted there with the old Chief's blessing.

SECTION FIFTH

THE EXILE.

I.

His separation from his friends at the steamboat, was a touching scene. He was a young man, for he had not passed his thirty-fifth year. He was in the vigor and strength of early manhood. He had filled the highest stations, and been crowned with the highest honors his State could give. They knew the history of his early life, and they felt pride in his character. He was literally a man of the people, and they looked forward to his future advancement with all the pride of kindred feelings. A storm had suddenly burst upon his path ; but they knew it would soon sweep by, bearing him to a higher and fairer eminence than before. He seemed to be casting from him the palm of victory ; to be stepping down from his glory to obscurity, and his friends (and they were *the people of Tennessee*) parted from him with sorrow and in sadness.

II.

And it *was* a strange sight to see one so young, around whose brow the myrtle wreath of fame was twining, cast aside the robes of office and give up a bright future for a home in the wilderness. It was no flight of a criminal ; it was not even a necessary retirement from turbulence and excitement, for even

before he left, the fury of his enemies had abated and his real
strength was greater than ever. But it was a voluntary exile
from scenes which only harrowed his feelings while he stayed,
and the Almighty Providence, which had shaped out his future
life, was leading him in a mysterious way through the forests to
found a new empire. Let those who laugh at a Divine Providence, which watches over its chosen instruments, sneer as they
read this ; they may sneer on—they are welcome to their creed.

III.

Landing at the mouth of the White River, he ascended the
Arkansas to Little Rock, and then on, alternately by land and
water to the Falls of the Arkansas, four hundred miles to the
northwest. The old chief's wigwam was built near the mouth of
the Illinois, on the east side of the Arkansas, and the Cherokees
were settled on both sides of the river above Fort Smith.

It was night when the steamboat, which carried Houston,
arrived at the Falls, two miles distant from the dwelling of the
Cherokee chief. As the boat passed the mouth of the river,
intelligence was communicated to the old man that his adopted
son *Colonéh* (the Rover—the name given him on adoption) was
on board. In a short time the chief came down to meet his son,
bringing with him all his family.

IV.

This venerable old chief, Oolooteka, had not seen less than
sixty-five years, and yet he measured full six feet in height, and
indicated no symptom of the feebleness of age. He had the
most courtly carriage in the world, and never prince sat on a
throne with more peerless grace than he presided at the council
fire of his people. His wigwam was large and comfortable, and

"The old chief threw his arms around him, and embraced him with
great affection."   page 51.

he lived in patriarchal simplicity and abundance. He had ten or twelve servants, a large plantation, and not less than five hundred head of cattle. The wigwam of this aged chieftain was always open to visitors, and his bountiful board was always surrounded by welcome guests. He never slaughtered less than one beef a week, throughout the year, for his table—a tax on royalty, in a country, too, where no tithes are paid.

V.

Such was the home Houston found waiting for him in the forests. The old chief threw his arms around him and embraced him with great affection. "My son," said he, "eleven winters have passed since we met. My heart has wandered often where you were ; and I heard you were a great chief among your people. Since we parted at the Falls, as you went up the river, I have heard that a dark cloud had fallen on the white path you were walking, and when it fell in your way you turned your thoughts to my wigwam. I am glad of it—it was done by the Great Spirit. There are many wise men among your people, and they have many councillors in your nation. We are in trouble, and the Great Spirit has sent you to us to give us council, and take trouble away from us. I know you will be our friend, for our hearts are near to you, and you will tell our sorrows to the great father, General Jackson. My wigwam is yours—my home is yours—my people are yours—rest with us."

VI.

Such was the touching greeting the old chieftain gave him; and Houston has often been heard to say, that when he laid himself down to sleep that night, after the gloom and the sorrows of the past few weeks, he felt like a weary wanderer, returned at last to his father's house.

Houston now passed nearly three years among the Cherokees. His history during this period is filled with stirring and beautiful incidents, many of which have come to our knowledge, well worthy of being related, since they would afford the finest pictures of the lights and shadows of forest life. But they would only illustrate more fully those characteristics of stern courage and wild heroism for which he has, throughout his life, been so distinguished, and of which the world will require no better proofs than he has already given. We shall, therefore, pass by the romance of his forest life, at this period, and speak only of his untiring and magnanimous efforts and sacrifices for several years, in behalf of the oppressed and outraged Indians.

The Red man on this continent has had few better friends than Houston. From his youth he loved the children of the forest, and among their wigwams, and around their council fires, he studied the mysteries of their nature. He has declared that, during an intercourse with them of many years, he never was betrayed or deceived by a Red man. Long familiarity with them had made him acquainted with their wrongs and their sufferings, and he knew why they looked upon the white man as their foe. He had robbed them of their forests and game—he had laid waste their wigwams, and introduced discord at their council fires—he had, with the glittering bribe of gold and rifles, enticed them away from their ancient haunts, and even driven them at the point of the bayonet from the graves of their fathers —and, worse than all, he had brought among them his accursed *fire-water*, which had melted down the lofty chivalry and unbending strength of their primitive nature, and by that infernal agency degraded and enfeebled a power which, without it, they could never have subdued. This was the forerunner, and the hand-maid of his conquests—this was the magic wand he had raised over their stern chieftains, and they had melted away. Was it any wonder that the stricken few who were left of those bold, untameable tribes, that once possessed the fair lands of this broad continent, should know any other feelings towards their usurpers than revenge !

Houston knew all their wrongs, and sympathized in all their sufferings. He was now determined to devote himself to their interests, and be the guardian of their rights. He knew that General Jackson, who was then President, felt towards him the affection and confidence of an old and tried friend, and he was resolved to scrutinize the actions of the Indian agents, and sub-agents, with the greatest severity, and report the result of his observations to the President.

VII.

He was always invited to mingle in the Councils of the Cherokees during his residence among them, but while he often met them as a friend, he never entered their Councils, or joined in their deliberations. The chief counselled with him often about his people, nor was he long in becoming acquainted with the oppressions and glaring injustice which had been inflicted on them by the agents to whom their affairs had been intrusted in their migration to that country. In exchange for the territory they had occupied lower down on the Arkansas, they were, by treaty, to receive twenty-eight dollars *per capita*, which amounted, in the aggregate, to a vast sum. Instead of paying this money, as they should have done, certificates were issued by the agents, under the pretence they had no money, and as paper is always considered worthless by the Indians, merchants, who had connections with the agents, purchased up these certificates in a fraudulent manner for a mere song, representing that it was very uncertain whether the Government ever could send them money. A Mackinaw blanket, a flask of powder, and even a bottle of whisky, was often all these defrauded exiles ever got for the plighted faith of our Government.

VIII.

In this manner, whole tribes were preyed upon by abandoned speculators, and so completely despoiled of the munificent appropriations of Congress, that it is more than doubtful if a fifth part of the money, secured to them by solemn treaty, ever got into their hands ; and even the fraction which went to them only proved a curse. In speaking on this subject, General Houston once said :—

"During the period of my residence among the Indians, in the Arkansas region, I had every facility for gaining a complete knowledge of the flagrant outrages practised upon the poor Red men by the agents of the government. I saw, every year, vast sums squandered and consumed without the Indians deriving the least benefit, and the government, in very many instances, utterly ignorant of the wrongs that were perpetrated. Had one-third of the money advanced by the government been usefully, honorably and wisely applied, all those tribes might have been now in possession of the arts, and the enjoyments of civilization. I care not what dreamers, and politicians, and travellers, and writers say to the contrary, I know the Indian character, and I confidently avow, that if one-third of the many millions of dollars our government has appropriated within the last twenty-five years, for the benefit of the Indian population, had been honestly and judiciously applied, there would not have been at this time a single tribe within the limits of our States and Territories, but what would have been in the complete enjoyment of all the arts and all the comforts of civilized life. But there is not a tribe but has been outraged and defrauded ; and nearly all the wars we have prosecuted against the Indians, have grown out of the bold frauds and the cruel injustice played off upon them by our Indian agents and their accomplices. But the purposes for which these vast annuities and enormous contingent advances were made have only led to the destruction of the constitutions of thousands, and the increase of immorality among the Indians. We cannot measure the desolating effects of intoxicating liquors among the Indians by any analogy drawn from civilized life. With the Red man the consequences are a thousand times more frightful. Strong drink, when once introduced among the Indians, unnerves the purposes of the good, and gives energy to the passions of the vicious; it saps the constitution with fearful rapidity, and inflames all the ferocity of the savage nature. The remoteness of their situation excludes them from all the benefits that might arise from a thorough knowledge of their condition by the President, who only hears one side of the story, and that, too, told by his own creatures, whose motives in seeking for such stations are often only to be able to gratify their cupidity and avarice. The President should be careful to whom Indian agencies are given. If there are trusts under our government where honest and just men are needed, they are needed in such places; where peculation and fraud can be more easily perpetrated than anywhere else. For in the far-off forests beyond the Mississippi, where we have exiled those unfortunate tribes, they can perpetrate their crimes and their outrages, and no eye but the Almighty's sees them."

During the entire period he resided in that region, he was unceasing in his efforts to prevent the introduction of ardent spirits among the Indians; and though, for more than a year, he had a trading establishment between the Grand River and the Verdigris, he never introduced or trafficked in those destructive drinks. This, too, was at a period when he was far from being a practically temperate man himself. But, whatever might be his own occasional indulgences during his visits to Fort Gibson and other white settlements, he had too much humanity and love for the Red men, ever to contribute to their crimes or their misfortunes by introducing or trafficking in those damnable poisons.

Cognizant of the frauds practised on these various tribes by the agents of the Government, he could not endure such intolerable acts of outrage upon the rights and the sympathies of those whom he could not but esteem a generous and a good people; and he determined their conduct should be known at the seat of

Government, not doubting they would be instantly removed. He visited Washington early in 1832, and made such representations as caused an investigation into their conduct, and not less than five agents and sub-agents were promptly removed.

IX.

These disgraced men were, some of them, *highly respectable*, and they had powerful friends in Congress. Their dismissal from office was, therefore, the signal of a general attack upon Houston from every quarter, where mortified pride or disappointment was aroused ; and even to this day these attacks are made. Before leaving Arkansas, the swindlers, whose conduct he had exposed, had crowded the journals of that region with the basest and most infamous libels against Houston's character. He had been the friend of the despoiled Red man ; and when he saw a band of land pirates leagued together to rob the poor Indian, his humanity was stirred, and he fearlessly tore off the mask which covered these perpetrators of such high-handed injustice. But it was a crime for which they never forgave him —and all that money, lavishly used, and friends in high stations, who shared the spoils of the robbers, and a venal Press, all moved by untiring malignity, could accomplish, to cover Houston with infamy—*was done.*

X.

At that time, hostility against General Jackson had reached its culminating point. There was a majority against him in Congress, and this majority were bent upon his ruin as a public man. All the agencies that are resorted to, to crush a great man who is rising into fame, had been tried. Calumny had exhausted its venom, and hatred had belched forth all its malignity. But the heroic old man had gone through it all unscathed, and he now sat calm and high above the shafts of his foes.

XI.

But Houston was the sworn friend of the old General, and being a young man he could be more easily crushed. A desperate effort was made, to rally against him all the foes of General Jackson, and the effort was successful. One charge which he had made against the agents, and proved incontrovertibly, seemed to increase their former malignity a hundredfold. They had been contractors for furnishing Indian rations ; and through their injustice or delinquency, some of the Indians had *died of starvation*, and to multitudes only a scanty and insufficient supply of food had been issued. These rations were issued at but one point in the two Nations (Creeks and Cherokees), which compelled the emigrants, as they had not had the benefit of a crop, to locate in the most unhealthy parts of the country, for there only their rations could be obtained. This prevented their establishment and creation of homes in the new country, to which they had emigrated.

When the mask was torn off from this den of iniquity, by the bold, humane hand of Houston, he was attacked and pursued with ferocious malignity.

XI.

But it was not enough to have stirred up the Press of the Nation against a lofty-minded and upright man : *Now*, all Congress was to be moved against him. It was necessary in this last desperate crusade, to hit upon a file-leader, who had distinguished himself for his malignant personal hatred of General Jackson, and, at the same time, he must have no

3*

scruples against being the supple tool of wiser, but not better men, who pulled the wires behind the scenes.   Characters of this description were not wanting in the Congress that waged this THIRD PUNIC WAR against the old man of the Hermitage ; but the most supple, brazen-faced, shameless of all, was a certain politician, who had been elected as a friend of Jackson. He was chosen as the best instrument they could find, to use for their purposes.   In his place in the House of Representatives, he assailed Houston, and charged him with an attempt to obtain a fraudulent contract for Indian Rations, and he boldly intimated that the Secretary of War, and even General Jackson himself, were implicated in the attempt to defraud.

XV.

A crisis had now come.   Houston had suffered all sorts of abuse before, and borne it in silence : but when he saw the fame, and even the integrity of Gen. Jackson, ruthlessly assailed *on his account*, by a member of Congress, he was determined to chastise him for his cowardly insolence to the President.   He knew Houston's determination, and was careful not so cross his path.   At last, one evening, when he knew, by positive information, that Houston was *not armed*, he crossed over to the other side of Pennsylvania Avenue (where Houston was walking), for the purpose of perpetrating some foul deed in the dark, we have a right to suppose, since it was proved on the trial that he was armed, and did attempt the life of Houston, who had no weapon about him but a hickory cane.

XVI.

As soon as Houston recognized his antagonist, through the moonlight, he asked him if his name was ———, of Ohio.   The

answer had no sooner escaped his lips, than Houston, who knew
he had no time to lose, since he was unarmed, levelled him to
the ground, and shivered his hickory cane upon his head. In
the meantime, he had snapped a pistol at Houston, but it missed
fire, or he had been a dead man, for it was held to his breast.
Houston spared his life; and the politician crawled off to his
bed, which he kept some days.

XVII.

The chastised member now caused four processes to be commenced against Houston, by which he expected to crush
and disgrace him for ever. He was arrested by the sergeant-at-
arms, and brought before the House of Representatives, which
resolved itself into a judicial tribunal, to try him on the
charge of violation of the rights of one of the members, whom
Houston had held responsible for words uttered in debate. The
court sat nearly thirty days, and no means were spared to condemn the accused man. It was argued, and with great ability,
by his friends, that the House had no jurisdiction in the case;
that by the Constitution, Congress had been made a Legislative
Assembly, but clothed with no judicial powers over American
citizens. In this opinion, too, it is but just to add, some of
Gen. Jackson's political opponents concurred. The matter
dragged on nearly a month; and as the conduct, the character,
and the winning personal appearance of Houston, were continually gaining him friends, and the public were becoming
indignant that Congress should abandon the business of the
country, to prosecute and lacerate an unfortunate and self-
exiled man, who had bled in its service; even his foes themselves became tired of the prosecution. On the trial, Houston
spoke in his own defence, at great length, and with consummate
eloquence and ability. It was a touching spectacle, to see a man

who had been four years a member of that body, the Governor of a great State, the bosom friend of Gen. Jackson, one who bore on his body the deep wounds received in fighting under the flag waving from the top of the Capitol, arraigned by *party politicians* before their bar, for having, in protecting himself, while unarmed, from the stealthy attack of an armed coward, chastised a renegade demagogue, who had dared to charge the President of the United States with a bold fraud, because he thought he could, in his place in Congress, do it with impunity. Politicians of a certain class will at last learn, that in their attempts *to crush* those bold and magnanimous men who stand by the masses of the people, and have, from the very beginning of the Government, led the popular majorities—they are only hastening the advancement of such men to power.

XVIII.

What turned the popular feeling in favor of Houston at the time, and made him dear to the people, just in proportion as he was persecuted, was the undeniable fact that he was brought to the rack and tortured there, *because of his enthusiastic love for his old General, who was then President.*

This protracted and august trial, ended in a party vote of instructions to the Speaker, to reprimand the prisoner at the bar of the House. But the reprimand was delivered in so courteous and delicate a manner, it carried with it more of the tone of an approval than a reprimand. It was everywhere regarded as a signal triumph for Houston, since few men ever had so mighty a power marshalled against them.

XIX.

The second process was to move for a committee to be appointed to investigate the truth of the charge that member had made against Houston, of fraud in procuring a contract for furnishing Indian rations. A committee was raised and *the demagogue was appointed chairman*, which threw into his hands power to crush his enemy, if the fraud could be proved. Houston, conscious of his innocence, had procured this measure to be adopted himself. And what was the result of this second attempt to ruin this man, who had come from his distant exile only on the humane mission—which an angel might have undertaken—of procuring justice for the outraged Indians. After a tedious and thorough investigation—after marshalling every circumstance they could to his prejudice, the committee was *compelled* to report that *not the slightest evidence had appeared to sustain the charge.*

XX.

Houston was still triumphant, and his foes made *another* effort. They introduced a resolution to exclude him for ever from the lobby of the House, where, as an ex-Member of Congress, and the Governor of a State, he had a right to go. But this also failed!

Every process that could either injure or disgrace him, had now been tried in Congress, and so far from crushing him, he had been steadily rising. The fourth and last act in this disgraceful drama then opened. At the instance of this same demagogue, who, by being flogged by Houston, had now won, what was doubtless to him, a very gratifying notoriety, he was indicted and held to bail in a criminal process of $20,000. He could have evaded the trial by leaving the District, but he met his enemy once more, and after twenty days he was fined $500 and costs. But no enforcement of the sentence of the Court was ever attempted. It is worthy of remark, that the last act but one of Gen. Jackson's administration, was to remit the fine.

XXI.

Seldom, if ever, in the history of this country, has so malignant a persecution been waged against a public man. Seldom, in the history of the world, has a man been able to withstand so mighty a conspiracy. But Houston came off triumphantly. During this entire period of attack and abuse, he had displayed no cowardice nor shunned the most searching scrutiny. He had bared his breast to his foes, and invited their weapons. And now, when they had given over the contest, and retired from it loaded with mortification and contempt, this hunted and persecuted man deliberately abandoned once more the haunts of civilization, and went voluntarily where his foes never could have driven him—back to his exile.

XXII.

He returned by the way of Tennessee, and wherever he went he was received with every demonstration of regard. Years had passed since other painful occurrences had taken place—and with them had passed, too, the storm they had raised. Reason had resumed it sway over the public mind, and a strong desire was manifested that he should again take up his abode in Tennessee. The recent persecutions he had just passed through, had only won for him a deeper sympathy than ever, and all the pride of the State was aroused to protect and honor the man it had lost. But he could not be dissuaded from his purpose of returning once more to the forest. A sight of the spot where he had seen the bright hopes that had greeted his early manhood, crushed in a single hour, only awakened associations he wished to forget; and he once more turned his face towards the distant wigwam of the old Indian Chief, where, after a year of persecution from Christian men, he found repose by the hearth-stone of a savage King—a biting satire upon civilized life.

XXIII.

It is not difficult to imagine the effect that such unrelenting persecution must have produced upon a sensitive, a proud and a magnanimous man. He had escaped civilized life, and gone where its pestiferous and calumny-loaded breath could not reach him.

He had no more ambition to gratify. Posts of honor and emolument proffered by Gen. Jackson, he rejected—for he would never suffer the foes of the old Warrior and Statesman to heap opprobrium upon his name, for showing favor to a proscribed man.

SECTION SIXTH.

TEXAS—THE NEW FIELD.

I.

His intention was now to become a herdsman, and spend the rest of his life in the tranquillity of the prairie solitudes. A fondness for rural pursuits was now the only passion he had to gratify. Leaving his wigwam, which was situated on the margin of a prairie between the Verdigris and the Grand River, a short distance from its junction with the Arkansas, he set out on the 1st of December, 1832, with a few companions, through the wilderness to Fort Towson. At Nacogdoches he reported himself to the authorities, and a few days after went on to San Felipe de Austin, the seat of government of Austin's Colony ; after reporting to the authorities, he prosecuted his journey to San Antonio de Bexar.

Here he held an interview with a delegation of the Camanche Indians on a visit to that place. In all his intercourse with the authorities and citizens, his conduct was marked by great respect for law and the institutions of the country. After some days he returned with two companions to San Felipe de Austin. At Nacogdoches he was now warmly solicited to establish his permanent residence, and allow his name to be used as candidate for election to a Convention which was to meet in the following April.*

* In 1832, in view of the probable necessity of revolutionizing Texas, the people of the country openly and generally expressed themselves in favor of inviting either Houston or Carroll to come among them, and head any revolutionary movement that might be determined on.

II.

He was now slow to yield to their request, for his purpose had been formally settled to abandon public life and enjoy the repose and solitude of a forest home. But a single glance at the resources of this new country, and the character and condition of its population, satisfied him that a great destiny awaited them, and in imagination he already saw a new commonwealth rising into power. He was still in the morning of life—here was a new field for achievement, where all the bold elements of his character could find full play. Once embarked on the stream of a revolution, the world would learn, at last, the character of the man it had hunted from society, and history and time would pronounce his eulogy. Sober reflection convinced him that his public life was hardly yet begun, and he permitted them to use his name for the suffrages of the people, who seemed at once to recognize his great qualities as a civil and military leader.

III.

While the election was going on, he returned to Natchitoches, in Louisiana, and made a report to the Government of the United States. Its origin is supposed to have been in the fact of his having been requested by Gen Jackson to ascertain the disposition of the Camanches to make peace with our Government, and to prevail upon a delegation of that numerous and warlike nation to visit Fort Gibson on the Arkansas, and afterwards proceed to Washington. Gen. Jackson thought that the emigration of the Choctaws, the Chicasaws, and the Creeks, would be promoted by a Treaty of Peace with the Camanches, whose power and hostile disposition they dreaded, in establishing themselves in their new home. As this was a confidential mission, little is known of its history. But it is certain that in

Houston's interviews with the Camanches at Bexar, the objects were accomplished which had been contemplated by the mission.

On his return to Nacogdoches, he learned that during his absence he had been elected by a unanimous vote. He took up his residence among his new constituents, who had extended towards him so generous a greeting.

IV.

This Convention, which was composed of more than fifty members, assembled at San Felipe de Austin, the first of April, 1833. It was the first deliberate assembly made up of men descended from the Anglo-Saxon race, which had ever assembled within the limits of the ancient dominions of Cortez, and the first step in that stupendous movement, which has already swept across the Cordillera Mountains to the green shores of the Pacific, where thousands of young riflemen from New York and New England have gone to plant fortresses of protection, and institutions of learning, like those which are now overshadowing the crumbling despotisms of two hemispheres.

The Convention met in a rude, narrow apartment—as the first colonists of the Grecian States are said to have organized those famous Republics of antiquity, under rude tents in the forests, robed in the skins of wild beasts. But there were men there, whose deliberations involved the fate of many millions.

V.

As the delegates had their own expenses to pay, they proceeded forthwith to the business which had called them together, and in thirteen days, they completed one of the best models extant, for a State Constitution. It was signed by the members, and a Memorial adopted by the Convention. Stephen F.

Austin, William H. Wharton, President of the Convention, and James B. Miller, were appointed commissioners to bear the Constitution and Memorial to the Supreme Government of Mexico, and obtain the recognition of Texas as one of the States of the Confederacy. The Memorial set forth various reasons why Texas should become one of the States of Mexico ; amongst others, that it would enable her to negotiate terms with the hostile Indian tribes, and secure their rights to land previously promised by the General Government. Encroachments had been made on the Indian territory, subsequent to the rupture between the colonists and the Mexican soldiers, stationed at Nacogdoches, Velasco, and Anahuac. This rupture had taken place in the summer of 1832, in consequence of a difference between Bustamente and Santa Anna. The former had attempted to subvert the Constitution of 1824, and the military throughout Texas had pronounced in his favor. Santa Anna declared himself the friend and supporter of the Constitution, and the colonists siding with him in the civil revolution, which had begun in Mexico and spread to Texas, had expelled the military, whose usurpations, up to that time, had been submitted to without murmuring. Santa Anna was now in power, and the colonists doubted not that Austin and his colleagues would be received with favor, and their Constitution ratified by the Federal authorities.

VI.

Austin alone finally went to the city of Mexico. He was received with some formality, but little encouragement was given to his mission. *In the meantime Santa Anna had resolved on establishing a military despotism, which was the only reason that could have been urged against accepting the Constitution.*

In the formation of that instrument, the greatest care had been taken to render it entirely acceptable to the Central

Government. In the organization of the States of Mexico, under the Federal Constitution of 1824, the Provinces of Texas and Coahuila formed one State, but the right had been reserved to Texas, of constituting herself a distinct State when her population would justify the measure. The Federal Government and Coahuila had for some time pursued towards Texas a policy which rendered it necessary for her to become a separate State as soon as possible. They had granted away her territory in large tracts, under the pretence of raising funds to enable Mexico to defend her frontiers against the Indians, but she had .never appropriated one dollar to that object. For, whenever the Central Administration stationed any troops in Texas, it was in the towns nearest to the sea-board, where no hostile attack from the savages could be apprehended. Here, with a military force to overawe the citizens, a support of the Government, which would never otherwise have been conceded, could be extorted. The Frontiers were left without protection, and the colonists were obliged to protect themselves as best they could, against the hostile incursions of fifteen or twenty tribes of Indians.

VII.

We have already said that great care was taken to render the new Constitution acceptable to the Federal Government. Mexico, for example, had no banks. In the Convention, a measure had been brought forward, and an article proposed to be inserted, authorizing the Legislature of the State of Texas to create a bank or banks. This measure was introduced by Branch T. Archer, and supported by the principal men in the Convention. Houston was the only speaker who opposed the policy. In principle he was opposed to any system of banking, except one whose powers could be brought within very narrow limits; and he did not believe a more fatal precedent could be established in the infancy of the new State. The exigencies of cupidity and of business would prove stronger than the enactments of law, and he was persuaded that no sound system of banking could be hoped for in so new a community.

But he was opposed to the measure also, on the ground of policy. It would be a valid reason, if inserted, for Mexico to reject the Constitution, since it would be an innovation upon the Legislation of the General Government, and he was deeply anxious to preserve harmony, and wished Texas to defer to the prejudices and institutions of Mexico, rather than excite her jealousy by any of these new movements, which would at least be likely to excite suspicion, if not positive alarm. Houston spoke on this subject with great eloquence and convincing power. He caused the article in dispute to be stricken out, and one inserted prohibiting the establishment of all banks and banking Corporations, for a period of ninety-nine years, which passed the Convention by a large majority.

VIII.

This was the first illustration Houston gave of that wise and profound policy, which guided all his counsels during the long struggle Texas was obliged to pass, before she could be admitted to the full prerogatives of an American commonwealth. We shall have occasion to remark the difference between his policy, and that of other public men, who figured on the same scene. All new States are infested, more or less, by a class of noisy, second-rate men, who are always in favor of rash and extreme measures. But Texas was absolutely overrun by such men. There seemed to be few of that class who give character to the institutions of new States, which spring suddenly into power,— men who are brave enough for any trial, wise enough for any emergency, and cool enough for any crisis. But fortunately,

Texas had some such men, and she had a leader she depended on in the camp, and a Counsellor she relied on in the Senate. It is exceedingly doubtful what would have been her fate, but for him. And yet, we shall perceive, as we trace down Houston's history, involving, as it necessarily does, the history of Texas, that all his difficulties and all the dangers of the State, and the sufferings and sacrifices of her people, grew out of the rash and headstrong movements of a few men, whose judgments and counsels were generally precipitate, and ended, when followed, in embarrassing the State, or plunging it into danger.

IX.

Those who were present in the Convention, have always attributed to Houston the moulding influence which controlled the action of the Assembly, and gave tone to the political feelings and events that followed. They are also just as confident in the belief, that if restless and ambitious spirits, who will " rule or rend," had been willing to follow Houston's wise counsels, the Independence of Texas would have been achieved without much sacrifice of blood or treasure. We shall see how he at last triumphed, and how much sacrifice, care, and endurance, it cost him and his country.

X.

But to return to Austin, whom we left in Mexico, and in trouble. Finding his application fail, he concluded to return to Texas. On his way home, he was pursued by order of the Government, taken back to the Capital, and thrown into a dungeon, where he dragged out many months of gloom and suffering. He was an amiable, enlightened, excellent man, and a pure patriot. He was beloved and respected by the colonists, and his fame and virtues will be long cherished by the Texans. During his imprisonment, stories of his sufferings reached Texas, and everywhere they produced a deep sensation. The indignation of the colonists burst forth like the rage of a single man. There was, at that time, only one press in Texas [at Brazoria], but it gave utterance to the wrongs of the people ; and although few in numbers (for the entire population of Texas did not exceed 20,000 souls), yet, instead of exercising discretion, they spoke freely of the wrongs they endured, and the rights guaranteed to them under the Constitution of 1824. Houston discouraged such unrestrained ebullitions of feeling, since they would be likely to plunge Texas into a bloody struggle with Mexico, *before she was prepared for it*—while he was as anxious as any man, for the day of her political redemption.

XI.

Austin had been cast into prison, with no definite accusation alleged against him, and without even the form of a trial. At length he was liberated by Santa Anna, and permitted to return home. He had great confidence in Austin, for he had shown himself a friend of order on all occasions in Texas, and loyal to the principles recognized at the time. He had first migrated to that country with 300 families, as colonists—and thus introduced the materials of that vast political structure, which was subsequently wrought into form and beauty. When he returned to Texas, he found the public mind inflamed, and indignation had been expressed in municipal meetings. But when public feeling was subsiding, and few, if any, orderly men were thinking of extreme measures, Santa Anna showed clearly that nothing short of absolute power would satisfy him.

XII.

The colonists were alarmed, and precautionary measures were taken. They were ruled by Mexican laws, and governed by officers who followed blindly Mexican edicts. Rumors were constantly reaching Texas, that the colonists were laboring under the disapprobation of the Mexican government. The commerce of Texas, had been placed under restrictions of the most oppressive character, and the worst men had been set over the administration of the customs. Taxation had become oppressive. The people had been baffled in all their attempts to secure justice, and large sums of money had been extorted from them in obtaining titles to the lands they had improved, and which had been guaranteed to them by the Mexican government. An edict of Santa Anna had demanded of the people, the surrender of their private arms. This struck them like an *electric* shock. It not only exposed their wives and children to the fury of hostile Indians, but to all the horrors of starvation—for many families depended upon wild game for daily subsistence.

XIII.

At Gonzales, there was a piece of artillery for the defence of the place, which was called into almost weekly requisition by the incursions of the Indians. It was the capital of Dewitt's Colony, situated on the eastern bank of the Guadalupe, about seventy miles east of Bexar. In obedience to Santa Anna's edict, Ugartchea, a Colonel in the Mexican army, in command of several hundred dragoons, marched to Gonzales, from Bexar, to carry off the four-pounder. The colonists flocked together for the rescue of the little field-piece. Some skirmishing took place, without any serious consequences at the moment. But a great point had been won—*the first shot had been fired by the*

Mexican army, and the swords drawn that day, were to be returned no more to their scabbards, till the last link in the Mexican fetters, which had bound the youthful form of Texan Liberty, had been snapped asunder, and she stood erect among the nations.

XIV.

Austin arrived at the scene of the struggle, and was elected General of the Forces. The insurgents not only rescued their four-pounder, but resolved to pursue the enemy to Bexar, and drive the base myrmidons of the Mexican tyrant from their soil. A general alarm was spread to the banks of the Sabine. Eastern Texas had hitherto been disposed to remain tranquil, supposing all might not be so bad as rumor proclaimed it;— but the torch of war had now been lighted, and Texas rose everywhere like a single man.

Committees of Vigilance and Safety, had been constituted in the Municipalities of San Augustine and Nacogdoches, and a partial organization of the militia under their direction, had taken place. In the meantime, Houston had been chosen General of Texas, east of the Trinity. An invitation had been given by the people of the county of Brazoria, and responded to by other Municipalities, to elect delegates to meet in a General Consultation, to devise means of safety, in the event of danger; for they had now become pretty well satisfied that they had little to hope for from the despot of Mexico.

XV.

Austin had proceeded on to Bexar with his forces, and invested it. The colonists marched to him from all sections of the Province, till eight hundred armed men joined his standard. These

4

events occurred in October, 1835. The Consultation was to meet early in that month at Washington and at the specified time, fifty-six delegates assembled. At their first meeting, they conferred, and changed the place of deliberation to San Felipe, where they received an invitation from Gen. Austin to repair to Bexar, pledging himself, if they complied, that he would reduce the place in three days. After his advance upon Bexar, citizens residing near Matagorda and Victoria, formed a company, and under the command of Captain Collinsworth, reduced Goliad, and maintained possession of the town. On the first meeting of the Consultation, General Austin wrote to Houston, to send on his Division of troops. Houston took from his pocket the last five dollars he had in the world, and put it into the hand of a good rider, with dispatches to his Division, and in a short time the Redlanders were rapidly mustering for the scene of war. Immediately after having received the invitation of General Austin, Houston, with the major part of the Consultation, set out without delay for Austin's Camp, at the Salado, within three miles of Bexar.

XVI.

Soon after their arrival, General Austin, in whose pure and lofty mind, love of country outweighed all considerations of personal aggrandizement, feeling diffident to lead an army at such a time, proposed to surrender his command to Houston. Houston most positively declined his magnanimous offer, alleging, among other reasons, that the troops, then in the field, were either those who had elected Austin as their commander, or had marched to the camp in obedience to his requisition: and he believed it would furnish a pretext for the seditious and disaffected to abandon the service, and defeat the objects of the campaign. But he frankly offered to render General Austin any aid in his power, in organizing or drilling his command.

A Council of War was held in the camp, to which the principal officers and members of the Consultation were invited. A question arose as to the propriety, or rather necessity, of forming a Provisional Government, which could be done only by the re-assembling of the members of the Consultation at San Felipe. In this exigency, the Council of War determined to refer the subject to the Army. The following day the troops were drawn up, and their vote taken. They were unanimous in the opinion that the Consultation ought to re-assemble and form a Provisional Government, and devise ways and means for maintaining the army then in the field; and adopt such measures as would give Texas credit abroad.

XVII.

After General Austin had marched the army some ten or twelve miles below, to the Mission of Espada, the members of the Consultation repaired to San Felipe, where they re-organized, and once more opened their deliberations. They made a Provisional Declaration, exhorting all Mexicans to unite in maintaining the Constitution of 1824; and pledged their lives, property, and sacred honor, in support of its principles. They established an organic law for the Provisional Government of the Province, and organized a temporary administration for it. Houston was one of the Committee to frame the Declaration. A disposition existed on the part of the members of the Committee, to make a Declaration of absolute Independence, and such a resolution was adopted. Considering this movement premature and ill-judged, he got a member of the majority to move a reconsideration of the vote. By one of the ablest efforts of his life, he carried his point: and on the trial, there was found to be a considerable majority in favor of the *Provisional* Declaration.

XVIII.

These deliberations were held in a little framed building of one floor—without ceiling or plaster—whose only apartment was the narrow room where they assembled. Houston, as was his custom in those days, was dressed in buckskin breeches, and a Mexican blanket. But the appearance of the room, and the costume of the members, had little to do with their deliberations. In regard to this freak of Houston, of dressing for years, *à la sauvage*, General Jackson is reported to have said, he "thanked God there was one man, at least, in Texas, who was made by the Almighty, and not by a tailor." When Houston took up his abode in the forests, he assumed the simple and picturesque costume of the proud race among whom he dwelt; that portion of the world, which had poured gall into his lacerated bosom, and finally hunted him into the forests, now invaded the solitude of his new home. One of his crimes was, that he had become an Indian—even in his dress. Certainly these men "the tailors had made"—and he must have been an outlaw, whose dress was more like a Roman Senator's than the dandy's of Broadway.

Some of Napoleon's officers were once laughing, on the morning of one of his great battles, at the gay dress of Murat as he rode by, decked in ribbons and plumes.

"You may smile, *Messieurs*," said Napoleon, "at my dandy Marshal, but take care that when the columns are shot down to-day, you keep your eye upon him—for where you see Murat's gaudy plumes, there will be the hottest of the fight. Let a hero have *one* folly, gentlemen." Diogenes lived in a tub, but from all accounts, the world felt a good deal more disturbed about it than the old philosopher himself.

Yes, Houston, the adopted son of an Indian Chief, wore the dress of his tribe; but he carried a brave heart under his blanket. He refused to be a candidate for any office ; what he could do, however, he was ready to do. A Governor and Lieutenant-Governor were elected. A Council was also created—one member from each Municipality—and the requisite number of officers appointed for the administration of such a government. The Council was to continue in session till they should be superseded by officers elected by the people. Measures were also taken for raising a Regular Army, and organizing the militia.

XIX.

Another event took place, which decided the fate of Texas. The man in buckskin, and the Mexican blanket, was, with only one dissenting voice among more than fifty members, elected COMMANDER-IN-CHIEF OF THE ARMIES OF TEXAS.

There was no alternative for Houston but to accept the office. There was no one else gifted with those great qualities which nature lavishes on men born to command. He accepted the appointment, and proceeded to appoint his staff, and draw up the necessary bills for the organization of the Army, and the appointment of the officers of the line—embracing a competent organization of the forces to be raised.

XX.

Texas had not a dollar at this time ; and previous to Houston's election, Commissioners had been appointed to visit the United States to forward her interests, and procure a loan to sustain her under the pressure of her bold undertaking. Austin, Wharton, and Archer, were appointed Commissioners, and they were already on their way. Houston's hopes of money were not sanguine. He regarded Texas as thrown upon her own resources, and such aids as could be afforded by individuals whom the spirit of patriotism might inspire with generosity. At that moment, there were few men in the United States who had any adequate conception of the importance of those early movements, or dreamed of the results that were to follow. Even now, as these grand events of the last twenty years pass in review before us, we seem, in the soberness of solitary reflection, to be tracing the progress of one of the States of Antiquity. But there are few men who understand great social or political changes, till they have become matters of history. We shall, in the sequel, glance at some of the causes which have operated to cloud and prejudice the minds of the people of this country on the entire subject of Texas.

XXI.

In the meantime, General Houston issued a proclamation, inviting five thousand volunteers to unite in the cause of Texas. The Army still remained in the field under Burleson, who had succeeded to the command, after General Austin had left for the United States. He was an early settler of Texas, and a good man ; but destitute of those great qualities which fit men for military control. Before General Austin left the army, Fannin and Bowie, with about one hundred men, encountered five hundred Mexicans at the Mission Conception. The action was sustained gallantly by the Americans, and the Mexicans retreated, leaving some dead on the field, and carrying with them many wounded. The victors then marched to the neighborhood of Bexar, and posted themselves above the town. Colonel Benj. R. Milam, who had then no command in the Army, proposed that volunteers should turn out, who were willing to enter the town of Bexar, and storm the place. About two hundred flocked to his banner ; and led by the gallant Milan, whose chivalry entitled him to the confidence

of such brave men, entered the town at night ; and taking possession of certain buildings, made their way with crowbars
through the walls, from house to house. After performing acts
of singular bravery for several days, the heroic Milam fell, his
head pierced by a rifle-ball ; and, shortly after their leader's
death, the troops got entire possession of the town, and the
Alamo (the enemy's fortress) capitulated.

XXII.

A singular spectacle was presented on the morning of the
capitulation. Not less than eleven hundred Mexican soldiers,
passed before a little band of less than two hundred Texans, and
laid down their arms. They were released on their parole
of honor, and marched to Mexico by General Cos. This same
General violated his faith, and fought at San Jacinto. The
colonists were now generally discharged, and marched to their
homes, with the exception of the gallant Company which had
reduced the Alamo. During the siege of Bexar, a Company called
the New Orleans Greys, under Captain Morris, and another
Company from Mobile, under Captain Breeze, had arrived, as
volunteers from the United States. They bore a gallant part
in the siege, and every man engaged in the town, deserved and
secured renown.

XXIII.

While the troops were before Bexar, a Dr. Grant arrived, and
joined the Army. He had been concerned with an English Mining
Company, at Parras, but he had fallen under the displeasure of
the Mexican Government, and was obliged to fly. He was a
Scotchman by birth, but did not seem to possess much of the
methodical shrewdness which characterizes that nation. He
was a man of much more than ordinary capacity, but, in all

military affairs, seemed to be destitute of judgment and discretion. As one of the aids of General Austin, he claimed the command of the troops remaining, after Burleson had retired with most of the Army. He immediately projected the invasion of Matamoras, for he entertained a single-hearted hatred of the Mexicans, and he induced the New Orleans Greys, and Capt. Breeze's Company from Mobile, to join him in the expedition. These two Companies accordingly took up their march for Matamoras, by the way of Goliad. At the same time, Grant opened a correspondence with the General Council, which unfortunately at the time contained some men of capacity utterly destitute of moral principle, and carrying on machinations which were in the end to terminate most disastrously for Texas. The members of the Military Committee of the General Council coincided with Grant's plan of attack upon Matamoras, and thought it necessary, in effecting its capture, to destroy Houston's influence, and create a power that would supersede him.

XXIV.

In the appointment of his staff, General Houston had chosen J. W. Fannin, Jr., his Inspector General. He had held command at the battle of the Mission of Conception, and arriving at the Council of San Felipe, Houston, who felt that he deserved an appointment in the line of the Army, obtained for him the Colonelcy of the Regiment of Artillery, which placed him next in command to himself.

The Council—to effect their designs without reference to the safety of the country—thought proper to direct the headquarters of the army to be established at Washington, fifty miles distant from the sessions of the Council. This, of necessity, removed Houston's station, and it was evident they believed the success of their intrigues depended upon getting him as far off as possible. About the middle of December, he repaired to Washington, and continued there, engaged in his arduous duties. Meantime he had assigned the officers of the Regular Army to their several recruiting stations, and directed them to make such reports as would enable him, at any time, to know the number and condition of the regular force.

Fannin was ordered to Brazoria, the principal recruiting rendezvous, and Houston supposed, of course, that his orders would be carried out with a strict regard for his authority But his dispatches were utterly disregarded. At this time, letters were circulated through the country, to create a suspicion, that Houston's design was to establish a military government, by raising five-thousand volunteers, through the sanction of the General Council.

XXV.

Houston bore this in silence, but endeavored to counteract it by the efficiency of his conduct. About the 1st of January, he received orders from Governor Smith,—who had detected the secret intrigues of the council, with Grant, Fannin, and others, to repair to San Felipe, while the General had been at Washington. Colonel Ward's command from Georgia, and the Alabamians, had arrived at the mouth of the Brazos. Houston had taken precautions, and issued his orders for all troops that might arrive in the country; requiring them to report to the Governor as nominal Commander-in-Chief, and to himself as Commander of the Army, on their arrival. Fannin being in the neighborhood of the United States volunteers when they landed, paid no attention to the orders of General Houston; and abandoning his post as an officer of the Regular Army, became a candidate for the Colonelcy of the regiment that was to be formed, by the union of the Georgia and Alabama troops.

4*

Governor Smith no sooner detected the treasonable conspiracy of the Council, than he manifested the highest disapprobation of their conduct, and of course excited their hottest displeasure. Fannin treated all General Houston's dispatches with cool contempt, and looked only to the orders of the Council. He had made known to them his desire to be elected Colonel of the new Regiment ; and in accordance with their views, he was chosen to the new post, Ward being put second in command. They were then ordered to sail from Velasco, to Copano, and thence to march to Refugio Mission, twenty miles distant from their landing, where Grant was to join them with his command, on their way to Matamoras.

XXVI.

In obedience to his orders, Houston reported to the Governor at San Felipe ; and was ordered to repair to Refugio, where a juncture of the troops was to be effected. He returned forthwith to Washington ; and after arranging matters at headquarters, proceeded to the execution of the Governor's orders. He reached Goliad about the middle of January, 1836, and found Grant and his troops on the eve of departure for Refugio. General Houston made known to the troops the orders under which he was acting, and urged obedience to his authority. Ignorant of the extent to which the Council had gone in thwarting his intentions to save the country by routing the enemy on their first engagement, and knowing it was impossible for the troops at Bexar to maintain the place, he dispatched Colonels Bowie, and Bonham (of South Carolina) on the 15th of January, with an escort to Bexar, directing the commanding officer to blow up the Alamo, and fall back to Gonzalez on the Guadalupe, which he intended to make the line of defence.

XXVII.

Grant and Morris refused obedience to the orders of the Governor, while Houston was left without the power of accounting for their extraordinary conduct. He marched with them twenty-five miles to Refugio Mission, leaving a few Regulars to maintain the post at Goliad, with no subsistence but the cattle of the country. He arrived at Refugio, but no intelligence had come of Fannin's landing.

The Governor, refusing to concur in their lawless measures, had been deposed by the Council—although under the Organic Law, which required a certain number to constitute the Council or transact business, they had ceased to be a lawful Body. The conduct of the stormy spirits in that Council, had disgusted and enraged their more patriotic and rational colleagues ; and unwilling to concur in their high-handed and treacherous movements, they had withdrawn, reducing their ambitious associates to an incompetent number. But they were nevertheless determined to brave it out, and "rule or rend."

XXVIII.

Houston did not wish to be the cause of insubordination, for he was aware that it would require all the harmony and union possible, to save the country. Yet knowing that all the troops from the United States had left with the expectation of serving under himself, he used every persuasive he thought convincing, against the expedition to Matamoras ; and then resolved to return and report in person to the Governor. The only object of the Council in directing the campaign upon Matamoras, was to command the revenues of the place. Houston at once discovered the absurdity of such a plan, since the possession of

Matamoras by an enemy, would cut off all intercourse with the interior, and prevent all communication with the sea ; and he had forecast enough to know, that, if an army could reach Matamoras without opposition, they could not keep it a single week, with a force of only seven hundred men. But they could never reach the sight of its walls. They had an area of several hundred miles to pass, with no means of transportation—they had not three days of breadstuffs, and the men were unprovided in every respect for a campaign.

XXIX.

Houston remonstrated with the officers in a friendly manner ; representing the great difficulties they would have to encounter —the futility of the project—and the disasters attendant on a failure. So careful was he to avoid exciting sedition among the troops, who bowed very reluctantly to the command of any other General—that he set out from Refugio in the night, with a few of his staff, for San Felipe.

On the road he received news that the Council had deposed the Governor, and superseded his own authority—also, letters of Colonel Fannin, which had been published, showing his reliance on the Council, and disregarding all other authorities. This opened Houston's eyes to the true situation of the country, and he saw that unless something was done, without delay, to repair the evil, and to prepare the nation for the trying struggle she must pass, in wading through a Revolution—all would be lost. The hopes, which had greeted the first dawning of Anglo-Saxon Liberty in the fair Province of New Estramadura, seemed likely to be extinguished, and it is not strange that a man who had been prevailed on to exchange the tranquillity of a forest life—where he could find repose from persecution—

to mingle in the struggles of a Nation emerging into a free existence, should, when he saw himself still hunted down by malignant rivals, and his hopes clouded, feel his great-heart dejected by sadness.

XXX.

But men whom God raises up to become leaders of Nations, cannot be crushed—in the midst of their adversities they may seem, for a moment, to bow before the blast, yet they never despair. For not more sure was Columbus to surmount at last all opposition, and plant his feet upon the green shores of the New World, than are such men in the end, to overcome all their foes and triumph over even the malignity of fortune. All the way to San Felipe, he was troubled by the most painful suspense— whether to withdraw once more from the treacheries and persecutions of the world, and bury himself deep in the solitude of nature, and pass a life of communion with the Great Spirit, and his beautiful creations—or whether he should boldly mark out a track for himself, and in leading a new people to Independence, trample down all opposition. During most of the day he rode along in silence, and none of his companions disturbed his reveries. Towards evening he addressed them—he made a rapid but clear survey of events that had passed—contemplated the present state of affairs, and dwelt with enthusiasm upon the future prospects of Texas. He seemed to read her future, as the prophets did the unwritten history of Judah. He had fixed his purpose, and the world could not move him. After making an official report to the Governor, he proceeded with his Aide-de-Camp, Major Hockley, to the Cherokee Nation—in pursuance of instructions received from the Consultation—to form Treaties with them and other tribes. He met the Indians in Council—and having been returned as a delegate to the Convention which was to meet in Washington on the 1st of March, he arrived there the day previous. The Convention assembled and organized—the following day, the 2d of March, 1836, the DECLARATION OF INDEPENDENCE was adopted and signed.

SECTION SEVENTH.

THE GENERAL.

I.

THE Declaration of Independence, for which public feeling had been precipitately matured, was adopted unanimously, and hailed throughout Texas with joy and acclamation. So was it received, too, by the people of the United States, wherever they had even a faint conception of the issue made in the struggle, or the vast magnitude of the consequences that were to follow.

II.

But, from the hour the news that Texas had declared herself free and independent reached the United States, a feeling of hostility was excited against the Infant Republic, without a parallel in the history of the world. Losing sight of the grand moral results that were to flow from that event, and unmindful even of the hour of our own need, when we extended our feeble hands to France for help, a loud burst of indignation went up from a thousand newspapers, and everywhere the Declaration of Texan Independence was declared to be an act of high-handed robbery, perpetrated by a band of bold outlaws. To have emigrated to that part of the world, was enough to brand a man with infamy ; and those who gave the little they could afford, to help on the struggle, cast their mite into the Texan Treasury in silence. All recollection of our fathers, and the days of their dark struggles, seemed to be as completely obliterated from the memory of many of our countrymen, as though they had been swept by the waters of oblivion. We forgot that many of the men who were fighting those battles, were descended from the early settlers of Jamestown and Plymouth ; that hearts were nerved there for the defence of liberty, whose fathers had poured out their blood at Yorktown, and Saratoga, and Bennington, and Bunker's Hill ! And who were the men who joined in this ten years' crusade against the liberties of a Sister Republic ? And how would the victors of San Jacinto have been laughed by them in scorn, away from our altars of confederate freedom, if they had not themselves been crushed by the simultaneous rising of an indignant people at the Elections which soon followed.

III.

Some days before the Declaration was adopted, letters had been received from Travis, in command of the Alamo, at Bexar, notifying the *people* of Texas,—for there were then no chief authorities of the country—that he was invested by a numerous force in the Alamo, calling loudly for help. Houston, it will be remembered, anticipating this very result, had given orders to the commanding officer to abandon and blow up the Alamo; but his orders had been disobeyed by the officer, and treated with contempt by the General Council, who had ordered the commander to defend the place to the last, promising to reinforce him. And now the brave men in the Alamo were to atone for the treachery and low ambition of a few selfish men. The promised reinforcement was limited to *thirty men*, making Travis' whole effective force not more than one hundred and eighty-five, and without a month's provisions—detached from all Texan

settlements more than seventy miles, and the intervening territory swept by the Mexican cavalry.

IV.

As the Provisional Government, by which Houston had
been elected Commander-in-Chief, had ceased when the Convention assembled, he resigned his Major-Generalship.   But, there
was no other man in Texas to whom the people could look in
this emergency. The Convention went into the election of
a Commander-in-Chief, and out of fifty-six votes, Houston, who
was not present, received all but one vote. Texas had no organization of forces, and the few gallant men from Georgia and
Alabama in the field, were detached beyond the southern settlements, under the command of a man who had treated the orders
of the Commander-in-Chief with contempt. The treatment
Houston had received from the Council was known, and
the people feared he would decline the office. A deep gloom
now hung over the public mind. Apprehension and alarm were
written on every face, and the conviction became almost universal, that the cause of Texan Independence was lost, unless
Houston would accept the command of the Army. Impressed
with the general feeling, and stirred by the heroic spirit
which has always guided him, he resolved to peril everything, and stake life itself upon the issue. He accepted the
command.

V.

On Sunday, the 6th of March, a letter was received from Col.
Travis, addressed to the President of the Convention, brought
by the last express that ever left the Alamo. The intelligence
it conveyed was no sooner known, than an electric terror flashed
through the community.- The members, and a crowd of spec-

tators, rushed to the Hall of the Convention, the President to his chair, the members to their seats, without summons or signal. The President rose, and announced the receipt of a document of "the most important character ever received by any assembly of men." He then read a letter from Col. Travis, of the most thrilling character. It was written in all the fervor of patriotic and devoted courage; but it breathed the language of despair. Robert Potter rose, and moved that "the Convention do immediately adjourn, arm, and march to the relief of the Alamo." Houston, feeling that the next movement made in the Convention would be likely to decide the fate of Texas, determined what should be done by the Convention, as well as by himself.

VI.

All eyes were turned upon him, and as he rose from his seat, it would seem that, for a moment, every heart in the assembly stopped beating. He opposed the motion, and denounced it as madness, worse than treason, to the people. They had, to be sure, declared themselves independent, but they had yet no organization. There must be a government, and it must have organic form—without it, they would be nothing but outlaws, and could hope neither for the sympathy nor respect of mankind. He spoke nearly an hour, and his appeal, if he ever was eloquent, was eloquence itself. He admonished the Convention of the peril of the country; he advised them to sit calmly, and firmly and coolly pursue their deliberation; to be wise and patriotic; to feel no alarm, and he pledged himself instantly to repair to Gonzalez, where he had heard that a small corps of militia had rallied, and interpose them between the Convention and the enemy; and while they chose to sit in Convention, the Mexicans should never approach them unless they marched over his dead body. In the meantime, if mortal power could avail, he would relieve the brave men in the Alamo.

VII.

Houston stopped speaking, and walked immediately out of the Convention. In less than an hour he was mounted on his battle-horse, and with three or four brave companions was on his way to the Alamo. Men looked upon it as an idle and desperate attempt, or surely more would have followed him. The party rode hard that day, and only stopped late at night, to rest their horses. They were now in the open prairie. At break of day, Houston retired some distance from the party, and listened intensely, as if expecting a distant signal. Col. Travis had stated in his letters, that as long as the Alamo could hold out against the invaders, signal guns would be fired at sunrise. It is a well authenticated fact, that for many successive days, these guns had been heard at a distance of over one hundred miles across the prairie—and being now within the reach of their sound, Houston was anxiously waiting for the expected signal. The day before, like many preceding it, a dull, rumbling murmur had come booming over the prairie like distant thunder. He listened with an acuteness of sense, which no man can understand whose hearing has not been sharpened by the teachings of the dwellers of the forest, and who is awaiting a signal of life or death from brave men. He listened in vain. Not the faintest murmur came floating on the calm, morning air. He knew the Alamo had fallen, and he returned to tell his companions. The event confirmed his convictions, for the Alamo had fired its last gun the morning he left Washington; and at the very moment he was speaking in the Convention, those brave men were meeting their fate.

VIII.

After returning to his companions, who were preparing to pursue their march, he wrote a letter to the Convention recommending them to adopt a resolution *declaring Texas a part of Louisiana under the Treaty of* 2803. His suggestion was not adopted, but if he had been there to enforce it by his commanding eloquence, it would doubtless have been passed— for in those deliberative assemblies he was as absolute as ever Cromwell was in the Rump Parliament, with a thousand bayonets at his back. In this case, too, he would have had the the means of conviction in the policy he proposed. Such a measure would have won for them the sympathies of Legislatures, as well as peoples. They would not then have been regarded as a separate people. It would have matured the Republic and its institutions ; it would have shortened the period of her struggles. Neither the question of recognition nor annexation would have been raised—she would have been *adopted* at once. Houston looked at the whole matter with the eye of a statesman, and the heart of a soldier. He knew that Mexico would have withdrawn *at once* from the conflict, if Texas had at once been constituted a part of Louisiana.

IX.

If, then, it be asked, why Mexico, at last, not only made war upon Texas, after the Great Powers recognized her independence, but against the United States after annexation, we answer, that there is no man who knows enough about this subject to qualify him to hazard an opinion, who does not understand and believe, that Mexico was emboldened to provoke the war, only because of the long, powerful, persevering, and desperate hostility with which a thousand newspapers and

N. ORR

"THEY WERE NOW IN THE OPEN PRAIRIE, AT BREAK OF DAY. HOUSTON RETIRED SOME DISTANCE FROM THE PARTY, AND LISTENED INTENSELY, AS IF EXPECTING A DISTANT SIGNAL.—THESE GUNS (FROM THE ALAMO) HAD BEEN HEARD AT A DISTANCE OF OVER ONE HUNDRED MILES ACROSS THE PRAIRIE."

page 91.

a thousand public men, in this country, resisted the annexation. These presses and these public men held the very same language, and displayed the very same spirit towards Texas, that Santa Anna, and Bravo, and Bustamente, and Almonte, and Herrera, and Paredes, and their hireling presses exhibited. In fact, the hopes of these military despots all rested upon the efforts of the enemies of Texas in the United States, and not upon their popularity at home, or the power of their cannon, or the justice of their cause. In New York and Philadelphia, and Boston, they stationed their most trustworthy and confidential agents ; here they expended their money, and here their battles were fought. Who of those bold impudent tyrants would have dared to tread upon a single fold of the mantle that wrapped the youthful form of Texan Liberty, if its very name had not been made a by-word among the children of the Heroes of '76 ? It is known that Paredes never apprehended any danger of being brought to battle ; he never expected he would be called on to make good his braggart threats. And later, when this mad hostility against Texas had been frowned down by the American people, its grand movers were glad enough of the first chance offered to redeem their American character. They threw off the Mexican disguise, voted the ten millions and the fifty thousand volunteers with loud huzzas, threw up their caps to the hero of Palo Alto and La Resaca de la Palma, and made him President of the United States.

X.

The Alamo had fired its last gun, and its brave defenders had met their fate. But Houston proceeded to Gonzalez, although not a man joined him on the road. On setting out from the Convention, he dispatched an express to Fannin, directing him to form a junction with him on the Cibolo, a small river between

Gonzalez and San Antonio, intending with the united forces to march to the relief of the Alamo. About the 10th of March, (1836) he reached Gonzalez, where he found 374 men. They were without organization, and destitute of supplies—they were neither armed nor clad for the campaign. He at once had them assembled and organized, the men electing their own officers. Scouts who had been dispatched to the neighborhood of San Antonio, returned about the time of Houston's arrival, under the impression that the Alamo had fallen. This created some sensation among the troops, and immediately afterwards two Mexicans, whose families had resided among the American colonists, came in from the region of San Antonio and confirmed the general apprehension. Houston, who was satisfied that their statement was correct, had it written down. It represented that the Alamo had been taken on the morning of the 6th of March, and every human being in it slaughtered, except a woman, her child, and a negro ; that after their slaughter, the dead had been dragged out and piled together with wood, in one vast hecatomb, and burned to ashes !

XI.

When the news of this act of cold-blooded barbarity flew through the colonies, it stirred up a spirit that would never sleep again. But the day of vengeance was rapidly coming—the hour of San Jacinto was not far off. Houston immediately sent another express to Fannin (March 11th), apprising him of the fall of the Alamo, and ordering him to evacuate Goliad, blow up the fortress, and fall back without delay upon Victoria and the Guadalupe. This would unite all the forces then in the field, which Houston regarded as the only means of saving Texas. Fannin's force, the General estimated at over 500, and once joined to his own, the army would number at least 900 effective men, since Fannin had a fine supply of arms brought from the United States.

XII.

This order reached Fannin some eight days before he attempted a retreat; indeed he did not attempt it at all, till he had been surrounded by the Mexicans several days. In reply to the orders of the commander-in-chief, Fannin sent an express, saying he had held a council of war, and had concluded to defend the place, and had named it Fort Defiance. He also said, he was prepared to abide the consequences of disobeying his orders. The sequel showed but too well how prophetic was the glance Houston cast over the future.

XIII.

On the twelfth (we believe) of March, about eight o'clock in the evening, Mrs. Dickinson arrived with her child at Gen. Houston's camp, accompanied by two negro guides, sent to attend her by Santa Anna, and also to bring a proclamation of pardon to the insurgent colonists, if they would lay down their arms. The proclamation was, of course, treated as such papers had been by our fathers, when they were sent to their camps of suffering by the myrmidon generals of a British king. Mrs. Dickinson was the wife of one of the brave officers whose bones had crumbled on the sacrificial pyre of the Alamo. Houston was walking alone, a few hundred yards from the camp, at the moment this stricken and bereaved messenger arrived. He returned soon after, and found that her fearful narrative of the butchering and burning, with some of the most stirring details of that dark tragedy, had already struck the soldiers with a chill of horror; and when she told them that 5,000 men were advancing by forced marches, and their artillery would soon be

heard at Gonzalez, the wildest consternation spread through the
camp. Their alarm soon reached a pitch of desperation. Some
were stunned with silence—others were wild with lamentations
—and even officers had set fire to their tents.

XIV.

When Houston came up, he ordered silence, and the fires to
be extinguished. He then addressed the soldiery in the most
fervid manner, and they all gathered around him, except a few
who had at the first impulse fled for their horses. He detached
a guard instantly to intercept fugitives, and more than twenty
were brought back to the camp. But a few good runners made
their escape to the settlements, and carried panic in every
direction.

XV.

The General announced to his comrades that he should that
night fall back to a more secure position, as they were in a bend
of the river, where the enemy, by crossing, could cut off all
possible retreat. Accordingly, about eleven o'clock that night,
Houston ordered every light in Gonzalez to be extinguished,
and leaving a rear-guard with orders to use the utmost vigilance,
and give information of the first approach of the enemy, he
ordered the camp to be struck, and the little band took up their
line of march in good order. On reaching Gonzalez, feeling
assured that the disasters which finally followed, were inevitable,
he had ordered all the women and children to be transported to
the interior settlements; for throughout the entire Texan
struggle, he was resolved that the helpless should never be left
to the tender mercies of the Mexicans. Before the crisis came,
he hoped the transports would return, but in this he was disap-

pointed, and that night the entire army was followed by only one baggage waggon, which was drawn by four oxen.

XVI.

He continued his march that night to Peach Creek, ten miles from Gonzalez, and halted to refresh the troops. He was there met by a reinforcement of a hundred men, which increased his army to upwards of four hundred and fifty. The fugitives from Gonzalez had met this company and given them the news from the Alamo, and so anxious had they become, that nearly one quarter of them had left their officers to hurry on to the camp. About day-break, an hour after the arrival of the army at the Creek, an explosion was heard in the direction of Gonzalez. It produced an electrical effect upon the army, and many exclaimed it was the enemy's cannon. Another and a third explosion were heard in quick succession. Houston afterwards said, that they were the most agreeable sounds he had ever heard. On the march that night, he was informed that several barrels of intoxicating liquors, left in a store at Gonzalez, had been poisoned by arsenic, and he denounced it as a monstrous act, and not to be justified even by the barbarities of their savage foe. Understanding at once the cause of the explosions, Houston quieted their apprehensions by announcing the reason. It has been stated that Houston had ordered the town of Gonzalez to be reduced to ashes ; but credible men who were there, declared that the charge was not only false, but that he was angry when he heard the fact. The gallant Captain Karnes, who had been left in command of the rear-guard, believing its destruction would be an annoyance to the enemy, and deprive them of the merchandise and other supplies, had set the town on fire. After a halt of three hours, the army continued their march to the Brazos. At the La Baca he

5

received the letter from Colonel Fannin, which has already been referred to, and he is said to have turned to his aide-de-camp, Major Hockley, and pointing to the little band which seemed but a speck on the vast prairie, said ; " Hockley, there is the last hope of Texas. We shall never see Fannin nor his men— with these soldiers we must achieve our independence, or perish in the attempt." It was a sad and gloomy march. Over the fatal tragedy of the Alamo seemed to come the dirge of 500 more devoted men.

XVII.

Towards evening, they perceived, at a distance, a small moving mass in advance, which soon proved to be a company of some thirty volunteers, from the Brazos, under Captain Splann. Even this diffused some cheerfulness, and added to the lustre of the setting sun an additional ray.

At night they encamped on the La Baca, where Houston created a volunteer aide-de-camp of Major Wm. T. Austin, and dispatched him to the settlements of the Brazos, to meet him with supplies of cannon, &c., on the Colorado, where he intended to make a stand against the enemy. A person present has given a graphic account of a scene that occurred that night in a little shantee. Hockley was sitting on a block, writing out the orders for Austin, as they were dictated by General Houston, who was feeding a little fire with oak splinters, to furnish the only light their extremities allowed.

XVIII.

On the assurance of Austin that supplies could be obtained, Houston had directed him to bring not less than seven pieces of mounted cannon, with mules sufficient for draught, and at least twelve good horses for his spies, with ammunition sufficient for

"Hockley was sitting on a block, writing out the orders for Austin, as they were dictated by Gen. Houston, who was feeding a little fire with oak splinters, to furnish the only light their extremities allowed."

page 98.

the artillery. The march was continued to the Navidad—where intelligence reached him that a blind woman and her seven children had been passed by, and were not apprised that the enemy was approaching. The General immediately detached a company of fifty men, under two confidential officers, and delayed his march till the woman and her little orphans were brought safely to the camp.

XIX.

We have before us a dispatch written by Houston, "from the camp on the Navidad," to the chairman of the Military Committee, dated March 15, from which we make a few extracts :

"My morning report, on my arrival at the camp, showed 374 men, without two days' provisions ; many without arms, and others without ammunition. We could have met the enemy and avenged some of our wrongs ; but, as we were, without supplies for men in the camp, either of provisions, ammunition, or artillery, and remote from succor, it would have been madness to have hazarded a contest. * * The first principles of the drill had not been taught the men. * * If the camp had once been broken up there would have been no hope for the future. * * *I am fearful Goliad is besieged by the enemy. All orders to Col. Fannin, directing the place to be blown up, and the cannon to be sunk in the river, and to fall back on Victoria, would reach him before the enemy could advance.* * * *I directed, on the 16th of January last, that the artillery should be moved and the* ALAMO *blown up ; but it was prevented by the expedition upon Matamoras, the cause of all our misfortunes.*"

These extracts show, beyond a question, that the horrid slaughter at the Alamo was foreseen by Houston, and caused by *violating his orders.* Also, that the still more bloody tragedy of Goliad was in the commander's eye before it happened, and caused in like manner by disobeing his orders. The lives of hundreds of the bravest men paid the penalty: and Texas did not recover from the fatal consequences for many years.

XX.

From the Navidad he marched on to the Colorado, where he halted till all the women and children, and non-combatants, with their cattle and horses, had safely crossed over. Leaving a guard on his rear, he went over the Colorado with the main army. On this day, 17th of March, he thus writes the Military Committee: "To-day, at half past four P. M., we reached this Point (Burnham's). * * It pains me at heart that such consternation should be spread by a few deserters from the camp, but we are here, and if only three hundred men remain on this side the Brazos, I will die with them or conquer our enemies. * * Send agents to the United States. Appeal to them in the holy names of Liberty and Humanity. * * Let the men from the East of the Trinity rush to us. Let all the disposable force of Texas fly to arms."

XXI.

On the following day he marched down the eastern bank of the Colorado, about twelve miles, and encamped opposite Beason's, to await the arrival of Austin with his supplies. During this period he had to keep pickets for more than thirty miles up and down the river to prevent surprise. Shortly after his arrival, it was ascertained that General Sezma had advanced to the opposite side of the river, and taken a position a few miles above the Texan Camp, which caused Houston's rearguard to fall back over the river. They had, without authority from their General, set fire to Burnham's premises, as the enemy had encamped near by.

Houston now sent a detachment with orders to secrete themselves in a strong position, supposing that the army would be likely to pass the river with a strong advance guard, and the position of the Texans being well chosen, would enable them to discomfit five times their number. As he had anticipated, the enemy crossed the river with upwards of fifty cavalry, unconscious of the ambuscade, and would have been completely cut off, had it not been for the imprudence of one man, who fired upon them too soon, and thus advertised them of their danger. No other attempt was made to cross.

Some few reinforcements and supplies reached the camp about this time. But his entire force, including all his detachments, did not exceed 650 men: and his artillery not arriving, he was unable to cross the river and give battle to General Sezma. Austin had limited his arrival with the supplies and artillery to twelve days, and although the time had passed, nothing had yet been heard from him. A slight skirmish had taken place between a party of riflemen and an advance guard of the enemy, but without any decisive result.

On the 23d March, Houston wrote to Mr. Rusk:

"You know I am not easily depressed, but, before my God, since we parted, I have found the darkest hours of my life. For forty-eight hours I have neither eaten an ounce of anything, nor have I slept. All who saw the deserters, breathed the poison and fled. It was a poor compliment to me to suppose I would not advise the Convention of any necessity that might have arisen for the removal."

XXII.

In the midst of all this gloom and suspense, the news came, which burst like a bolt of thunder over the little army—*Colonel Fannin's Regiment has all been massacred!* A Mexican, by the name of Peter Kerr, had brought the intelligence, and although he had not a shadow of doubt the man's story was true, yet such was the alarm it had created, the General was obliged to throw miscredit upon the messenger, to prevent his camp from being deserted. The fall of the Alamo had well-nigh dispersed the little army, and when they heard that 500 brave comrades, fully armed and equipped, had all been cut off, their consternation was redoubled. The last barrier between them and a slaughtering army seemed swept away, and it was not strange that this last sad news had unnerved their courage.

XXIII.

Houston had his part to play that night, and he played it well. In such exigencies all the difficulties have to be overcome *at once*. He instantly called for the sergeant of the guard, and denouncing Kerr as an incendiary of the Mexicans, sent to his camp to produce distraction, declared in a furious passion he would have the spy shot the next morning at nine o'clock. An order was immediately given to have the man arrested and placed under a strong guard. He then addressed the soldiery, and adduced many reasons why the news could not be true. His apparent disbelief calmed the excitement, which had reached a fearful pitch. Houston would not see the prisoner, till the camp had retired to rest. He then went to the guard-fire and heard his story. He knew that his worst apprehensions had become history. He gave private orders to have his prisoner treated kindly, and the next morning he forgot to have him executed! The excitement had passed away with the dreams of the soldiers—but the prisoner could not be released at once, since everything which savored of the Mexicans was odious to the army, and Houston would have been charged with turning loose a spy, and perhaps collusion with the enemy.

XXIV.

Houston struck his camp that evening, and marched towards the Brazos. The army reached San Felipe the next night, effecting a march of about twenty-eight miles in less than twenty-four hours. We find in one of the General's dispatches, dated

" Camp, West of Brazos, March 31st.

"My intention was to have attacked the enemy on the second night after the day Fannin's destruction was reported by Kerr. * * Send me daily expresses, and let me know what to rely on. I must let the camp know something, and I want everything promised, to be realized by them, and I can keep them together. I have thus far succeeded beyond my hopes. I will do the best I can ; but be assured, the fame of Jackson could never compensate me for my anxiety and mental pain. Two nights since, when it was reported that the enemy was on this side of the Colorado, the citizens of San Felipe reduced it to ashes. There was no order from me for it."

On the 3d of April, Houston again writes the Secretary of War. After describing the massacre of Fannin's command, he says :—

" Humanity must recoil at the perfidy which has been exercised towards brave and heroic men, who have perished in the unequal conflicts with the enemy, when they were always more than six to one. Will not our friends rush to the conflict, and at once avenge the wrongs which have been inflicted on our dauntless comrades? The day of just retribution ought not to be deferred."

Again, on the 6th of April, he says :—

" The enemy shall be closely looked to, and the first favorable moment seized with avidity, to effect his total defeat."

XXV.

The army encamped on the night of the 29th of March at Mill Creek, and the following day reached their destination opposite Groces. The steamboat Yellow Stone, which was lying at the landing, was at once pressed into the service, and a company of troops stationed on board to prevent the boat or its engineers from *running off*. The army remained in the same position till the 11th of April. During this time, the river had swollen by the spring rains, and as Houston's camp lay on an island of the Brazos, where he was secure from the enemy, he constructed a narrow bridge, by which communication was maintained with the enemy's country, over which the Texan scouts could pass, to gather information, and hold a keen vigilance of the movements and designs of the Mexicans.

XXVI.

Before the waters reached their greatest height, General Houston had designed, as soon as the enemy should approach San Felipe, to march with all his force, and surprise them at night, believing that their confidence, inspired by numbers, discipline, and success, would have completely thrown them off their guard, which would give an easy victory to the Texan commander. But when he learned of the arrival of the enemy at San Felipe, the freshet was at its height, and having three creeks without fords, to pass in his march, this boldly conceived plan failed. Although no fortunate result followed many of these designs of Houston, yet they will show to the reader the sleepless vigilance and bold daring, of the man upon whose movements was suspended the fate of the young Commonwealth. We also deem their relation important, because they serve to render the reader familiar with the chances and changes of warfare, and the qualities necessary in the citizen who leads an army to the field.

XXVII.

The company left in charge of San Felipe, having retired to the east side of the river, and thrown up a partial fortification of timber, the enemy immediately opened the artillery upon their breastworks, and the noise of their cannon announced to Houston the first *certainty* of their approach. A company of eighty men, which had just arrived at the camp from Eastern Texas, was detached with another body to succor Captain Baker, while, by means of expresses, the Commander-in-Chief kept up communication with the troops at San Felipe and Fort Bend.

His entire force at Groces, where the main body of the army lay, did not now exceed five hundred and twenty men. He had been encouraged to expect not less than five hundred men from the Redlands, and they could have been furnished; for they were already in the field, and many of them had advanced their march to the banks of the Trinity. But some turbulent men, who where willing to ruin the country rather than fail in Houston's destruction, raised rumors of Indian hostilities, which prevented them from joining him. Amongst them was General Quitman's command from Natchez—a fine company of southern chivalry, who were thus prevented from participating in the triumphs of San Jacinto. They arrived at the camp two days after the victory. The country behind Houston was entirely depopulated. He never fell back till the women and children were secure from danger—always interposing the army between the enemy and the helpless.

XXVIII.

He had now become apprised of the strength, position, and designs of the enemy. They were marching upon him in three Divisions. The *Centre* was to advance from San Antonio to Gonzalez, Beason's, and by San Felipe or Washington, and Robbins' Ferry to Nacogdoches—led by Santa Anna himself. The *Second Division*, under General Urrea, was to march from Goliad by the way of Victoria to Brazoria and Harrisburg, while the upper or *Third Division* advanced by Bastrap to Tenoxtitlan on the Brazos, and thence to the Camanche, crossing the Trinity, on to Nacogdoches. The plan of the campaign gave evidence of the superior ability of Santa Anna, and showed Houston the man he had to deal with. At the same time the entire scheme had to be broken up in less than thirty days, or Texas would be swept by three rolling streams of fire, which would cover the land with desolation, and blot out the last hope of the Republic. How this almost impossible work was to be achieved, no one knew but Houston. There was a painful feeling of suspense throughout the little army, and all eyes were turned anxiously upon their bold leader. There was no longer a doubt in the mind of any who knew the position of affairs, that the salvation of Texas, under God, had been thrown entirely upon Houston's arm.

XXIX.

What was his policy ? Apprised of all this, he believed that the Divisions were sufficiently detached to be managed in detail, if the succors he had a right to expect should reach him in time. His position on the Brazos, enabled him to cover a larger extent of country than any other he could have selected, and was one of the most eligible for supplies. During his entire

encampment there, he was sending frequent expresses to Eastern
Texas, and while he represented his true situation in his confidential dispatches to the Committee of Vigilance and Safety at
Nacogdoches, he was in the habit, we have heard, of endorsing
the envelopes with certain postscripts, that all might see that
his force did not exceed *twenty-five hundred men;* for he
believed if his real situation was known, it would deter all
succors from coming to his aid. This is the only origin we have
discovered for the report of his having so large a command.

XXX.

About the 11th of April, news came from Fort Bend that
the Centre Division, under Santa Anna, had already crossed the
river at that place. The company stationed there, not maintaining the vigilance enjoined, the ferry-boat was taken over by
a negro to the western side. By this means they were enabled
at once to pass the river. Had it not been for this circumstance, the Brazos being at high flood, they could not have
passed for a month, and Houston could have maintained his
position till his safety inspired a confidence that would have
reinforced his army.

XXXI.

A fortunate combination of circumstances enabled Houston
to maintain himself against the influence that seemed to be
marking his destiny. The Upper Division of the Mexican
army, under Gaono, became bewildered in their march, and
ascended the Colorado. The South Division, under Urrea, was
delayed by high waters, and never passed the Brazos at all.
Santa Anna had, doubtless, learned that Harrisburg had
become the seat of Government, after the adjournment of the
Convention, which took place on the 17th of March, and was

prepared to take advantage of the alarm which this flight of the officers of the Republic had spread over the colonies. The Convention had broken up in utter consternation and dismay, and only seven of its members ever found their way to the army. None but those who were on the ground can have any conception of the fatal consequences that attended this movement. It is safe, probably, to say that to it, more than any other cause, was it owing that Houston received no more reinforcements in that trying crisis. A constitutional act had been passed by the Convention, creating a Government *ad interim*, consisting of a President, and Secretaries of War, Navy, and the Treasury, with all powers incident to a Government, except the law-making. They had adjourned to Harrisburg, not less than seventy miles from the scene of war. This flight of the wise men and the worthies of the nation, was calculated to alarm the old, the young, and the helpless, to afford an excuse to the timid, and sanction the skulking of the cowardly. Many brave men, who had joined Houston, hearing of the general consternation which had followed the adjournment of the Convention, could not resist their natural impulses to go and render protection to their abandoned flying wives and children. Houston has often declared that this was one of the most appalling circumstances that ever befell him while struggling for Texas, and we find it confirmed by his dispatches.

XXXII.

But the event proved it was fortunate for him, that Santa Anna had heard that Harrisburg had become the seat of Government, for it caused him to abandon his general plan of invasion, and diverge from his route to Nacogdoches, with a view to capture the self-preserving administration of the new Republic. As soon as General Houston received intelligence that Santa

Anna was crossing the Brazos, he dispatched without delay his orders for all the troops, scattered up and down the river, from Washington to Fort Bend, a distance of more than eighty miles, to join him on his march to Harrisburg. While he lay on the Brazos, General Rusk, now Senator from Texas, and then newly-appointed Secretary of War, instead of flying from the scene of danger, when the rest of the cabinet fled, hastened to the Commander-in-Chief on the Brazos. They advised together cordially on all matters connected with the welfare of Texas, and harmonized most perfectly in the means necessary to be adopted. The steamboat Yellow Stone was put in motion, and in two days the entire army, with their baggage-wagons and horses, was transported to the eastern side of the Brazos. On the shore, Houston met the first artillery which had been under his control. They were two six-pounders (a present from some patriotic men in Cincinnati), but they were without equipments necessary for use, except that they were mounted. There being a smith's shop and gunsmiths there, who had been employed in repairing the arms of the troops, the two field-pieces were immediately made ready for effective use, and all the old iron in the neighbor-hood cut into slugs, and formed into cartridges. The little army halted a few miles from the Ferry, and encamped for the night.

XXXIII.

After the Commander-in-Chief had, as was his uniform custom, examined in person the state of the camp, and seen that every-thing necessary for an early march had been done, he inquired the route for Harrisburg. Houston had never before been in that region ; but he took the precaution to inform himself perfectly of the geography of the country, well knowing that he was liable to be surprised any hour by a superior force. One road led to Nacog-doches, crossing the Trinity at Robbins' Ferry ; and Houston

knew that this was the road Santa Anna must have taken
in his march upon Harrisburg. The main army, amounting to
between seven and eight hundred men, was now put in motion.
They marched that day (16th April) to McArley's, a fatiguing
march of eighteen miles, through a prairie. There were fourteen
baggage-wagons, and two pieces of artillery in the train. Excessive rains had made the prairie boggy, and in many places the
wagons had to be unloaded, and the dismounted field-pieces carried, or rolled, through the mire. This brought into requisition
the entire physical strength of the army. Houston had, early in
the march, foreseen what lay before his men, and on the first
emergency, he stripped off his coat, dismounted, and set the example of unloading and transporting baggage and guns, and so
continued throughout the day, commanding and aiding the
soldiers with his personal strength. The brave little army halted
at sun-set, and laid themselves down to sleep in the open field,
without covering, for there was not a tent in the camp. About
dark, a cold rain set in, and continued for twenty-four hours. Such
were the hardships those men were compelled to undergo, while
working out the emancipation of their country.

XXXIV.

The second day (17th) they pursued their exhausting march
through the rain, twelve miles, to Burnett's settlement, which
they found deserted. Another night followed—the soldiers slept
on the wet ground, with their arms in their hands, ready to
answer in a single moment the three taps of the drum, which
was the only instrument of martial music in the camp, and which
was never touched but by the General himself. The third day's
march (18th), through the prairie, of eighteen miles, brought
them to Post Oak Bayou, where they encamped for the night.
Their toilsome march through the prairie was now over, and

they were only six or eight miles from Harrisburg. But Santa Anna had been there before them, and reduced the town to ashes, on his march to New Washington.

XXXV.

The army had marched up within two miles of the stream, and almost in sight of the ruin, and prepared to cross the Buffalo Bayou, which lay between them and the scene of desolation. The gallant Karnes, and Deaf Smith, swam over the stream with several companions, and in a short time brought back over the Bayou two expresses that bore most important intelligence. On the person of the courier, who was a Mexican officer, were found dispatches from Filisola to Santa Anna, so recently written, that the reader remarked : " The ink, sir, is hardly dry." The Texan commander now had the most positive assurance that Santa Anna was in command of the advance of the enemy. The second express contained the mail from the capital, filled with letters of congratulation, recognizing Santa Anna as Emperor of Mexico, &c.

XXXVI.

Mr. Rusk, the Secretary of War, and General Houston, immediately retired for a private conference. Very few words passed between them : the facts were before them, and they could come to but one decision.

" We need not talk," said the General; " you think we ought to fight, and I think so too." The battle was decided on, and the fate of Texas was to be settled as soon as the enemy could be found. Shortly after this conference, General Houston was informed by Colonel Hockley that he had overheard an officer in command of a regiment saying to the men about him, over whom he supposed himself to possess the greatest influence,

"Boys, Houston don't intend to fight—follow me and you shall have enough of it." Houston at once remarked to Hockley, "I'll cure this mischief directly." He ordered the two Colonels to be sent for.

"Gentlemen, have you rations of beef in the camp, for three days?"

"Yes sir."

"You will then see that each man is supplied with three days' cooked rations, and hold the camp in readiness to march. We will see if we can find Santa Anna: good morning, gentlemen." Turning off with Hockley, Houston remarked, "There is no excuse for sedition now, if they wish to fight." At the same time orders were given to prepare for crossing the Bayou—that the army might commence their march upon the enemy the next morning.

XXXVII.

Night passed, and daylight came—but no preparations had been made for the march. The orders of the Commanding Officer had been disregarded, and not a soldier was prepared with his rations. Not a moment was to be lost. Instead of taking his rest, as was his custom early in the morning, the General issued his orders himself to the men, and the camp was soon busy with the note of preparation. But it was nine o'clock before he could get his column under arms. When the army arrived at the Bayou, two miles from the encampment, they found the boat nearly filled with water. Houston at once dismounted, called for an axe, and went to hewing oars out of rails.

XXXVIII.

The passage was a difficult and perilous undertaking, and yet Houston was determined to make it that morning. The Bayou

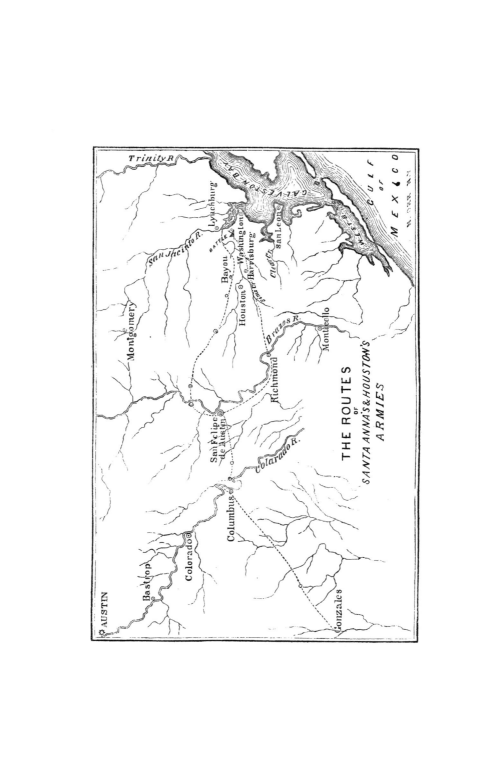

THE ROUTES
OF
*SANTA ANNA'S & HOUSTON'S
ARMIES*

was about fifty yards wide, and more than twenty feet deep.
As the Pioneers, a small company, were going aboard, an accident occurred which damaged the boat. Houston leaped aboard
at once ; and his faithful horse, that he had left pawing on the
bank, plunged in after his master, and swam to the opposite
shore. A rope was soon constructed out of cabriestas (a rope
of horse hair) and raw tugs, and fastened to both sides of the
stream, which enabled the boat to make more rapid trips, and
kept it from floating down the stream. The passage was now
being made with great rapidity, but it was an hour of intense anxiety to the commander and his intelligent counsellor,
the Secretary of War. General Houston had crossed and stood
on one side, while Mr. Rusk remained on the other, both watching the perilous movement of their little army, in whose brave-
hearts the hopes of Texas were now all gathered. A single
accident ! No one knew but the next moment the enemy's
column might come in sight, and if they came up while that
deep stream divided the army of Texas, the result would be fore-
told before it happened.

XXXIX.

Half the army had now passed, and it was the moment of the
deepest peril. The boat was giving way ; four strong men were
bailing out the water continually. The body of cavalry was
now to be risked. They were goaded to plunge into the deep
stream, and they at once disappeared. But they rose again in
their strength and strained for the steep bank. They reached it,
and when they struck the solid ground, they sprang from the
water and shook their tired limbs. The passage was made.
Mr. Rusk went over on the last boat. It was an affecting spectacle to see these two brave men seize each other's hands when
they met on the left bank of the stream ; and it is not difficult to

believe what is indeed said, that the same expression of gratitude fell from their lips together—" Thank God—we are at last safely over." While the lines were forming, General Houston drew from his pocket a scrap of paper, and with a pencil (here was his only portfolio) wrote the following letter.

Camp at Harrisburg, April 19th, 1836.

To COLONEL RUSK, IN THE FIELD.

This morning we are in preparation to meet Santa Anna. It is the only chance of saving Texas. From time to time I have looked for reinforcements in vain. The Convention's adjourning to Harrisburg struck panic throughout the country. Texas could have started at least four thousand men. We will only be about seven hundred to march, besides the camp guard. *But we go to conquest.* It is wisdom growing out of necessity to meet and fight the enemy *now.* Every consideration enforces it. The troops are in fine spirits, and now is the time for action. We will use our best efforts to fight the enemy to such advantage as will insure victory, though the odds are greatly against us. I leave the result in the hands of an all-wise God, and I rely confidently upon His providence. My country will do justice to those who serve her. The right for which we fight will be secured, and Texas shall be free.

SAM HOUSTON, COMMANDER-IN-CHIEF.

(Certified copy from the Department of War, of the Republic of Texas.)

XL.

The lines were now formed, and Houston rode up and addressed the soldiers. Those who heard him, say that he made the most impassioned and eloquent appeal they ever listened to. The words seemed to flow along the lines like streams of electric fluid, and when he gave them for their watchword, REMEMBER THE ALAMO, it struck like a bolt of fire. The watchword had no sooner fallen from his lips, than it was caught up by every man in the army, and one simultaneous shout broke up into the sky—*Remember the Alamo—Remember the Alamo,* was repeated, and the green islands of trees in the prairie sent back the echo. The Secretary of War also spoke in the most happy and stirring manner. The men seemed inspired with the spirit of chivalry, and were impatient for the order of "March" to be given.

XLI.

The order came, and the column got under way. As it moved on over the prairie, the golden sun shone out full and clear from mid-heaven, as it never shines even in that beautiful climate, except after a long, cold rain. It seemed to be the signal of God's approval, and they felt that the Heavens themselves smiled on the struggle. No martial strains fell upon the ear—no rich bugle rang out its full, clear blast—no gorgeous banners waved over the embattled host. Their march was not measured even by "the thrilling fife, the pealing drum." There was little of the pomp or circumstance of glorious war; but there was the firm purpose, the strained muscle, the compressed lip, and the heavy tramp of seven hundred men, determined to be free.

XLII.

In a narrow woodland not far from the stream, the army halted till sun-down, to avoid being seen in the open prairie. The column was now once more in motion, and a forced march made to a point not more than four or five miles distant from the ground which was to witness the main struggle. They took shelter under the covert of a grove off from the line of march, and the weary men laid down on their rifles to sleep for an hour.

At daylight General Houston rose from the ground where he had been resting his head on a coil of rope used in dragging the artillery, and roused the camp by his well known three taps of the drum—for a reveille or tattoo had never been beaten from the day he took the command. Their artillery was never fired till it was fired in the face of the enemy.

Pickets were advanced in every direction. The scouts sent on ahead soon returned with information which satisfied the Commander the enemy was not far distant. A small party had been fallen in with, and chase given to them—but they were well mounted, and effected their escape. On the return of the scouting party, the army halted to take refreshment, beeves were dressed, and the roasting-fires kindled.

XLIII.

But little progress had been made when, about seven o'clock that same morning, news came that the enemy was marching up from New Washington to cross the San Jacinto, which, if effected, would have enabled Santa Anna to carry desolation to the Sabine. Houston immediately ordered the line to be taken up for the crossing of the San Jacinto at Lynchburg. The issue of the entire struggle hinged on cutting off Santa Anna's retreat. The army saw it at once. The soldiers, with alacrity, abandoned their meat half-cooked, flew to their arms as one man, and as soon as the horses could be harnessed to the artillery, the march began. The column did not halt till the Ferry at the junction of Buffalo Bayou, and the San Jacinto was reached, where, to the great joy of the Texans, they learned that Santa Anna had not yet come up. Houston took possession of a new boat which Santa Anna had forced some Americans to construct, and had it rowed up opposite the first grove on the Bayou. In the meantime, having arrived first, he could choose his own position, and he posted himself in a beautiful copse of trees which grew on a bend in the stream—and lay in a semicircular form on the margin of the Prairie. The trees and the undergrowth enabled him to conceal his forces on the bank of the river, and plant his artillery on the brow of the copse.

XLIV.

The Texan army was now ready to go into battle at a moment's warning. But as the enemy had not yet come up, they again lighted their fires to complete their culinary operations, which had been so suddenly interrupted a few hours previously. But they had scarcely laid aside their arms and kindled their fires, before Houston's scouts came flying into the camp, with news that the Mexicans were in sight—and shortly after Santa Anna's bugles were heard over the Prairie, sounding the charge of the Mexican army.

XLV.

Whatever may have been said to the contrary, it is perfectly certain that Santa Anna knew the position of the Texan General, and so far from his being *surprised* by a discharge from the Texan artillery, he intended to surprise the enemy himself. Accordingly he opened his "brass twelve-pounder" upon the Texan position, intending to sustain the Artillery by his Infantry and Cavalry. But a well directed fire of grape-shot and canister from Houston's two six-pounders drove back the Infantry column, which took shelter in a piece of timber within rifle shot of the left wing of the Texan army. In the meantime, the Mexican field-piece was kept playing, but with no other result than that Col. Neill, the gallant officer of the Artillery, received a grape-shot in his thigh, which disabled him from service. These events took place about ten o'clock in the morning. Col. Sherman, of the 2d Regiment, requested of the Commander permission, with a detachment, to drive the infantry from their covert. Houston, who had already decided (for reasons known then only to himself, but apparent enough the next day) his plan and time for action, complied with Col. Sherman's request, although he gave him positive orders not to advance beyond the piece of timber, or endanger the safety of his men. Houston directed him to take two companies of his Regiment. He preferred charging on horseback. Houston gratified him. He was repulsed, and the circumstance produced no good effect upon the men.

XLVI.

General Houston, as appears from his dispatch, which we have already given, was resolved to choose his own time for fighting, and compensate for his want of numbers, by military skill and superior advantage in position. In other words, he was resolved to watch his opportunity, and "fight the enemy to such advantage as would insure victory, though the odds were greatly against him."

Some slight skirmishing followed, which ended in Santa Anna's retiring with his army to a swell in the Prairie, with timber and water in his rear. His position was near the bank of the Bay of San Jacinto, about three-quarters of a mile from the Texan camp, where he commenced a fortification.

XLVII.

Houston was well satisfied with the business of the day ; and he declared to one of his confidential officers that evening, that, although he did not doubt he would that day have won a victory, if he had pursued the enemy, yet it would have been attended with a heavy loss of men—"While, to-morrow," said he, "I will *conquer, slaughter, and put to flight* the entire Mexican army —and it shall not cost me a dozen of my brave men." Those who clamored then, and have clamored since, about Houston's

losing so fine an opportunity of fighting on the day before the
battle of San Jacinto, were, without doubt, brave men—but if
they could have had their way at any *one* time after Houston
took the command at Gonzalez, it is certain that it would
have cost another Alamo or Goliad tragedy, and the day of San
Jacinto would never have come.

XLVIII.

Evening came on, and Houston was about to withdraw his
army from the field, to give them time for refreshment and repose,
and to prepare for the following day. The flight of the enemy,
in the first instance, and Santa Anna's rather precipitate retreat
afterwards, had inspirited the Texan army. But Col. Sherman,
who was determined to resort to a *ruse* for the purpose of forcing General Houston into a general engagement that day—now
pressed the General most earnestly for leave to advance with his
Cavalry, and attempt the capture of the Mexican field-piece.
Houston discountenanced the movement altogether—for he felt
sure that his plan of giving battle to the enemy the next day
would succeed, and he was reluctant to peril unnecessarily the
life of a single man. He also had some reason to apprehend a
similar result to that which followed Sherman's ill-advised movement that morning. But he importuned him till the General
consented to have him go out with the Cavalry and *reconnoitre*
the enemy's position and forces ; but he peremptorily ordered
him by no means to go within gun-shot of the Mexicans, nor
court a conflict. Houston ordered out the artillery and the
infantry battalion behind an island of timber, to remain concealed, and if the enemy should attack Sherman's command, to
be in readiness to meet and check their advances. Sherman disappeared with his Cavalry behind the timber the enemy had
occupied in the morning, and Houston and his staff awaited the

result, utterly ignorant of the *ruse* of Sherman to force the Texan commander into a general engagement, and therefore unconscious of their imminent peril.

XLIX.

The reconnoitering party had hardly disappeared, before the sound of firing in that direction was heard. In a single moment a suspicion of Sherman's *real* design flashed over Houston's mind ; he mounted his horse and rode straight to the scene of action. He met Col. Sherman coming in. Although he had *not* succeeded in perilling the entire army by forcing them into a general engagement, yet he had succeeded in sacrificing the life of the brave Trask, and disabling the intrepid Woodliff, both of whom were now being borne back. Houston was incensed, for all this had been done in direct violation of his orders, and two of his Spartan soldiers borne bleeding by, were the only fruits that had followed. Gen. Foote's History (vol. ii. p. 301) declares that this was "a bold and well-conceived *ruse* to delude the Commander-in-Chief into a conflict, in spite of the monitions of his cooler judgment," though Sherman has since had the effrontery to declare that Gen. Houston sent him to be *cut off !* This would seem rather a singular charge, without remembering the circumstances, since Houston had lost neither a man nor a beast in his retreat to the Brazos, or in his advance to San Jacinto ; and on the night before the battle, he certainly had no men to spare. We only allude to the circumstance, however, as a fair sample of the countless calumnies which disappointed and factious men have heaped upon the name of Houston. The best way to kill falsehood is to publish plain truth—and we shall not trouble ourselves to deny in detail the thousand and one false statements which have been published against the **Texan Senator.**

L.

The Texan army now retired to their camp, and refreshed themselves for the first time in two days.. "The enemy in the meantime extended the right flank of their infantry, so as to occupy the extreme point of a skirt of timber on the bank of the San Jacinto, and secured their left by a fortification about five feet high, constructed of packs and baggage, leaving an opening in the centre of their breastwork, in which their artillery was placed—the cavalry upon the left wing." (Extract from Gen. H.'s official report.)

Such was the position of the Mexican army, and they maintained it till the charge was made the next day.

SECTION EIGHTH.

THE HERO OF SAN JACINTO.

I.

DURING the entire presence of the enemy, on the day that witnessed the first meeting of the hostile armies, Houston had remained on horseback, exposed to their artillery, as a target. Branches were cut down over his head by cannon balls, and one shot struck the bit of his horse's bridle. After he had doubled the vigilance of his encampment, to render surprise impossible, he was prevailed on by his staff to take some rest, for he had scarcely eaten or slept for several days. It was now evening twilight, and the men were enjoying a hasty repast of the beef they had found so difficult to cook.

Houston laid himself down under an old oak, with the coil of the artillery rope for his pillow. From the day he took command of the army, he had never been known to have one hour's sound rest. His *only* time of repose had been after four o'clock in the morning, when he beat three taps on the drum, which he had done every morning till that day. At four o'clock, the line was always formed, and every man kept under arms till daylight. He then lay down, and got what rest he could till the men had taken their breakfast, and were ready to march. In one of his letters to Mr. Rusk, during this period, in speaking of the solicitude he suffered, he says : "I will do the best I can ; but, be assured, the fame of Jackson could never compensate

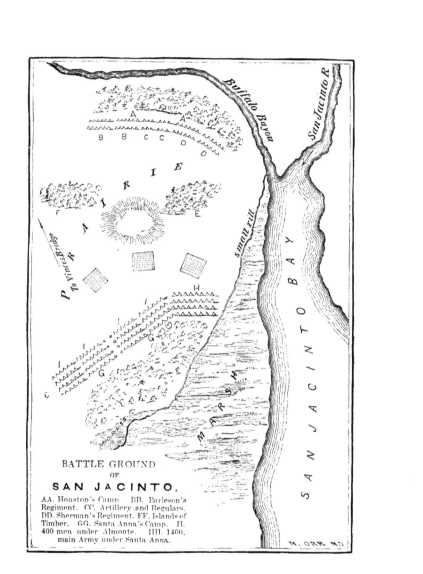

BATTLE GROUND
OF
SAN JACINTO.

AA. Houston's Camp. BB. Burleson's
Regiment. CC. Artillery and Regulars.
DD. Sherman's Regiment. FF. Islands of
Timber. GG. Santa Anna's Camp. H.
400 men under Almonte. HH. 1400.
main Army under Santa Anna.

M. ORR N.Y.

me for my anxiety and mental pain." All this suffering arose from uncertainty. He had expected troops and supplies, and waited for them in vain. The fall of the Alamo, and the massacre of Fannin's command, had 'dispirited his men, and caused desertions. The Government itself had fled from the scene of danger, and consternation had spread through Texas ; he was in a new country, without the means of subsistence or transport ; his men were but half clad and half armed ; he was in the neighborhood of a powerful army, whose picket-guards outnumbered all the men in his camp, and he could decide neither the day nor the scene of battle. He had slept on the wet ground, without covering ; his only dress was the garb of a hunter, and his food only kept him alive.

It is not strange, therefore, when the harrowings of suspense were over, and in the presence of the enemy, he had posted his faithful guards and fixed his iron purpose, that this man could lie down and sleep calmly and profoundly throughout the entire night. But he was probably the only man in that camp over whose mind flitted no anxious vision.

II.

The night which preceded the bloody slaughter of San Jacinto, rolled anxiously away, and brightly broke forth the morning of the last day of Texan servitude. Before the first grey lines shot up the East, three strange taps of a drum were heard in the camp, and 700 soldiers sprang to their feet as one man. The camp was busy with the soldier-hum of preparation for battle; but in the midst of it all, Houston slept on calmly and profoundly. The soldiers had eaten the last meal they were to eat till they had won their independence. They were under arms, ready for the struggle.

III.

At last the glorious sun came up over the Prairie, without a single cloud. It shone full and clear in the face of the Hero, and it waked him to battle. He sprang to his feet, and exclaimed, " the sun of Austerlitz has risen again." His face was calm, and for the first time in many weeks, every shade of trouble had moved away from his brow. He ordered his Commissary General, Col. John Forbes, to provide two good axes, and then sent for Deaf Smith. He took this faithful and intrepid man aside, and ordered him to conceal the axes in a safe place near by, where he could lay his hands on them at a moment's warning, and not to pass the lines of the sentinels that day without his special orders, nor to be out of his call.

IV.

Morning wore away, and about nine o'clock, a large body of men was seen moving over a swell of the prairie in the direction of Santa Anna's camp. They were believed to be a powerful force which had come to join the Mexicans, and the spectacle produced no little excitement in the Texan lines. Houston saw it at a glance, and quelled the apprehension by coolly remarking, that " they were the same men they had seen the day before—they had marched round the swell in the prairie and returned in sight of the Texan camp to alarm their foe, with the appearance of an immense reinforcement—for it was very evident Santa Anna did not wish to fight. But it was all a *ruse de guerre* that could be easily seen through—a *mere Mexican trick.*"

V.

All this did very well, and yet Houston, of course, had quite a different notion on the subject. He sent Deaf Smith and a comrade, with confidential orders, as spies on their rearward march. They soon returned, and reported publicly that "the General was right—it was all a humbug." A few minutes after, Deaf Smith whispered quite another story in the private ear of the commander. The enemy seen was a reinforcement of 540 men, under Gen. Cos, who had heard Santa Anna's cannon the day before on the Brazos, and come on by forced marches to join his standard. But the secret was kept till it did no harm to reveal it.

At this juncture, a council of war, consisting of six field officers was called, at their suggestion. The General in Chief, seated on the grass beneath a post oak tree, submitted the proposition whether they should attack the enemy in his position, or whether they should wait for him to attack them in theirs? The two juniors in rank were in favor of attack, but the four seniors objected, alleging that such a movement as charging a disciplined army in position by a raw soldiery, advancing in an open prairie, without the cover of artillery, and with only two hundred bayonets, was an unheard-of thing. The council was dismissed. The troops were sounded as to an attack, and were found to be favorable, and the General at once determined, on his own responsibility, to give battle.

A proposition was made to the General to construct a floating bridge over Buffalo Bayou, "which might be used in the event of danger." Houston ordered his Adjutant and Inspector Generals and an Aide to ascertain if the necessary materials could be obtained. They reported that by tearing down a house in the neighborhood, they could. "We will postpone it awhile at all events," was Houston's reply.

VI.

In the meantime, he had ordered Deaf Smith to report to him,

with a companion, well mounted. He retired with them to the
spot where the axes had been deposited in the morning. Taking
one in either hand, and examining them carefully, he handed
them to the two trusty fellows, saying, " Now, my friends, take
these axes, mount, and make the best of your way to Vince's
bridge; cut it down, and burn it up, and come back like eagles,
or you will be too late for the day." This was the bridge over
which both armies had crossed in their march to the battle-
ground of San Jacinto, and it cut off all chance of escape for
the vanquished.

" This," said Deaf Smith, in his droll way, " looks a good
deal like fight, General."

VII.

The reader will not fail to notice the difference between
Houston's calculations of the results of that day, and those of
some of his officers. *They* bethought themselves of building a
new bridge––*he* of cutting down and burning up the *only* bridge
in the neighborhood. The fact was, Houston was determined
his army should come off victorious that day, or leave their
bodies on the field.

VIII.

The day was now wearing away ; it was three o'clock in the
afternoon, and yet the enemy kept concealed behind his breastworks, and manifested no disposition to come to an engagement.
Events had taken just such a current as Houston expected and
desired, and he began to prepare for battle.

In describing his plan of attack, we borrow the language of
his official report, after the battle was over. " The 1st Regiment, commanded by Col. Burleson, was assigned the centre.
The 2d Regiment, under the command of Col. Sherman, formed

the left wing of the army. The artillery, under the special command of Col. George W. Hockley, Inspector-general, was
placed on the right of the 1st Regiment, and four companies of
infantry, under the command of Lieut. Col. Henry Millard, sustained the artillery upon the right. Our cavalry, sixty-one in
number, commanded by Col. Mirabeau B. Lamar, placed on our
extreme right, completed our line. Our cavalry was first dispatched to the front of the enemy's left, for the purpose of
attracting their notice, whilst an extensive island of timber
afforded us an opportunity of concentrating our forces and
displaying from that point, agreeably to the previous design of
the troops. Every evolution was performed with alacrity, the
whole advancing rapidly in a line, and through an open prairie,
without any protection whatever for our men. The artillery
advanced and took station within two hundred yards of the
enemy's breastwork."

IX.

Those who expect a minute and accurate account of this
engagement, from the writer, or any one else, must be disappointed ; for no such description can ever be written. It was a
slaughter, more than a *battle*. We can only give the reader an
idea of the position of both armies when the engagement began
—fill up the interval of the next few minutes with blood, and
smoke, and cries, and slaughter, and then tell the almost incredible result. The two armies were now drawn up in complete
order. There were 700 Texans on the field, and Santa Anna's
troops numbered *over eighteen hundred*. Houston had informed
Mr. Rusk of the plan of the battle, and he approved of it as
perfect. The Secretary, it is true, had never been a soldier—he
understood little of military evolutions or the discipline of an
army ;—but Houston knew he carried a lion-heart in his bosom,

and he assigned him the command of the left wing. The General of course led the centre.

X.

Everything was now ready, and every man at his post waiting for the charge. The two six-pounders had commenced a well-directed fire of grape and canister, and they shattered bones and baggage where they struck. The moment had at last come. Houston ordered the CHARGE, and sounded out the war cry, REMEMBER THE ALAMO. These magic words struck the ear of every soldier at the same instant, and "the Alamo !" "the Alamo !" went up from the army in one wild scream, which sent terror through the Mexican host. At that moment a rider came up on a horse covered with mire and foam, swinging an axe over his head, and dashed along the Texan lines, crying out, as he had been instructed to do, "*I have cut down Vince's bridge—now fight for your lives and remember the* ALAMO,"—and then the solid phalanx, which had been held back for a moment at the announcement, launched forward upon the breastworks like an avalanche of fire. Houston spurred his horse on at the head of the centre column right into the face of the foe.

XI.

The Mexican army was drawn up in perfect order, ready to receive the attack, and when the Texans were within about sixty paces, and before they had fired a rifle, a general flash was seen along the Mexican lines, and a storm of bullets went flying over the Texan army. They fired too high, but several balls struck Houston's horse in the breast, and one ball shattered the General's ankle. The noble animal staggered for a moment, but Houston spurred him on. If the first discharge of the Mexicans had been well directed, it would have thinned the Texan ranks. But they pressed on, reserving their fire till each man could choose some particular soldier for his target : and before the Mexicans could reload, a murderous discharge of rifle balls was poured into their very bosoms. The Texan soldiers rushed on. They were without bayonets, but they converted their rifles into war-clubs and levelled them upon the heads of Santa Anna's men. Along the breastwork there was little more firing of muskets or rifles—it was a desperate struggle hand to hand. The Texans, when they had broken off their rifles at the breech, by smashing in the skulls of their enemies, flung them down, and drew their pistols. They fired them once, and having no time to reload, hurled them against the heads of their foes ; and then drawing forth their bowie-knives, literally cut their way through dense masses of living flesh.

XII.

It would be a gross mistake to suppose that the Mexicans played the coward that day—for they were slain by hundreds in the ranks where they stood when the battle began—but the fierce vengeance of the Texans could not be resisted. They fought as none but men can fight, when they are striking for their homes, their families and their dead kindred. The Mexican officers and men stood firm for a time, but the Texans stamped on them as fast as they fell, and trampled the prostrate and the dying down with the dead, and clambering over the groaning, bleeding mass, plunged their knives into the bosoms of those in the rear. When they saw that the dreadful onset of their foe could not be resisted, they either attempted to fly, and were stabbed in the back, or fell on their knees to plead for mercy, crying, " *me no Alamo !*" " *me no Alamo !*" " *me no Alamo!*" These unfortunate slaves of the Mexican tyrant had witnessed

that brutal massacre of brave men, and now they could think of
no other claim for mercy, but the plea that they were not there:
for they knew the day of vengeance for the Alamo had at last
come.

But before the centre breastwork had been carried, the right
and left wings of the enemy had been put to the rout, or the
slaughter. The Mexicans, however, not only stood their
ground at first, but made several bold charges upon the
Texan lines.

XIII.

A division of their Infantry, of more than five hundred men,
made a gallant and well-directed charge, upon the Battalion
of Texan Infantry. Seeing them hard pressed, by a force of
three to one, the Commander-in-chief dashed between them and
the enemy's column, exclaiming :—

"Come on, my brave fellows, your General leads you."

The Battalion halted and wheeled into perfect order, like
a veteran corps, and Houston gave the order to fire. If the
guns of the Texans had all been moved by machinery, they
could not have been fired nearer the same instant. There was
a single explosion—the Battalion rushed through the smoke, and
those who had not been prostrated by the bullets were struck
down by the cleaving blows of uplifted rifles ; and the levelled
column was trampled into the mire together. Of the five
hundred, only thirty-two lived, even to surrender as prisoners
of war.

XIV.

In the meantime, although Houston's wound was bleeding
profusely, and his dying horse could scarce stagger his way over
the slain, yet the Commander-in-chief saw every movement of

his army, and followed the tide of battle as it rolled over the field. Wherever his eye fell, he saw the Mexicans staggering back under the resistless shock of his heroic soldiers. Regiments and Battalions, Cavalry and Infantry, horses and men, were hurled together ; and every officer and every man seemed to be bent upon a work of slaughter for himself.

XV.

The Mexican army had now been driven from their position, and were flying before their pursuers. Houston saw that the battle was won, and he rode over the field and gave his orders to stop the carnage if the enemy would surrender. But he had given *the Alamo* for their war-cry, and the magic word could not be recalled. The ghosts of brave men, massacred at Goliad and the Alamo, flitted through the smoke of battle, and the uplifted hand could not be stayed.

XVI.

" While the battle was in progress," says General Rusk, " the celebrated Deaf Smith, although on horseback, was fighting with the infantry. When they had nearly reached the enemy, Smith galloped on ahead, and dashed directly up to the Mexican line. Just as he reached it, his horse stumbled and fell, throwing him on his head among the enemy. Having dropped his sword in the fall, he drew one of his belt-pistols, presented it at the head of a Mexican, who was attempting to bayonet him, and it missed fire. Smith then hurled the pistol itself at the head of the Mexican, and, as he staggered back, he seized his gun, and began his work of destruction. A young man, by the name of Robbins, dropped his gun in the confusion of the battle, and happening to run directly in contact with a Mexican soldier who had also lost his musket, the Mexican seized Robbins, and both being stout men, rolled to the ground. But Robbins drew out his bowie-knife, and ended the contest by cutting the Mexican's throat. On starting out from our camp, to enter upon the attack, I saw an old man, by the name of Curtis, carrying *two* guns. I asked him what reason he had for carrying more than one gun. He answered : 'D—n the Mexicans ; they killed my son and son-in-law in the Alamo, and I intend to kill two of them for it, or be killed myself.' I saw the old man again during the fight, and he told me 'he had killed his two men ; and if he could find Santa Anna himself he would cut out *a razor-strap from his back.*'"

XVII.

Such was the day of vengeance. It was not strange that no *invading* army, however brave, could long withstand so dreadful an onset. "When the Mexicans were first driven from the point of woods where we encountered them," continues General Rusk, "their officers tried to rally them, but the men cried 'It's no use, it's no use, there are a *thousand* Americans in the woods.' When Santa Anna saw Almonte's Division running past him, he called a drummer, and ordered him to beat his drum. The drummer held up his hands and told him he was shot. He called then to a trumpeter near him to sound his horn. The trumpeter replied that he, also, was shot. Just at that instant a ball from one of our cannon struck a man who was standing near Santa Anna, taking off one side of his head. Santa Anna then exclaimed, 'D—n these Americans ; I believe they will shoot us all.' He immediately mounted his horse, and commenced his flight."

XVIII.

The flight had now become universal. The Texans had left on the ground, where the battle began, more than their entire number, dying and dead ; and far away over the Prairie they were chasing the flying, and following up the slaughter. Multitudes were overtaken and killed as they were making their escape through the deep grass. The Mexican cavalry were well mounted, and after the event they struck deep their spurs into their fleet horses, and turned their heads towards Vince's Bridge. They were hotly pursued by the victors, and when the latter came up, the most appalling spectacle, perhaps, of the entire day, was witnessed. When the fugitive horsemen saw that the bridge was gone, some of them, in their desperation, spurred their horses down the steep bank ; others dismounted and plunged in the stream ; some were entangled in their trappings, and were dragged down with their struggling steeds ; others sunk at once to the bottom ; while those whose horses reached the opposite bank fell backwards into the river. In the meantime, while they were struggling with the flood, their pursuers, who had come up, were pouring down upon them a deadly fire, which cut off all escape. Horses and men, by hundreds, rolled down together ; the waters were red with their blood, and filled with their dying gurgles. The deep, turbid stream, was literally choked with the dead !

XIX.

A similar spectacle was witnessed on the Southern verge of the Island of Trees, near the Mexican encampment, in the rear of the battle-ground. There was little chance of escape in this quarter, for a deep morass was to be passed ; and yet multitudes, in their desperation, had rushed to this spot as a forlorn hope. They had plunged into the mire and water with horses and mules, and, in attempting to pass, had been completely sub-merged ; every one who seemed likely to escape soon received a ball from the murderous aim of a practiced rifleman, and the morass was literally bridged over with carcasses of dead mules, horses, and men.

XX.

The conquerors rode slowly off from the field of fame, and the resting-place of the dead, and returned to the oak, at whose foot the hero of San Jacinto had slept till the " Sun of Auster-litz" had woke him that morning. All resistance to the arms of Texas ceased. The pursuers returned to the camp, where a command was left to guard the spoils taken from the enemy. As the Commander-in-Chief was riding across the field, the vic-torious soldiers came up in crowds, and slapping him rudely on the wounded leg, exclaimed—

"Do you like our work to-day, General ?"

" Yes, boys, you have covered yourselves with glory, and I decree to you the spoils of victory ; I will reward valor. I only claim to share the *honors* of our triumph with you. I shall not take my share of the spoils." He did not.

XXI.

While he was giving his orders, after he reached the Texan encampment, and before he dismounted, General Rusk came in and presented his prisoner Almonte. It was the first time these two men had ever met. This seemed to give a finishing stroke to the victory; and Houston, who was completely exhausted from fatigue and loss of blood, fell from his horse. Colonel Hockley caught him in his arms, and laid him at the foot of the oak.

XXII.

Thus ended the bloody day of San Jacinto—a battle that has scarcely a parallel in the annals of war. Its *immediate fruits* were not small—for the spoils were of great value to men who had nothing in the morning but the arms they carried, scanty, coarse clothing, and the determination to be free. About 900 stand of English muskets (besides a vast number that were lost in the Morass and Bayou), 300 sabres, and 200 pistols, 300 valuable mules, a hundred fine horses, a good lot of provisions, clothing, tents, and paraphernalia for officers and men, and twelve thousand dollars in silver, constituted the *principal* spoils.

XXIII.

But the booty was esteemed meaner than nothing, in comparison with the great moral and political consequences that attended the victory. On that well-fought field Texan Independence was won. A brave, but an outraged people, in imitation of their fathers of the last age, had entrusted their cause to the adjudication of battle, and God took care of the issue. For our own part, we can find in the whole range of History no spectacle more sublime. It was not a struggle for the aggrandizement of some military chieftain—nor was it a strife for empire—the soldiers, who marched under the " Lone Star" into that engagement, were free, brave, self-relying men. Some of them, indeed, had come from a neighboring Republic, as Lafayette crossed the sea, to join in the struggles of freedom, but most of the Texan army were men who cultivated the soil they fought on, and had paid for it with their money or their labor. Hundreds of them had abandoned their fugitive wives to achieve everlasting freedom for their children. They were fighting for all that makes life worth having, or gives value to its possession.

And when the victors laid themselves down to rest that night, and Heaven folded its blue curtains kindly around them, and they thought that their troubles and anxieties were over—that they could now return to the embrace of their happy families with the hope of a long and peaceful life of earnest and manly endeavor, and a quiet old age, when they should hold their grandchildrens on their knee, and tell them the story of the bloody day of San Jacinto—it is not strange that they felt more than compensated for all their privations and all their sufferings.

XXIV.

But the sublimity of the spectacle is lost, unless the eye has scope for a wider field of vision. There *are* events whose consequences can be measured by no estimate into whose calculation *centuries* do not come. If the historian of the Plymouth Colony could have lived a century longer, he might have perceived clearly what is now reduced only to a question of *time*, that from the day the Mayflower swung round to her mooring on the rock of Plymouth, the sceptre of the New World passed for ever into the imperial hand of the Anglo-Saxon race. But for a long period this grand result seemed impossible, and he who should have proclaimed that it would one day take place, would have been called a dreamer. Spain and Portugal, France and England, had divided the Northern aud Southern Hemisphere of the new-found World. But the French empire in America received a fatal shock when England wrested from it the Canadas in 1763 ; and she afterwards lost by diplomacy what could not be wrested from her in battle. *One dominion then disappeared.*

XXV.

At last, when it became apparent that even Englishmen in

America could not develop their strength under British sway, the drama of '76 began, and all that was valuable in the New Continent that belonged to England, became the heritage of her American children. *This was the second great act.*

XXVI.

In the meantime the powerful savage tribes, whose wigwams served as beacon fires to the earliest voyagers along the Atlantic coast, melted away before the steady advance of European population, and the *Indian dominion passed away.*

XXVII.

At last, the American people,—*this new form of humanity,* which concentrated in itself nearly *all* those qualities, which, in past times, had given empire to separate nations, began to cross the frontiers of that ancient power which, for three hundred years, had made the fair valley of the Montezumas the seat of their dominion. But this began in *no encroachment—no invasion upon the rights or soil of a neighboring State.* Mexico, although she had caught enough of the all-pervading spirit of the Anglo-Saxon to rise and shake off the foul mantle of Spanish despotism, had not vital energy enough left within herself to work out her own political regeneration. She had been too long bowed into the dust by the foreign tyrant—she had been too long steeped in the besotted bigotry of superstition—she had never thought or acted for herself—she had no clear perception of human rights—no intelligent idea of liberty. She did not know that a nation never can grow rich by abandoning the cultivation of the soil, and digging gold and silver from the mine—she could not understand why it was that six vigorous republics had grown up into power on the cold barren hills of

New England, while *she* had become feeble and impoverished in the midst of the very garden of the world. And yet she believed, if she could once introduce that northern population into her limits, she could borrow from them the secret of their magic power. Her statesmen were told that New Englanders, when they found they could not get their bread from their rocky, frozen soil, made commerce of stones and grew rich by exporting their granite, and lime, and cobble-stones, during the summer, and sent off ship-loads of their surplus water as soon as it froze in winter, albeit they had to find their market for it on the other side of the globe. These, said the Mexican statesmen, are the men we must get to colonize our vast garden-province of Texas—for we have for three centuries tried in vain to do it ourselves.

XXVIII.

So that fertile territory was thrown open to the people of the United States, and they were plied by all those motives of gain and pledges of protection which, in the mind of the pioneer settler, prove too strong for the allurements of home. A band of choice spirits, hardy, working men, who had been trained in the district schools of New York and New England, and cultivated their cold, ungrateful soil, were led out to find their new homes in the fair province of New Estramadura, where all nature was blushing under the purple light of the tropics. At their head went STEPHEN F. AUSTIN; one of those few men upon whose incorruptible, dauntless truth, a young nation finds it her salvation to repose. In his rare and great character, all that was lofty in the Cavalier and uncompromising in the Puritan was mingled.

XXIX.

He entered into his obligations with the Mexican Government, and conducted all his negotiations and redeemed all his pledges, in good faith, For a time, Mexico stood by her engagements, and the infant colony struck its roots deep into the soil. At last Mexico discovered that the very qualities from which she promised herself so much advantage—the industry, the enterprise, the inventions of the new colonists,— were all owing to that intelligent love of liberty which she so little understood, and yet so much dreaded. She saw that men who had energy enough to be good settlers, where Spaniards had failed, had too much independence ever to be governed as Spaniards. But she found out her mistake only when it was too late to correct it. Like the ancient Britons, she had invited a superior race into her country, unconscious that her sceptre would one day be transferred to their hands.

XXX.

This was the point upon which the destiny of the old Spanish empire hinged. Mexico might now have borrowed from her new subjects the elements of an entire political regeneration. These colonists were not ambitious men—they went there *only to cultivate the soil*—but they had carried, of necessity, their civilization and love of liberty with them, and they could not brook the tyranny of Mexican Dictators. They went prepared to stand by the Federal Constitution of 1824, and up to the 2d of March, 1836, when the Declaration of Independence was signed, all the protests and discontent, all the demands and petitions of the Texans, were *limited to a concession of the rights secured to all the States of Mexico by that Constitution!*

XXXI.

But Mexico was now under the sway of selfish, ambitious

military chieftains, who, in the struggle for supremacy, had trampled the Constitution of 1824 into the dust. And let it never be forgotten, that when the political agitations of Texas began, and the will of the entire people had been declared, *all they asked for, and all they desired then, was to see the Constitution of* 1824 *preserved inviolate.* But men, who are driven to the wall, and compelled to fight for life, sometimes fight for victory. Mr. Austin was then Commissioner to Mexico, and he went to the Capital with his memorial. His very appearance in that city with the prayer of his colony, that the Mexicans would abide by their own Constitution, under whose solemn pledges he had led his people to their new home—was too bitter a sarcasm upon the corrupt tyrants who had trampled down that high compact, and he was plunged into a foul dungeon, where for many months he never saw a beam of sunshine, nor even the hand that fed him.

XXXII.

How was all this tampering with Anglo-Saxon men to end? Who, that knows what plighted faith means, or has any notion of the obligations growing out of a political compact, will pretend to say that Texas was bound to submit to the decrees of a Dictator who had committed high treason against his government—treason for which he would have been brought to the block by the people of Mexico, had he not had 20,000 bayonets at his back. The Federal compact had now been broken, and by the highest law of nations, every State of the Union not only had the right, but was bound in duty to take care of itself. An *immediate* Declaration of Independence would have been justified by the world. But Texas still remonstrated, and still prayed. *All she wanted, was a return to the Constitution of* 1824. But that Constitution lay bleeding under the hoofs of

Santa Anna's battle-horse, and his myrmidon soldiers had possession of the Capital. War was proclaimed against Texas by Mexico, *because she would not acknowledge a Dictator*— and an invading army was sent across the Rio Grande, to "*lay waste the infant colony, and slaughter all its inhabitants.*"

XXXIII.

This was the position of Texas—and if those men were not justified in defending their wives and children from slaughter, and their dwellings from fire, there never was a people who had a right to smite the arm of a tyrant. The heroes of '76 rebelled against a constitutional government, with its parliament and king, because they were required to pay a stamp tax. *The Texans never rebelled at all.* They would not bow to a Dictator who had stamped the free Constitution of his country under his feet ;—and now a war of extermination was proclaimed. Seven hundred brave men were slaughtered and burned to ashes, after they had, under a solemn pledge that their lives should be spared, surrendered themselves prisoners of war.

The red flame of exterminating war was now rolling over the very bosom of the young Republic, whose only crime was her loyalty to the Federal Constitution of Mexico.

XXXIV.

At last the slaughter-day of San Jacinto came, and the Texans who went into battle, knew that every one of them would have been put to death in cold blood, if the enemy had conquered. Such had been the case at Goliad and the Alamo, and such was the watchword of the advancing Dictator. But high over the smoke and screams of the field of San Jacinto, we seem to see, and do see, the hand of the God of Freedom and of Vengeance. His purposes were unknown to man, but they could not be overthrown. The wing of his Almighty Providence had sheltered the bark of the Pilgrims, and his strong arm had been thrown around the rude homes of Plymouth. Over the deliberations of the Provincial Congress, He again presided, and in the Declaration of Independence His will was done. And now, having decreed, that the broad prairies and shining rivers of that vast land, which had groaned under the tramp of despotic power, and been blasted by the withering blight of superstition for ages, should be regenerated by a nobler and better race, He had begun to reveal his great purposes.

XXXV.

The *last* act of this drama, which had begun on the shore of New England, was to be opened on the field of San Jacinto. And although the sun gleamed on the armor of eighteen hundred Mexicans that morning, and when the Commander's bugles sounded the charge, he was, to all human appearances, sure of a victory ; yet the result proved that the battle is not always to the strong—that " God rules among the nations of the earth, and giveth its kingdoms to whomsoever He will." A decree had gone forth against that army, and against the long-abused reign of Spanish power in Mexico—" thy dominion is taken from thee."

And the future historian will, one day, open his scroll by announcing that when the sun went down over the groans and the slaughter of San Jacinto, the dominion of Mexico passed for ever away. Such had been the first four acts of the drama of the New World.

> " The Fifth, then closed the Drama with the day,
> Time's noblest offspring was the last."

"HOUSTON, WHO WAS COMPLETELY EXHAUSTED FROM FATIGUE AND LOSS OF BLOOD, FELL FROM HIS HORSE."

page 184

SECTION NINTH.

I.

THE battle of Independence had been fought.   Seven hundred soldiers had met nearly three times their number, and come off victorious.   Six hundred and thirty men were left dead on the field ; among them were, one general officer, four colonels, two lieutenant-colonels, seven captains, and twelve lieutenants. Multitudes had perished in the morass and the bayous.   Of the surviving, upwards of two hundred and eighty were wounded, and there were nearly eight 'hundred prisoners.   Only seven men are known to have escaped from the field.   And yet, incredible as it may seem, this bloody engagement had cost the Texans the lives of only seven men, and less than thirty had been wounded.   It *was* incredible, and when the Commander-in-Chief awoke the next morning, and heard the facts, he asked, "Is this so, or is it only my dream ?"

II.

At ten o'clock in the morning, Gen. Houston sent a detachment of men to bury the enemy's dead who had fallen in battle ; but decomposition had taken place so rapidly, the troops returned and reported they could not execute his order !   This extraordinary circumstance excited the greatest surprise, and the Mexican prisoners accounted for it by resolving it, like the defeat of the previous day, into "a malignant blast of destiny."

III.

In the meantime, a large number of Texans were scouring the prairie throughout the day, and bringing in prisoners. The grass was everywhere four or five feet high, and those who had not been taken the day before, were now crawling away on their hands and knees, hoping thus to effect their escape. Santa Anna had not yet been taken, but the victors were scouring every part of the field in search of the Dictator. "You will find the Hero of Tampico," said Houston, "if you find him at all, making his retreat *on all fours*, and he will be dressed as bad at least as a common soldier. Examine closely every man you find."

IV.

Lieutenant Sylvester, a volunteer from Cincinnati, was riding over the prairie, on a fine horse, about three o'clock in the afternoon, when he saw a man making his way towards Vince's bridge. The moment he found himself pursued, the fugitive fell down in the grass. Sylvester dashed on in that direction, and his horse came very near trampling him down. The man sprang to his feet, and apparently without the slightest surprise, looked his captor full in the face. He was disguised in a miserable rustic dress. He wore a skin-cap, a round jacket, and pantaloons of blue domestic cotton, with a pair of coarse soldier's shoes. But his face and his manners bespoke, too plainly, that he belonged to a different class than his garb betokened; and underneath his coarse disguise, Sylvester saw that he wore a shirt of the finest linen cambric. "You are an officer, I perceive, sir," said the horseman, raising his cap politely. "No, soldier," was his reply; and he drew out a letter in Spanish, addressed to Almonte. When he saw there was no hope of escape, he inquired for General Houston. By this time, Sylvester had been joined by several of his comrades, and mounting his prisoner behind him, they rode off together, on the same horse, to the camp, several miles distant. As he passed the Mexican prisoners, they exclaimed with the greatest surprise as they lifted their caps, "*El Presidente!*"

V.

In a single moment, the news spread through the camp that Gen. Santa Anna was a prisoner, and the Dictator was taken to Houston. The General was lying on the ground, and having slept little during the night, in consequence of his wound, had now fallen into a doze. Santa Anna came up behind him, and took his hand. Houston roused himself, and turning over, gazed up in the face of the Mexican, who extended his left arm, and laying his right hand on his heart, said, "*I am General Antonio Lopez de Santa Anna, President of the Mexican Republic, and I claim to be your prisoner of war.*" Houston waved his hand to a box,—for it was the only seat in the camp—and asked his prisoner to be seated. He then sent for Almonte, who spoke English perfectly, and requested him to act as interpreter.

VI.

In the meantime, Santa Anna had taken his seat, and glancing his keen eye occasionally around the camp, with a timid expression, pressed the sides of his breasts with both hands, and gave two or three half-suppressed groans, like a man who was suffering deep pain. An interesting incident took place about this time, which is thus related by Gen. Rusk: "At the time Santa Anna was brought into our camp, I was walking with

7

young Zavala. (The reader will recognize in this youthful character, the son of the noble and venerable Zavala, who distinguished himself as the friend of Texan independence.) We approached him together. Santa Anna recognized young Zavala at once, and advanced to meet him with great apparent cordiality, uttering many expressions of kindness, such as are customary among the Mexicans on such occasions, several of which I remember. Among other things, he exclaimed " Oh ! my *friend*, my *friend*, the son of my *early* friend ;" with which, and other exclamations in the same strain, he embraced young Zavala, with high indications of *apparent* feeling, and I think, *dropping a tear.* Young Zavala returned his greeting with that deference which would have been due to his former rank and power ; but at the same time, emitting from his countenance an expression I have scarcely seen equalled on any occasion. His look seemed to wither Santa Anna, and staring him full in the face, he replied immediately, with great modesty, 'It *has* been so, sir.' Santa Anna evinced plainly that he was much mortified."

VII.

Almonte approached his captive General with evident respect and grief, and the following conversation took place between the two commanders ; Houston, in the meantime, lying on the ground, resting on his elbow. Great pains has been taken to get as nearly as possible the exact words used by the speakers, and those who were present at the interview, have assured us, that all here related they *do* remember, and they recollect nothing else of importance.

VIII.

Santa Anna (after embracing Almonte, and recovering per-

"His look seemed to wither Santa Anna—Houston in the meantime lying on the ground resting on his elbow."

page 146.

fectly from his embarrassment, rose, and advancing with the air of one born to command, said to General Houston—"That man may consider himself born to no common destiny, who has conquered the Napoleon of the West ; and it now remains for him to be generous to the vanquished."

Houston.—" You should have remembered that at the Alamo."

S. A.—" You must be aware that I was justified in my course by the usages of war. I had summoned a surrender, and they had refused. The place was then taken by storm, and the usages of war justified the slaughter of the vanquished."

H.—" That *was* the case once, but it is now obsolete. Such usages among civilized nations have yielded to the influences of humanity."

S. A.—" However this may be, I was acting under the orders of my Government."

H.—" Why, YOU *are the Government* of Mexico."

S. A.—" I have orders in my possession commanding me so to act."

H.—" A Dictator, sir, has no superior."

S. A.—" I have orders, General Houston, from my Government, commanding me to exterminate every man found in arms in the province of Texas, and treat all such as pirates ; for they have no Government, and are fighting under no recognized flag. This will account for the positive orders of my Government."

H.—" So far as the first point is concerned, the Texans flatter themselves they have a Government already, and they will probably be able to make a flag. But if you feel excused for your conduct at San Antonio, you have not the same excuse for the massacre of Colonel Fannin's command. They had capitulated on terms proffered by your General. And yet, after the capitulation, they were all perfidiously massacred, without the privilege of even dying with arms in their hands."

Those who were present say that when Houston came to speak

of the Goliad tragedy, it seemed impossible for him to restrain his indignation. His eye flashed like a wild beast's, and in his gigantic effort to curb in his wrath, cold sweat ran off from his brow in streams.

S. A.—"I declare to you, General (laying his hand on his heart), that I was not apprised of the fact that they had capitulated. General Urrea informed me that he had conquered them in a battle, and under this impression I ordered their execution."

H.—"I *know*, General, that the men had capitulated."

S. A.—"Then I was ignorant of it. And after your asseveration I should not have a shadow of doubt, if it were not that *General Urrea had no authority whatever to receive their capitulation.* And if the day ever comes that I can get Urrea into my hands, I will execute him for his duplicity in not giving me information of the facts."

IX.

Here the conversation was suspended for a while, and Santa Anna requested a small piece of opium. It was ordered by Houston, who asked him if he would desire his marquee and luggage, and the attendance of his aides and servants. Santa Anna thanked him very politely, and said "it would make him very happy, since they were proffered by his captor."

While the order was being given, Almonte manifested a disposition to continue the conversation with Houston. After remarking to the Texan General that fortune had indeed favored him, he asked why he had not attacked the Mexicans the first day the armies met. "You had reason to suppose we should be reinforced. And yet if you had risked a battle that day you would have had another story to tell, perhaps, for our men were *then* ready to fight, and so anxious for the battle to come on, that we could hardly keep them in their ranks. Why did you wait till the next morning, General ?"

"Well," replied Houston, "I see I was right. I *knew* you expected I should bring on the battle that day, and were consequently prepared for it. Now if I *must* be questioned by an inferior officer in the presence of his General, I will say *that was just the reason why I did not fight;* and besides, I thought there was no use in having two bites at one cherry." After some remark of Almonte, which irritated Houston, and which, in the opinion of all who heard it, ill-befitted the occasion, he said—" You have come a great way to give us a great deal of trouble—and you have made the sacrifice of the lives of a great many brave men necessary." "Oh," flippantly replied Almonte, "what of six or eight hundred men ! And, from all accounts, only half a dozen of your *brave* men have fallen."

Houston replied : " We estimate the lives of our men, I perceive, somewhat higher than you do," and he gave him a look which seemed to say, "taunt me again, and you don't live an hour." Almonte very politely changed his tone. "You talk about reinforcements, sir," said Houston, raising himself up, " it matters not how many reinforcements you have, sir, you *never* can conquer freemen." And taking from his pocket an ear of dry corn which he had carried for four days, only a part of it being consumed, he held it up and said, " Sir, do you *ever* expect to conquer men who fight for freedom, when their General can march four days with one ear of corn for his rations ?"

X.

The exhibition of the ear of corn stirred up all the enthusiasm of the Texan soldiers, and they gathered round their General, and asked him to allow them to divide the corn. " We'll plant it," said they, " and call it the Houston corn." " Oh, yes, my brave fellows," said the General, smiling, "take it along if you care anything about it, and divide it among you—give each one a kernel as far as it will go, and take it home to your own fields, where I hope you may long cultivate the arts of peace as nobly as you have shown yourselves masters of the art of war. You have achieved your independence—now see if you cannot make as good farmers as you have proved yourselves gallant soldiers. You may not call it Houston corn ; but call it *San Jacinto* corn—for then it will remind you of your own bravery." It is also said that in one of his dispatches that day to the people of the Sabine, the General said to those who had fled from their homes, " return and plant corn." The soldiers distributed their corn, and it now waves over a thousand green fields in Texas.

XI.

Santa Anna had become interested in the conversation, and Almonte related to him what had been said. The Mexican General seemed to be transported with rage, and he cursed Almonte for losing the battle. He was mortified beyond measure to think that his large army, perfectly armed and munitioned, with officers whose camp was filled with every luxury, should have been conquered by an undisciplined band of raw troops, incompletely armed, and whose officers were destitute of most, even, of the necessaries of life. It is worthy of remark, also, that Santa Anna afterwards said *" that this was the first moment he had ever understood the American character ; and that what he had witnessed, convinced him that Americans never could be conquered."*

XII.

Santa Anna's marquee was set near the spot where Houston

was lying. His trunks were not examined, nor any portion of his baggage molested. The Texan General knew that there was hardly a man in his army who did not wish to see Santa Anna expiate his crimes with his blood, and very few believed it would be possible even for Houston to protect him from assassination. But he knew the eyes of the civilized world would be turned upon the Texan camp, and that however guilty Santa Anna may have been, the name of Texas would be given over to execration if any violence was offered to the Captive. He therefore took the necessary precautions to see that not only no violence, but no indignity, should be offered to his prisoner. The course he took in this matter entitles him to the regard of mankind. The feeling that prevailed in the army could not be mistaken, and various circumstances have come to our knowledge which serve to illustrate not only Houston's extreme vigilance, but his superior shrewdness in detecting insubordination, and his address in putting it down. One example we will allude to.

XIII.

An officer had resolved to shoot Santa Anna, and had prepared himself for the work. His design, however, he had kept to himself, and Houston could have had no intimation of it from any quarter. But as the officer was passing Houston on the day of the night he had fixed for the execution of his purpose, the General, who saw something wrong in his manner, beckoned him to approach. He conversed with him, privately and confidentially, on the subject of his fears ; and after depicting the horrible consequences that would follow Santa Anna's assassination, told the officer that he had made him his confidant in the matter, because he knew he would be more likely than any other man in the camp, to detect any murderous scheme projected, and he relied on his vigilance. The officer gave him his pledge he would act on his suggestion, and, more-over, declared that Santa Anna should never be assassinated while *he* was in the camp. He was as good as his word : and yet he afterwards declared he had, at the very time, the arms on his person with which he had sworn to kill Santa Anna. Such was one of the thousand expedients Houston was obliged to resort to, to maintain discipline over those wayward, reckless men. No one knew how he did it, and yet it passed into a proverb that *Houston was the only man in the world that could have kept the army in subjection, or achieved the independence of Texas, or preserved it after it was won.* Houston, therefore, exer-cised the keenest vigilance over the safety of his prisoner, and treated him as a guest and a gentleman, rather than as a captive.

XIV.

Night came. The guard was so disposed as to include Santa Anna's marquee, and he slept on his camp-bed with every com-fort he could have had if he had been the victor ; while, near by him, Houston lay upon the earth—his wonted bed in camp —with no respite from the intense agony of his wound. The ball had entered about one inch above the ankle joint, shatter-ing the bone, and severing the muscles and arteries. It pros-trated him for months, during which time he was worn down by fever and pain to the shadow of a man.

XV.

As Houston and Rusk were riding side by side from the battle-field, returning to camp, they discovered two ravens hovering over the field in the smoke which lingered over the battle scene. Some of the men proposed to shoot them, as they were near the earth. Houston said, "No—don't shoot them—it is a good omen. Their heads are pointing westward. 'Tis the course of empire. I own I am a little superstitious about the raven."

XVI.

The next morning Santa Anna asked leave to see General Houston, which was granted. He presented himself elegantly dressed in citizen's garb, and tendered a most respectful and cordial greeting to his "host," and inquired kindly for his health and the state of his wound. The difference in the dresses of the two men was striking. Houston had on a plain, old black coat, snuff-colored pantaloons, a black velvet vest, a fur cap, a worn-out pair of boots, and a scimitar of tried metal, with a plated scabbard—a gift from his friend Captain Joseph Bonnell, of Fort Jessup. He had worn it, hung by buckskin thongs. This constituted his wardrobe, and his armory. Santa Anna would have been taken for the victor, and Houston for the captive.

XVII.

The Texan commander received his prisoner with courtesy, and he immediately proposed negotiations for his liberty. Houston, *who, from the beginning to the end of Santa Anna's capture, never was alone with him a single moment*, immediately sent for the Secretary of War, and together they conversed some time with the prisoner. Santa Anna submitted a proposition. But General Houston informed the Mexican "President" that he could take no action on his proposals, as Texas was ruled by a Constitutional Government, whose members had been sent for immediately after the battle. Santa Anna naturally asked where the Government was—a question which he found could not be so easily answered.

7*

XVIII.

This "Government" had, as we have already stated, fled from the scene of danger, and scattered to the four winds of Heaven. Fortunately, it was known where the head of the Government was, or rather where he *had* been, for he had escaped to Galveston, and prepared to take passage on a little vessel called the Flash, before even the first flash of the enemy's guns. Houston thinking he might wait there till the news of the battle came—since even so *prudent* a man would perceive he could have plenty of time to get his craft under way before the victors could reach him—had dispatched his first express to that quarter.

XIX.

It is to be disclaimed that Houston, or the Secretary of War, in his presence, ever entertained any proposition of Santa Anna's, to enter into negotiations with him ; but referred him to the Cabinet. At the end of the first conversation with Santa Anna, Houston peremptorily ordered him to draw up a command to Gen. Filisola, second in command to him, to evacuate Texas, and fall back to Monterey, on the west side of the Rio Grande. And it was a peremptory command of Houston, without annexing any condition to it. Nor did Houston ever make any promise, nor was any made by any other person, so far as Houston was cognizant of it.

XX.

Santa Anna, who had a great aversion against any negotiations with civilians, manifested a perfect willingness to act with military men. But Houston and Rusk were immovable in their determination. A detachment of 250 Texans was then ordered to march with a dispatch from Santa Anna, and General Filisola was instructed to depart immediately, with all the Mexican troops, as far at least as Monterey,—this order had been exacted by General Houston without an intimation that even Santa Anna's life should be spared. Filisola was on the east side of the Brazos when he received news of the disaster of San Jacinto from an officer who had escaped from the battle-field on a fleet Andalusian courser, and succeeded in reaching his camp.

XXI.

It was night when he reached Filisola's head-quarters, when the camp broke up in confusion, and prepared for flight. They fired a large cotton gin, to have the benefit of the flames to light up their passage over the river. The Texan detachment pressed on by forced marches in pursuit of the rear-guard of the Mexican army. They found horses, mules, and baggage-wagons, with sick soldiers, scattered along the path of the flying Division, which indicated the utter consternation with which the retreat had been made. They had been obliged to march through a low, wet prairie, in reaching the Colorado. But they were overtaken by the pursuers, and Filisola received the messengers who bore the flag with every mark of respect, and pledged himself to execute General Santa Anna's orders without any delay. He asked leave only to take some cattle along his march : but he stretched his license far enough to rob every living thing he fell in with on his way. Filisola's Division marched, and the Texan Detachment returned to San Jacinto.

XXII.

Houston had given orders that a portion of the spoils should be divided equally among officers and men, and appointed three superior officers to execute his order.

A great number of incidents occurred during this period, which would serve to illustrate Houston's character. But we are obliged to omit their relation. A soldier, for example, had fled from the battle, declaring that all his comrades were killed at the first fire. When General Houston heard of the circumstance, he declared he would have him shot. His Captain importuned the Commander to let him go. "Why, yes, Captain," said the General, "I will let him off, but on condition that he will promise to marry into a valiant race and cross the breed. Under no other circumstances will I let him go."

XXIII.

The news of the victory spread by expresses all over the country, and not many days elapsed before the little steamboat Yellow Stone arrived from Galveston, bringing the (fugitive) "Government;" and they boldly marched right into the very presence of Santa Anna himself, who had been surrendered to them the moment of their arrival. But when they came from their hiding-places, they looked, of course, more like victors than fugitives. Houston, at once, surrendered everything into their hands but the money; this had been already divided among his gallant comrades.

Those who understand much of human nature, will not be surprised to hear that, from that day forward, these "fugitive statesmen" became the irrevocable foes of the brave man who had redeemed the nation which they had deserted in the hour of her darkest trial. They had fled, and Houston had fought; they knew the odium that would rest upon their names, and as Houston had been covered with the fame of a hero, they never could forgive him. An old philosopher once said, we never do forgive anybody whom we have injured. They did not express any aversion to, or condemnation of, Houston's acts—this would not have been entirely safe—but their future conduct showed most clearly, that, from that day, they were bent upon his destruction.

XXIV.

They began by treating him with manifest coolness. A proposition was even made by Robert Potter, Secretary of the Navy, to dismiss him from service, alleging no *cause*, but many *reasons*. Mr. Rusk, the Secretary of War, who, when the Cabinet fled to the sea-shore, had hurried to the camp, and toiled with its heroic soldiery, partaking of their privations and mingling in their perils—Mr. Rusk, the patriot-soldier, met the proposition in a spirited and indignant manner, and defeated their malicious machinations. The $12,000 had been distributed among the officers and men—Houston would receive no share— and this was a crime heavy enough to condemn him ; for the " Government" thought they needed it for their own purposes —and it is quite likely they did. But the " Government" did not dare to bring it forward as an accusation against the General, for they knew it would have roused the indignation of every man in the army.

XXV.

The Secretary of War wrote a letter to Houston, asking his views about the release of Santa Anna. He returned the following answer :

HEAD QUARTERS OF THE ARMY.
Camp San Jacinto, 3d May, 1836.

I have not the pleasure to know on what basis the Executive Government contemplate the arrangement with General Santa Anna, but I would respectfully suggest, that so far as I have been enabled to give my attention to the subject, the following points should have some weight :

The recognition of the Independence of Texas should be a *sine quâ non.* The limits of Texas should extend to the Rio Grande, and from the mouth, pursuing the stream to its most northwestern source, and from thence northeast to the line of the United States. Indemnity for all losses sustained by Texas during the war. Commissioners to be appointed for ascertaining the fact—one Mexican, one Texan, and one American. The guarantee to be obtained from the United States, for the fulfillment of the stipulation on the part of the contending parties. General Santa Anna to be retained as a hostage, with such other officers as the Government may think proper, until they are recognized or ratified by the Mexican Government. Immediate restoration of Texan or Mexican citizens, or those friendly to the cause of Texas, who may have been retained, with their property. Instantaneous withdrawal of all the Mexican troops from the limits of Texas. All property in Texas to be restored, and not molested by the troops or marauders in falling back. Cessation of all hostilities by sea and land. A guarantee for the safety and restoration of Mexican prisoners, so soon as the conditions shall be complied with. Agents to be sent to the United States to obtain the mediation of that government in the affairs of Mexico and Texas.

XXVI.

An attempt was made to heap upon Houston the odium both of Santa Anna's release and imprisonment after the treaty. But the attempt succeeded *only for a time, as falsehood always will,* and then these charges, with a thousand others, returned to plague their inventors. But in Texas they never were believed at all—there the facts were all known. It is a curious circumstance, that the report once so common in the United States, and even till now uncontradicted by Houston (for he never esteemed any lie worth contradicting), viz. that he played the coward at San Jacinto, and never would have fought at all if he had not been forced into battle by his soldiers ; that he fled from the field, or—as many had it—was never in the field at all,

—should have originated and been industriously circulated by the very men who had been the first to fly from danger, and leave the country in its darkest hour to take care of itself! And yet such was the case. But from all these "mountain lies" the name of Houston has come out fair and clear.

XXVII.

Volunteers had now rushed in from all quarters, where the news of the victory had spread ; and some brave men, who had come on by forced marches to join Houston's standard when he needed their help, had the misfortune, also, to reach the camp too late. Great activity, discipline and vigor became necessary. Houston was rendered perfectly helpless by his wound ; and it was believed that, even if he survived, he would not be again fit for service for many months. He signified his desire that General Rusk should succeed him in the command, and, as no other man would have been acceptable, he was selected by the Cabinet as Brigadier-General. From the arrival of the " Government," which, to the surprise of Santa Anna, had at last been found, the Mexican President had not been permitted to pay his customary morning visit to his courteous and humane captor ; and he had also been kept under the irritating and humiliating surveillance of the Cabinet. This unnecessary and indelicate severity (or, as Santa Anna himself termed it, " bad manners ") was a source of great pain and mortification to the captive General.

XXVIII.

Mr. Lamar was appointed Secretary of War, to fill the va-cancy in the Cabinet. After the failure to disgrace Houston, there was a cruel effort made to depress and harrow his feelings. Every petty artifice was resorted to, to torture the feelings of the enfeebled, wounded hero. A fine stallion, that had been

ridden in battle by Almonte, and captured by Karnes in the
pursuit of the enemy, had been presented by that gallant officer
to his General.   Although the animal was not of the spoils taken
on the field, Houston sent him to parade, and to be sold for the
benefit of the army.   By the united voice of the camp, he was
led up to his master, with an earnest entreaty that he would
retain him, and "they hoped, too," they said, "the General
would be able to ride him very soon."   He was a noble animal ; and as black as a raven.   After the army had confirmed the present of Karnes, the " Government " took the horse
from the Commander.   This was, certainly, a chivalrous act
towards a man who had saved the country, and was yet unable
to move, even on crutches.   We will state one more circumstance about these men, and then leave them to the odium which
rests on their name, for having tortured the feelings of a
brave and patriotic man.

XXIX.

When the army were taking up their line of march to the
west, with the settlements all broken up, and Houston was
without any of the comforts the wounded man so much needs;
when his surgeon had no medicine in the camp to give him, or
dress his wound with, and it became necessary for him to visit
New Orleans as the nearest place he could go to for medical aid
to save his life, and the steamboat Yellow Stone was ready to
sail for Galveston, with the Cabinet, and Santa Anna and suite ;
these gentlemen had, by common consent, agreed to leave the
wounded Commander-in-Chief to die—in sight of the field of San
Jacinto !   Houston could hardly believe this, and yet, when he
saw he was going to be left in his helplessness, he applied to the
Cabinet for a passage.   *The application was sternly refused !*
The captain of the boat, hearing of the circumstance, vowed it
should never leave the shore without it bore General Houston.

He tendered him a passage, and he was carried aboard by General Rusk and his brother David. He was also accompanied by a few of his staff ; among others his surgeon-general, Dr. Ewing. When the Doctor came on board, the Cabinet told him he could not accompany General Houston, and if he did, he would be discharged from the service, although they had not a shadow of authority to do it. The surgeon told Houston of this. "I am sorry, my dear fellow," said he, "for I have nothing to promise you in the future, and you know I am poor ; so you had better not incur the displeasure of the new Secretary of War." But the magnanimous man determined to follow his General, for he would not desert either a friend or a brave man in the hour of need. He went ; but the Cabinet was as good as its word ; he was dismissed at once from the army. He did not know then that Houston's star was so soon to come forth from its deep eclipse. When Santa Anna, who had wept when he was told that General Houston was not coming on board, saw him brought on, he ran to him, and embraced him with unfeigned joy.

XXX.

The boat reached Galveston Island, where, at the time, there was not a framed house, and remained there for the night. Some volunteers, who had arrived there from the United States, hearing the President, *ad interim*, as he went on shore, cast some reflections upon Houston, their officers immediately waited on the General, and offered to take him off, and do anything he might desire for his comfort or his honor. He was aware of the spirit the men felt, for they showed it too plainly to allow it to be mistaken, and he declined going just then. But he issued an order as he took leave of the men, and exhorted them to "render obedience to the authorities of the country, and not dishonor themselves by any disrespect to the Government, being assured that by honoring the ranks they would be qualified for the highest rights of citizenship." They discussed the subject of treating the Cabinet with great harshness ; but they at last yielded to Houston's commands and entreaties, and smothered their indignation. A single word from the wounded man would have crushed those restless and ambitious men, who had inflicted so much pain upon himself, and who afterwards brought so much misery and dishonor upon his country. But on this occasion, as on all others, he showed how well regard for law and order had fitted him to govern, and how easy it is for a truly great man to be magnanimous to his enemies.

XXXI.

We had nearly forgotten to mention the scene which was witnessed when Houston parted with the army. He was too feeble to speak to them, but he dictated the following touching address, which was read in camp as Army Orders.

Head Quarters, San Jacinto, May 5th, 1836.

COMRADES—Circumstances connected with the battle of the 21st render our separation, for the present, unavoidable. I need not express to you the many painful sensations which that necessity inflicts upon me. I am solaced, however, by the hope, that we shall soon be reunited in the great cause of Liberty. Brigadier-General Rusk is appointed to command the army for the present. I confide in his valor, his patriotism, his wisdom. His conduct in the battle of San Jacinto was sufficient to ensure your confidence and regard.

The enemy, though retreating, are still within the limits of Texas ; their situation being known to you, you cannot be taken by surprise. Discipline and subordination will render you invincible. Your valor and heroism have proved you unrivalled. Let not contempt for the enemy throw you off your guard. Vigilance is the first duty of a soldier, and glory the proudest reward of his toils.

You have patiently endured privations, hardships, and difficulties, unappalled; you have encountered odds of two to one of the enemy against you, and borne yourselves, in the onset and conflict of battle, in a manner unknown in the annals of modern warfare. While an enemy to your independence remains in Texas, the work is incomplete; but when liberty is firmly established by your patience and your valor, it will be fame enough to say, " I was a member of the army of San Jacinto."

In taking leave of my brave comrades in arms, I cannot suppress the expression of that pride which I so justly feel in having had the honor to command them in person, nor will I withhold the tribute of my warmest admiration and gratitude for the promptness with which my orders were executed, and union maintained through the army. At parting, my heart embraces you with gratitude and affection.

SAM HOUSTON, Commander-in-Chief.

It is said that when this touching and eloquent address was read to the army, the tears of the brave men fell upon the rifles on which they were leaning. Such was his parting with his companions in arms.

XXXII.

A small war vessel, belonging to the Republic, was sailing from Galveston to New Orleans. Houston applied for a passage with his staff. It was refused, although the war vessel carried several persons not belonging to the crew or the service. A little American schooner (the Flora) was also lying there. The General sent for the captain, and contracted with him for passage for himself and staff, to be paid when he could, for he had not a dollar of money to advance. During the entire campaign, neither he nor any one of his followers had received a shilling from the " Government," and all the funds he had of his own, he had generously devoted to the relief of the fugitive women and children, whose husbands and fathers had been slaughtered at the Alamo, or massacred with Fannin. Santa Anna now asked permission of the Cabinet to take leave of General Houston, but he was refused that privilege. Captain Chas. Hawkins, of the Texan Navy, stated these facts ; and he also said, that Santa Anna wept on the occasion.

XXXIII.

We pass over the long and tedious voyage of the little schooner. She arrived at the Balize in the night, and the next day, May 28th, was towed up to New Orleans. General Houston had now been nearly forty days without medicine or poultices; the bandages for his wound he had torn from the shirt he wore, till all but its bosom was gone—for he had given all he had away to the soldiers, as their necessities had before been greater than his own. He was now, as he supposed, in a dying state. He was so feeble, he could not even be raised up without fainting. In passing the English Turn, about eighteen miles below New Orleans, it was known by expresses in waiting, that Houston was on board, and it was the first confirmation of the news of the battle. It was Sunday, and the levee was black with the dense crowd which, as the intelligence spread through the city, had rushed together to see the wounded soldier., His friend, Colonel Wm. Christy, with whom he had served as lieutenant in his youth, had prepared for him in his house every comfort his situation required, and he was now eager to grasp the hand of his old comrade, and extend to him the most cordial welcome. Dr. Kerr, too, who had operated on his wounds just thirty years before, hastened to the vessel, where he found him lying on the deck. He fell upon him, and embraced him like a father. He, with Dr. Cenas, gave him every attention, and they saved his life; for they said if he had arrived a few hours later, he could not have been saved, since his wound had begun to show the first symptoms of mortification.

XXXIV.

The crowd on the boat was so great, it was in danger of sinking, and the throng so dense on the pier, it was a long time before he could be got ashore. An unsuccessful attempt had been made to lift him ashore, but it seemed he would die of torture before it could be done. At last, feeling that his strength was going, he rose on his crutches, and, by a desperate effort, got over the gunwale himself. He was immediately laid upon a litter, where he fainted away. In the meantime, bands of music had come down to the pier, and were playing martial airs, while the landing was being effected. The cot, which had been prepared, was brought up, and Houston, who seemed to be dying, was borne through the vast throng to the hospitable mansion of his friend, where this skeleton of disease and suffering at last found repose.

XXXV.

He remained about two weeks in New Orleans, and although he was far from being out of danger, yet his anxiety to return to Texas was so great, that he took passage to Nachitoches, on the Red River, this being the only practicable rout to his home in Eastern Texas. The fatigue and exposure of the journey were too much for his feeble health, and he was obliged to stop several days to recover his strength. But the first moment he was able, he travelled on to San Augustine, where he remained till the news came that the Cabinet had made a treaty with Santa Anna, and were resolved on his liberation. At the same time it was stated that the enemy was preparing for another campaign. Demonstrations of respect had been made, and dinners offered to him at New Orleans, Nachitoches, and San Augustine; but he declined all such compliments. The report

of the advance of the enemy had brought together a vast concourse of people at San Augustine.   Houston was taken to the
meeting, and, resting on his crutches, delivered an address,
which produced such an effect, that one hundred and sixty men,
in two days, took up their march for the frontier.

XXXVI.

Soon after, the General received intelligence that Colonels
Millard and Wheelock had been dispatched from the army then
at the Coleto, with a demand on the Cabinet that they should
deliver up Santa Anna into their hands for execution, reproach-
ing them for the neglect of their duty, and an order to arrest
President Burnet, and bring him to the Texan camp.   Houston
immediately dispatched by express to the army the following
Protest against their proceedings.

XXXVII.

Ayish Bayou, 26th July, 1836.

TO THE GENERAL COMMANDING THE ARMY OF TEXAS.

SIR,—I have just heard through a citizen, of the army, that it is the
intention to remove General Santa Anna to the army, and place him upon
his trial.   I cannot credit this statement; it is obviously contrary to the
true policy of Texas.   The advantages which his capture presented to us,
will be destroyed.   Disregard, if you will, our national character, and
place what construction you please upon the rules of civilized warfare,
we are compelled by every principle of humanity and morality, to abstain
from every act of passion or inconsideration that is to be unproductive of
positive good.   Execute Santa Anna, and what will be the fate of the
Texans who are held prisoners by the Mexicans—what will be the condition of the North Americans who are residing within the limits of
Mexico?   Death to them, and confiscation of their property is the least
that can be expected.   Doubtless, torture will be added to the catastrophe, when stimulated by ignorance, fanaticism, and the last expiring
struggle of the priesthood for power and dominion.   Texas, to be res-

pected, must be considerate, politic, and just in her actions. Santa Anna, living, and secured beyond all danger of escape, in the Eastern section of Texas (as I first suggested), may be of incalculable advantage to Texas in her present crisis. In cool blood to offer up the living to the manes of the departed, only finds an example in the religion and warfare of savages. Regard for one's departed friends should stimulate us in the hour of battle, and would excuse us, in the moment of victory, for partial excesses, at which our calmer feelings of humanity would relent.

The affairs of Texas connected with General Santa Anna, as President of the Republic of Mexico, have become matter of consideration to which the attention of the United States has been called, and for Texas, at this moment, to proceed to extreme measures, as to the merits or demerits of General Santa Anna, would be treating that Government with high disrespect, and I would respectfully add, in my opinion, it would be incurring the most unfortunate responsibility for Texas.

I, therefore, Commander-in-Chief of the army of the Republic, do solemnly protest against the trial, sentence, and execution of General Antonio Lopez de Santa Anna, President of the Republic of Mexico, until the relations in which we are to stand to the United States shall be ascertained.

SAM HOUSTON, COMMANDER-IN-CHIEF OF THE ARMY.

XXXVIII.

This protest had just the effect designed by the writer. The trial of Santa Anna was delayed, and Texas was saved from the disgrace and execration which so summary and barbarous a proceeding would have brought upon her name. Soon after this, Houston removed to Nacogdoches, where he remained under the influence of his wound till fall. But he was far from being idle, for the country was under a *quasi* state of martial law, and the exigency called for his constant vigilance and advice.

XXXIX.

In the mean time we must glance rapidly over the events

which were elsewhere taking place. The Cabinet perceiving that Houston's views, officially communicated to General Rusk, were founded upon the highest principles of policy, humanity, and justice, adopted them, in the main, in the treaty they made with Santa Anna, on the 14th of May. The President and his Cabinet were still at Velasco on the first of June, and the Texan schooner Invincible was anchored off the bar, in sight of the town, with Santa Anna and his suite on board, and the sailing orders of the vessel had been issued for her to proceed to Vera Cruz. Santa Anna wrote the following FAREWELL TO THE TEXAN ARMY.

XL.

" My friends! I have been a witness of your courage in the field of battle, and know you to be generous. Rely with confidence on my sincerity, and you shall never have cause to regret the kindness shown me. In returning to my native land, I beg you to receive the sincere thanks of your grateful friend. Farewell.

" ANT. LOPEZ DE SANTA ANNA.

" *Velasco, 1st June*, 1836."

XLI.

We know not what may be the opinions of others, but we are persuaded that Santa Anna never would have committed himself in *this* manner, when there was no necessity of doing it (for it was written *after* the vessel was under sailing orders), unless he really intended to redeem his pledge. For although he had entered into a solemn treaty, yet his own conscience and the whole world would have palliated any violation of that treaty (which was wrung from him by his captors ; for what will not a prisoner promise to buy his liberty ? they would have said), much sooner than they would have forgiven the violation of private pledges, voluntarily given by a *free* man. No such pledges were now necessary ; he was perfectly free to give or withhold them. Any bad faith subsequently manifested, would have been regarded as the blackest perfidy, and Texas would have gained more, perhaps (if she had *kept her* faith inviolate), by his treachery, than she would have lost ; for her honor and her magnanimity, and the perfidy of Santa Anna, would have won for her the sympathy of the civilized world ! But an event now took place which must be regarded as a public and lasting calamity to Texas.

XLII.

Several hundred volunteers from the United States arrived at Velasco, just as the Invincible was sailing. Their commander had not participated in the Texan struggle, and, in fact, he had yet no authority to order a drum beat in Texas. But he declared that the Invincible should not be allowed to lift her anchor. He was determined Santa Anna should be tried and executed ! It is unnecessary to indulge in any exclamations of censure for this use of military power. Popular feeling was on his side, and Mr. Lamar had already protested (in a voluminous paper) against Santa Anna's release. The President *ad interim* also yielded to this violation of the public faith, and although the treaty had been signed, sealed, and delivered, and Santa Anna had it with him on board, and the vessel was under sailing orders, yet he countermanded her orders, and sent a requisition on board for the Mexican President. Santa Anna was aware what had been the popular feeling towards him from the day of his capture ; and he undoubtedly believed that his life would be in danger in the hands of the President. Under such circumstances, he resolutely refused to go on shore. The order was repeated the next day, and it provoked a similar reply. On the afternoon of the third of June, armed men " visited the Invincible" (says Foote, 2 vol., p. 342), "for the purpose of

8

bringing off the Dictator, *dead or alive.*" Santa Anna remonstrated against the lawless outrage, and, like a brave man, declared he would die before he left. "All this time (p. 343) he lay on his back in his berth, and his respiration seemed to be exceedingly difficult." No wonder such a display of the boasted Anglo-Saxon faith should disturb the respiration even of a Mexican! All other means failing, a military commander ordered him to be *put in irons.* "When the irons were brought within his view, the prisoner jumped up, adjusted his collar, put on his hat, and stated his readiness to accompany us." (P. 343). And how else could a defenceless prisoner act, with a score of bayonets or bowie-knives at his breast? For our own part, we know of no circumstance in Santa Anna's history, so worthy of admiration as his conduct on this occasion ; nor do we know of any act of perfidy or cowardice equal to that evinced by his lawless aggressors.

Santa Anna was and is an ambitious, selfish, military chieftain, who has trampled on the Constitution, and blotted out the liberties of his country. But to his honor be it said, that *he* was not the first to violate the treaty of the 14th of May. Like a brave man, too, he boldly protested against the perfidy of the Texan cabinet.

XLIII.

He said : "I had embarked on the Texan schooner-of-war, the Invincible, on the 1st of June, after addressing a short farewell to the Texans, wherein I thanked them for their generous behavior, and offered my eternal gratitude. And I protest (5thly), for the act of violence committed on my person, and abuse to which I have been exposed, in being compelled to go on shore, merely because 130 volunteers, under the command of ———, recently landed on the beach at Velasco, from New Orleans, had with tumults and threats demanded that my person should be placed at their disposal, which took place on the very day the government received from Gen. Filisola the answer that he had strictly fulfilled what had been stipulated in the treaty. * * * Under these circumstances, I appeal to the judgment of civilized nations, to the consciences of the citizens who compose the Cabinet, and, above all, to the Supreme Ruler of the destinies of nations, who has placed the existence and happiness of nations on the faith of treaties and punctual fulfillment of engagements."

XLIV.

If Santa Anna is pointed to Goliad and the Alamo, his reply is, that such an appeal to the civilized world and to the Supreme Ruler of nations from the perpetrator of those massacres, only makes his sarcasm on the faith of the Texan Cabinet the more bitter.

If it be said that the President *ad interim* was *obliged* to yield to the clamor of the populace, who were thirsting for Santa Anna's blood, I reply that he could not have been *compelled*, by any mortal power, to write with his own hand the requisition for Santa Anna—had he been a man of nerve enough to fit him to hold the reins of power in revolutionary times. When Houston was asked what he would have done in the same circumstances, he said, " I would have regarded the faith of the nation under *any* circumstances, and before the mob should have laid hands on Santa Anna, they should have first drunk my blood." It now became perfectly certain that all the hopes of advantage for Texas, which Houston had borrowed from the treaty and the release of Santa Anna, were to be disappointed. He knew that the *only* reliance they had or could have, was upon his gratitude and sense of honor, and now the course his enemies had taken had dissolved all his obligations.

XLV.

After Mr. Lamar resigned his post as Secretary of War, the Cabinet appointed him Commander-in-Chief of the Army, over the heads of Generals Houston and Rusk. He immediately repaired to the army with his commission, and surrounded by his staff. The army was drawn up ; after addressing them, he requested an expression of their sentiments. They were anxious for Houston again to assume the command, and in the meantime were perfectly satisfied with General Rusk. But Mr Lamar wished some more decided demonstration, and they were ordered, by marching in different directions, to indicate their feelings towards the new commander. There were about 1800 troops in camp—less than one in eighteen voted for him, and the rest positively refused to serve under him ! He thus acquired the title of General, and got rid of the responsibilities of the command.

SECTION TENTH.

THE PRESIDENT.

I.

THE Government *ad interim* at last became disgusted with power. The people felt that when Houston was away, they had no one to repose on, and discontent became universal. Provision had been made by the Convention for the crisis, and writs were issued for the election of a President by the people of Texas.

II.

There were two candidates—General Stephen F. Austin, and Ex-Governor Henry Smith. They were both excellent men, particularly Gen. Austin, whom we have had occasion so often to mention with respect. Houston had been .importuned from the beginning to become a candidate ; but he had refused ; nor did he consent till twelve days before the election. He wished to retire from public life, for he believed there would be no necessity of firing another hostile gun in Texas, if the public councils were guided by firmness and wisdom. He had been unrelentingly persecuted, and his feelings outraged, just in proportion as he had devoted himself to the State. In retirement, he could be happy, and his country free. He was, therefore, disinclined to mingle in the turmoil of public life. But one motive at last overcame his objections. He believed the virulence of party to be such—that if either of the candidates should succeed, their cabinets would be made up exclusively of party men, which would endanger the stability of the administration. A government was to be created from chaos, without a dollar and without credit. The parties were pretty equally balanced, and there was great reason to fear that those out of power would so far embarrass the administration as to destroy its efficiency. He believed, that since he belonged to neither party, and possessed the confidence of the great mass of the people, he might still render signal service to the State, and he allowed his name to be used.

III.

At the announcement, the turbulence of party everywhere gave way to national enthusiasm. None but his enemies thought of opposing his election, and they were only a feeble clique of adventurers, who had rushed to Texas when her agitations began, hoping to win, in the turbulent scenes of Revolution, a notoriety they had in vain sought for in the calmer scenes of civic life. The Provisional Government of '35, and the Administration of '36, had proved they were incapable of holding the reins of Government over a frontier population. The people at last saw that they must place at the helm some man whose strong hand would steady the vessel through the boisterous surges. They knew there was but one man in Texas who could sway the mulitude, and when the hero of San Jacinto consented to accept the Presidency, they offered it to him by acclamation.

IV.

Houston had indeed displayed those rare qualities which make the great General. It now remained to be seen if he was endowed with those loftier and nobler qualities, which would fit him for the Cabinet—for a far more difficult task now remained,

"ADVANCING TO THE TABLE, HE DELIVERED AN EXTEMPORANEOUS INAUGURAL ADDRESS."

page 175

in the organization of a government which should secure peace, power, and prosperity at home, and command the respect of civilized nations—than it had been to win even the brilliant victory of San Jacinto. Senators and representatives were elected at the same time, and on the 3d of October (1836), the delegates assembled at Columbia, and the first Congress of the Republic of Texas was organized.

V.

On the morning of the 22d of the same month, the President *ad interim* tendered his resignation, and a resolution was immediately introduced, "that the inauguration take place at four o'clock this day." A committee from both houses waited upon the President elect, and at four o'clock, he was introduced within the bar of the House of Representatives. The Speaker " administered to him the oath of office, and then proclaimed Sam Houston President of the Republic of Texas." Advancing to the table, he delivered an extemporaneous Inaugural Address. We consider it important for the reader to be furnished with it entire, for it unfolds the policy of Houston's administration, and it could never have been spoken but by a statesman. It will be consulted by future times as the most important State paper that will be found in the early archives of Texas. We give it as it came from the reporter of the Congress.

VI.

MR. SPEAKER AND GENTLEMEN :

Deeply impressed with a sense of the responsibility devolving on me, I cannot, in justice to myself, repress the emotion of my heart, or restrain the feelings which my sense of obligation to my fellow citizens has inspired— their suffrage was gratuitously bestowed. Preferred to others, not unlikely superior in merit to myself, called to the most important station among mankind, by the voice of a free people, it is utterly impossible not to feel impressed with the deepest sensations of delicacy, in my present position before the world. It is not here alone, but our present attitude before all nations, has rendered my position, and that of my country, one of peculiar interest.

A spot of earth almost unknown to the geography of the age, destitute of all available resources, few in numbers, we remonstrated against oppression ; and when invaded by a numerous host, we dared to proclaim our Independence and to strike for freedom on the breast of the oppressor. As yet our course is onward. We are only in the outset of the campaign of liberty. Futurity has locked up the destiny which awaits our people. Who can contemplate with apathy a situation so imposing in the moral and physical world !

The relations among ourselves are peculiarly delicate and important ; for no matter what zeal or fidelity I may possess in the discharge of my official duties, if I do not obtain co-operation and an honest support from the co-ordinate departments of the government, wreck and ruin must be the inevitable consequences of my administration. If then, in the discharge of my duty, my competency should fail in the attainment of the great objects in view, it would become your sacred duty to correct my errors and sustain me by your superior wisdom. This much I anticipate— this much I demand.

I am perfectly aware of the difficulties that surround me, and the convulsive throes through which our country must pass. I have never been emulous of the civic wreath—when merited it crowns a happy destiny. A country, situated like ours, is environed with difficulties, its administration is fraught with perplexities. Had it been my destiny, I would infinitely have preferred the toils, privations, and perils of a soldier, to the duties of my present station. Nothing but zeal, stimulated by the holy spirit of patriotism, and guided by philosophy and reason. can give that impetus to our energies necessary to surmount the difficulties that obstruct our political progress. By the aid of your intelligence, I trust all impediments to our advancement will be removed ; that all wounds in the body politic will be healed, and the Constitution of the Republic derive strength and vigor equal to any emergency. I shall confidently anticipate the consolidation of Constitutional liberty. In the attainment of this object, we must regard our relative situation to other countries.

A subject of no small importance is the situation of an extensive frontier, bordered by Indians, and open to their depredations. Treaties of peace and amity and the maintenance of good faith with the Indians, seem to me the most rational means for winning their friendship. Let us abstain from aggression, establish commerce with the different tribes, supply their useful and necessary wants, maintain even-handed justice with them, and natural reason will teach them the utility of our friendship.

Admonished by the past, we cannot, in justice, disregard our national enemies. Vigilance will apprise us of their approach, a disciplined and valiant army will insure their discomfiture. Without discrimination and system, how unavailing would all the resources of an old and overflowing treasury prove to us. It would be as unprofitable to us in our present situation, as the rich diamond locked in the bosom of the adamant. We cannot hope that the bosom of our beautiful prairies will soon be visited by the healing breezes of peace. We may again look for the day when their verdure will be converted into dyes of crimson. We must keep all our energies alive, our army organized, disciplined, and increased to our present emergencies. With these preparations we can meet and vanquish despotic thousands. This is the attitude we at present must regard as our own. We are battling for human liberty ; reason and firmness must characterize our acts.

The course our enemies have pursued has been opposed to every principle of civilized warfare—bad faith, inhumanity and devastation marked their path of invasion. We were a little band, contending for liberty— they were thousands, well appointed, munitioned and provisioned, seeking to rivet chains upon us, or to extirpate us from the earth. Their cruelties have incurred the universal denunciation of Christendom. They will not pass from their nation during the present generation. The contrast of our conduct is manifest ; we were hunted down as the felon wolf, our little band driven from fastness to fastness, exasperated to the last extreme ; while the blood of our kindred and our friends, invoking the vengeance of an offended God, was smoking to high heaven, we met our enemy and vanquished them. They fell in battle, or suppliantly kneeled and were spared. We offered up our vengeance at the shrine of humanity, while Christianity rejoiced at the act and looked with pride at the sacrifice. The civilized world contemplated with proud emotions, conduct which reflected so much glory on the Anglo-Saxon race. The moral effect has done more towards our liberation, than the defeat of the army of veterans. Where our cause has been presented to our friends in the land of our origin, they have embraced it with their warmest sympathies. They have

8*

rendered us manly and efficient aids. They have rallied to our standard, they have fought side by side with our warriors. They have bled, and their dust is mingling with the ashes of our heroes. At this moment I discern numbers around me, who battled in the field of San Jacinto, and whose chivalry and valor have identified them with the glory of the country, its name, its soil, and its liberty. There sits a gentleman within my view, whose personal and political services to Texas have been invaluable. He was the first in the United States to respond to our cause. His purse was ever open to our necessities. His hand was extended in our aid. His presence among us, and his return to the embraces of our friends, will inspire new efforts in behalf of our cause.

[The attention of the Speaker and that of Congress was directed to Wm. Christy, Esq., of New Orleans, who sat by invitation within the bar.]

A circumstance of the highest import will claim the attention of the court at Washington. In our recent election, the important subject of annexation to the United States of America was submitted to the consideration of the people. They have expressed their feelings and their wishes on that momentous subject. They have, with a unanimity unparalleled, declared that they will be reunited to the Great Republican family of the North. The appeal is made by a willing people. Will our friends disregard it ? They have already bestowed upon us their warmest sympathies. Their manly and generous feelings have been enlisted on our behalf. We are cheered by the hope that they will receive us to participate in their civil, political, and religious rights, and hail us welcome into the great family of freemen. Our misfortunes have been their misfortunes—our sorrows, too, have been theirs, and their joy at our success has been irrepressible.

A thousand considerations press upon me ; each claims my attention. But the shortness of the notice of this emergency (for the speaker had only four hours' notice of the inauguration, and all this time was spent in conversation) will not enable me to do justice to those subjects, and will necessarily induce their postponement for the present.

[Here the President, says the reporter, paused for a few seconds and disengaged his sword.]

It now, sir, becomes my duty to make a presentation of this sword—this emblem of my past office. [The President was unable to proceed further ; but having firmly clenched it with both hands, as if with a farewell grasp, a tide of varied associations rushed upon him in the moment, his countenance bespoke the workings of the strongest emotions, his soul seemed to dwell momentarily on the glistening blade, and the greater part of the auditory gave outward proof of their congeniality of feeling. It was, in reality, a moment of deep and painful interest. After this pause, more eloquently impressive than the deepest pathos conveyed in language, the President proceeded.] I have worn it with some humble pretensions in defence of my country—and should the danger of my country again call for my services, I expect to resume it, and respond to that call, if needful, with my blood and my life.

VII.

The first step the President took in his administration, evinced his political forecast, and the broad national principles on which he intended to govern the country. He chose his two most important cabinet officers from his rivals for the Presidency ; General Austin, the incorruptible patriot, became Secretary of State, and Ex-Provisional Governor Henry Smith, Secretary of the Treasury. This selection was not only magnanimous, but it was high policy. The rancor of party subsided —the oil calmed the turbid waters. It evinced the important fact, that Houston had no party but country, and no aim bu' the public good.

VIII.

Everything was in chaos. The archives of the State were hurled loosely together in an old trunk—everything had to be done. Although the Cabinet was composed of apparently so discordant materials, yet all their proceedings were characterized by harmony, till Mr. Austin's death, which took place in a few months. He was deeply regretted by his people, for he was an upright, enlightened and purely patriotic man. Congress was now completely organized, and public business was being done in an orderly and efficient manner.

IX.

When Houston arrived at Columbia, for the inauguration, he found that his former captive, Santa Anna, was still retained a prisoner about twelve miles from the seat of government, under a guard of twenty men. Santa Anna sent word to Houston, that he would be glad if he could see him. He did not send to implore his release—for he seems to have given up nearly all hope of ever regaining his liberty. But in Houston he had found a magnanimous foe, and he wished to see his conqueror.

X.

The reader can readily imagine how Houston was affected by such a message from a prisoner, to whose release the government *ad interim* had pledged its most solemn faith, and then left him to drag out months of weary imprisonment. He still felt as he had in the beginning, and he determined to wipe out the stain of dishonor from the name of Texas.

"After a victory like San Jacinto," said he, " we could richly afford to be *magnanimous*—now the only question is, can we not afford to be just ?"

He knew, besides, that there were no means in the government to support captives. It had been in a state of *quasi* dissolution for months. Santa Anna and his friends had been living on a mere pittance, destitute of the comforts, and almost of the necessaries of life. Houston took with him several gentlemen to visit the prisoner. Those who were present have represented their meeting as affecting. Santa Anna, after the custom of his nation, opened his arms and came forward to meet his visitor. Houston, whose great heart was large enough to hold even his enemies, received him in like manner, and as the worn captive rested his head on Houston's broad breast (for he hardly came up to his shoulder), they say that the two generals wept together—the Mexican at the recollection of his reverses —the Virginian sympathizing with the man he had vanquished.

XI.

Through Almonte, who still acted as their interpreter, and in the presence of Patton and others, Santa Anna appealed to his conqueror to interpose his power in his behalf, and adverted to the letter he had himself written to Gen. Jackson, and inclosed to Houston at Nacogdoches. Jackson had answered his letter in very kind terms, and passed a high eulogium upon his friend Gen. Houston, for his magnanimity towards his captive. Indeed, Gen. Jackson often declared that Houston deserved and would receive as much honor from all great and good men, for his treatment of Santa Anna after the victory, as for the victory itself. "Let those who clamor for blood," said the brave old hero, " clamor on. The world will take care of Houston's fame."

XII.

Houston was not yet inaugurated, but he assured the Mexican general that he would remember him. Col. Christy (who bore Texas on his heart, and was jealous of her honor) and other generous men also, had sent some comforts to Santa Anna a short time before, and Houston and some of his friends dined with him that day, and then they parted. Santa Anna wrote to Houston after his return from Columbia. The communication was laid before Congress, and his release solicited. The matter was referred to committees of both houses, and a report was made of a most inflammatory character. In a secret session, the Senate passed a resolution requiring his detention as a prisoner. Houston responded in a calm, dignified veto, showing the impolicy of a longer detention—the probability of his being assassinated (as one attempt had already been made before Houston's arrival), and that if he were to die from violence or disease, Texas never would escape the odium of his death. The Senate reversed their decision, and referred the matter to the discretion of the President. He expressed the belief that if Santa Anna was restored to his country, he would keep Mexico in commotion for years, and Texas would be safe.

XIII.

Houston determined at once to release him on his own responsibility. He informed him that if he wished to visit Washington, as Gen. Jackson had requested, he should have an escort, chosen by himself. Santa Anna returned his thanks by the messenger, and requested that Cols. Hockley and Bee, and Major Patton, be allowed to attend him. About the 25th of November, the escort departed, and Houston went with them to take his final leave of the liberated captive. The parting took place—and the little party set out, on fine horses, for the Sabine. They lost their way in the prairie, and it so happened that they were compelled, in regaining it, to pass over the battle ground of San Jacinto ! When Santa Anna saw the bones of his soldiers whitening on the field, he was deeply affected, and the gentlemanly men who attended him, seeming not to observe his agitation, rode leisurely on and left the deserted General to indulge his feelings on the field of his slain.

XIV.

Santa Anna is a great man. He has a Mexican education and Mexican principles ; but an American intellect of high order.

He is a great General. He has a fine face—a rather long, but well-shaped head—black hair and eyes, and a *perfect form*—he is about five feet and eight or nine inches high—his elocution is rich, and characterized by considerable fire—his eye is quick, but firm, and his manners and address are worthy of a prince.

XV.

In the beginning of his Administration, the President appointed Colonel William H. Wharton, Minister to Washington, with instructions to commence negotiations with General Jackson for the annexation of Texas to the United States. Soon after, Memucan Hunt, Esq., was appointed to act in concert with him. During the summer of 1836, General Jackson had dispatched a confidential agent to Texas. He explored its Territory, scrutinized its Government, mingled in its society, made himself familiar with its resources, and reported fully to the President. His Report satisfied the President and his Cabinet, that Texas was entitled, by the Law of Nations, to a recognition of her Independence ; and although his own sympathies were with that people in their struggle, and from the hour they achieved their independence, he never had a doubt they would one day be annexed to the United States, yet he wisely withheld the expression of such an opinion, and did not even press upon Congress the Recognition. In his Message of the 5th of December, 1836, after assigning the most satisfactory reasons, he says, " Our character requires that we should neither anticipate events, nor attempt to control them." And alluding to the desire of Texas for annexation, he says : " Necessarily a work of time, and uncertain in itself, it is calculated to expose our conduct to misconstruction in the eyes of the world."

XVI.

On the twenty-second of the same month, the President, in another message, after discussing the question, expresses his opinion that it would be *impolitic*, yet, to recognize Texas as an Independent State, and then proposes to acquiesce in the decision of Congress. The question was not brought up again till the 12th of January, 1837, when Mr. Walker, Senator from Mississippi, introduced the following resolution :

Resolved, That the State of Texas having established and maintained an independent Government, is capable of performing those duties, foreign and domestic, which appertain to independent Governments; and it appearing that there is no longer any reasonable prospect of the successful prosecution of the war, by Mexico, against said State, it is expedient and proper, and in conformity with the Laws of Nations, and the practice of this Government in like cases, that the independent political existence of that State be acknowledged by the Government of the United States.

XVII.

The Senate was not prepared for immediate action on the question, and Mr. Walker knew it. He was aware that the strange and disgraceful war which the American, Press had so generally waged against the interests and advancement of Texan Liberty, had colored the prejudices, and would control the votes of Senators,—and he determined to bide his time. Mr. Walker moved that his Resolution be made the order of the day for the 18th of January ; but when the time came, it was crowded aside. Several ineffectual attempts were made to decide the question, and at last it was brought up on the 1st of March for final action. An able and brilliant debate followed ; "Messrs. Preston, Crittenden, Clay, and Calhoun, all sustained the Mississippi Senator with the persuasive power of their eloquence. Mr. Clay spoke of Texas with generous enthusiasm, and unhesitatingly declared that her Constitution, as a whole, was superior to that of the United States. How different might have been the political fortunes of that truly great and patriotic man, and the fortunes of his party, if he had, to the end, pursued the same high and sagacious policy towards that beautiful country! But his course, as well as Mr. Van Buren's, only furnishes us with another impressive illustration how few great men, even, are able to withstand the clamor of party in turbulent times. The measure prevailed by a small majority.

XVIII.

For the success of the measure, Texas was indebted to the efforts of Mr. Walker ; and his course in the affair entitled him to the regards of the entire nation. The day will come, too, when the mists that have obscured the gaze of the people and their statesmen, shall have cleared away, and the name of the Mississippi Senator will everywhere be mentioned with honor and with gratitude. Texas will build his monument, and give it a conspicuous place in the temple she will erect for those who proved themselves her friends in the day of trial. The grateful Republic commissioned the portrait of Mr. Preston, and the bust of Mr. Walker, for her Capitol.

XIX.

The last time General Jackson ever put his pen officially to paper, was to sign the Resolution recognizing Texas an Independent State. Such was the earliest fruit of the Mission of those intelligent and accomplished men whom General Houston commissioned to Washington. We have read their correspondence with the two Governments, and we have seldom perused abler State Papers.

XX.

In March, 1837, the seat of Government was removed from Columbia on the Brazos, to Houston, which stands on the highest point of navigation on the Bayou, that empties into Galveston Bay. There was but one house in Houston. It was a cabin just erected, and in it the President of the new nation took up his abode. His floor was the ground, where the grass was growing. But population rushed in, and in a short time comfortable public buildings were erected.

XXI.

Houston's policy in regard to the future, was to obtain annexation if possible. If this could not be done, he was determined to conduct the Government on principles that would secure confidence abroad, and inspire hope at home. The proposition for annexation had been rejected by our Government, and such was the state of feeling at the time in the United States, Houston had no expectation of the early success of that grand measure, in whose consummation the keen-sighted statesmen of both countries saw so many elements of mutual power and prosperity. He was therefore determined to lay the foundations of the Texan Republic deep and strong—to husband its resources—never to cripple the State with a public debt—to harmonize warring factions—to be the ruler of the Nation, and not of a party or a *clique*.

XXII.

The cultivation of friendly relations with the powerful and warlike savage tribes on the frontier, he regarded as one of the most important objects of his administration. This ferocious population not only outnumbered all the inhabitants of Texas, but they could not be conquered. The Camanches, the most numerous and savage tribe, live in the saddle. They can move with their women and children with great celerity whenever and wherever their necessities or their passions carry them ; they can make their incursions without the possibility of pursuit from their enemies. They are hordes of barbarians, as ferocious as Cossacks, and as fleet as the Bedouins of the desert. And yet, such was Houston's knowledge of the Indian character, and so rigidly did he regard the letter and spirit of his treaties with those fearful tribes, he saved the Republic from their incursions, and made them venerate and love his name.

XXIII.

In a former part of this work, we have given the views of Houston on the subject of our treatment of the Indians. Those views have been regarded by many as utterly chimerical ; and yet if we had space we could show, that during his two administrations in Texas, he carried them out successfully ; and he has often declared that, in no instance where he had an opportunity of giving the Indians evidence that he intended to treat them with good faith and with common justice, did he experience the slightest difficulty in winning their friendship, and preserving their perpetual alliance. In all these negotiations, the great secret of his power over those wily red men, consisted in two things. His associations with the Indians gave him a complete knowledge of their character—and he treated them on the great principles of humanity and justice.

XXIV.

And yet the Government was destitute of all ordinary means of support. It had not a dollar, nor could loans be obtained. An army was in the field, but it could not be maintained. When

Congress met at Houston, General Felix Huston, who commanded the army, hurried to the place. He had projected a grand campaign against Matamoras. Every man who felt jealous of the influence of the President joined in the scheme. The army now numbered over 2,400 men. The President foresaw the consequences of these movements. There was no money in the Treasury, or means, or currency except promissory notes, struck on common paper. It was clearly impossible to conduct a campaign. The President saw what the upshot of this matter would be, if something were not done at once, and he resorted to a sagacious expedient. Col. Rodgers, now left in command of the army, had caused it to be understood that, if the volunteers did not get justice, he would march with them to the Seat of Government, "chastise the President, kick Congress out of doors, and give laws to Texas."

XXV.

At this crisis the President determined to cut the evil up by the roots. General Felix Huston had occasionally indulged his men in what he called a *Saturnalia*, where murders had occurred in consequence of the brutal intoxication of the men. One evening, from intelligence of what was doing in Congress (for he never visited the House, except at the opening or close of the Session), Houston directed the Secretary of War to be ready to start the next morning, at two o'clock, for the Camp. He handed him sealed orders, to be opened in the Camp, and ordered him to go there with all possible dispatch. These orders required the Secretary to furlough the army by companies, until they were reduced to six hundred men. The first company was furloughed to march to Dimitt's Landing, on Matagorda Bay; the second to the mouth of the Brazos; the third to Galveston; and this process was continued till the reduction was made. His

object was to give them an opportunity to get to the United
States by water, and thus relieve the country from apprehensions.
The furloughs given to the men were unlimited, but they were
liable to be recalled at any time by Proclamation ; and if they
did not report themselves in thirty days after the Proclamation,
they were to be considered deserters, and treated as such.
Houston could not disband the army, for there was nothing to
pay them off with ; and he had been taught a lesson by the
attempt of General Washington to disband the army of the
North.   And yet, so entirely had all subordination been broken
down—daring scenes of violence were so constantly occurring
at the camp—so many lawless and desperate men were banded
together, to commit high-handed depredations—that the whole
country began to suffer the most serious apprehensions.   Houston
manifested no alarm, but the course he took bespoke his fears.
He was determined that the army should be disbanded, and he
accomplished his purpose in his own way.

XXVI.

When the various companies reached their destinations, no
longer held together by the bond which union had before given,
they thought they had seen enough of military life.   They had
fared roughly ; and their surplus chivalry had so completely
oozed out of the holes in their coats, that they no longer had
courage enough to be dangerous ; and—fearing they would not
get out of the country before the Proclamation was issued—
they made the best of their way to the United States.   In thirty
days they had all disappeared ; and when the *finale* was known
throughout the country, every man felt that Houston had saved
the nation from the deepest peril.   It was, in fact, a stroke of
bold, but sagacious policy, which none but a man like him would
have dared to attempt.   General Felix Huston was plotting

at the Capital; but before he knew what the President was doing, his army was disbanded.

XXVII.

About this time a Land Law was passed, under which all the troubles about *titles* have grown up. Its object was speculation, and many voted for it anticipating enormous gains. Houston vetoed it in one of his ablest state papers. But his veto was not supported, and the law went into operation. A few years showed its malign and fatal fruits. It opened the door to all sorts of frauds, and was a fruitful source of lasting litigation. This was but a single specimen of the recklessness of legislation in the Congress of Texas. (During Houston's two terms he issued not less than eighty vetoes.) Had there not been a firm and intelligent statesman at the head of the Government, no man can tell where such Congresses would have carried the Nation.

XXVIII.

Another Law was passed, authorizing an excessive issue of Promissory Notes. This also the President vetoed, and he declared that if the measure prevailed, the paper would soon depreciate ten to one. He arrested this fatal proceeding for a time. It passed under the administration of his successor, and his prophecy was abundantly fulfilled.

XXIX.

During the year 1837, the country was agitated by occasional alarms of Mexican and Indian invasions—but Houston was on the alert, and nothing of the kind took place. The utmost confidence in his administration prevailed among the people; and the beautiful spectacle was presented of an industrious and

increasing population, which had just recovered from the shock
and the devastation of a powerful invading army, and environed
with Mexican and Savage foes, quietly and successfully prose-
cuting the arts of peace. Houston proclaimed trade and intercourse between Mexico and Texas, and caused his Proclamation
to be printed and circulated in both languages. Trade grew up
rapidly ; the frontier counties were repopulated ; and the tide of
emigration was gradually flowing towards the Mexican borders.
Caravans of horses and mules came into Texas, with large
quantities of silver and merchandise ; good feeling was fast
growing up, and continued to increase. Men, on both sides of
the line, were now anxious for peace. The Mexican people had
nothing to gain in battle, and had the renewal of hostilities
depended on the vote of the Mexican population, both countries
would have been blessed with lasting peace.

XXX.

We must now close our brief account of Houston's first
administration. The proposition for annexation had been
steadily pressed upon the attention of the Government at
Washington. But the Texan ministers received little encouragement, and as Texas could promise herself no advantage
from further negotiations, Houston withdrew the proposition.
He believed that any further attempts to consummate that
great measure, would prejudice Texas in the eyes of other
nations ; and in withdrawing the proposal, his conduct met the
approval of the nation.

XXXI.

His Presidential term closed the 12th of December, 1838.
He went out of office, leaving a Government perfectly
organized ; with officers of ability, integrity, and economy in

every department of the State. The nation was not more than a million and a half in debt, with about $600,000 of Promissory Notes in circulation. Texas had peace with the Indians and commerce with Mexico. The feuds between the two nations were dying away, and the Promissory Notes were at par. This circumstance is, perhaps, the clearest and most convincing proof of the great ability and integrity with which Houston had conducted the Government. There was, little specie in the country—how these notes were ever to be redeemed the people did not know—but they said, "As long as Old Sam is at the helm the ship is safe." They were voyaging through stormy seas, but they knew they were sailing with Cæsar.

XXXII.

No man was ever confronted with greater difficulties in the beginning of his administration—for the mild but firm sway of Constitutional Law had to be substituted in the place of anarchy and confusion, over a reckless people who had long been accustomed to the unrestrained liberty of the frontier, where no man looked for protection but in his own right arm. During these revolutionary times, too, even in the older settlements, the ordinary course of justice had been suspended, and it was no strange thing that such men should not at once yield to the high supremacy of Constitutional Law. The very same elements of character, which have long made the Anglo-Saxons the most law-abiding people on the globe, have always made them the most lawless frontier-men. Men who choose their homes in the distant forest or prairie, are slow to transfer their protection from their rifles, which never miss fire, to tardy juries, which seldom mete out justice. How long was it before that wonderful People, that first scared the wild beasts from the solemn forests of the Tiber, voted to abide by the awards of the Temple of Justice ! And how many centuries did our ancestors roam over the beautiful Island of Britain, dressed in the skins of wild beasts, before they would listen to the stern utterances of Judicial Tribunals ! But Houston could sway those reckless frontier settlers by the mild sceptre of Civil Law, as easily as he had swayed them by the stern despotism of the camp.

XXXIII.

But while he was sucessfully accomplishing those benign changes, and rearing the noble structure of civil government, he was not only harassed by petty intrigues, but confronted with formidable combinations. The same clique of small but ambitious men, who had, from the beginning, busied themselves in inventing means to undermine the castle which they could not overthrow, while Houston was bleeding on the field, or toiling anxiously in the Cabinet, finding all their intrigues fruitless, at last cemented themselves as well as they could, into one organized conspiracy, bent upon his destruction. Their history would be a story of all that is low in faction, and mean in selfishness. But we have neither time nor inclination to chronicle their doings—nor would we snatch them from the oblivion to which they have hastened.

XXXIV.

Houston's conduct met with the warmest approval throughout the country, and he would have been the almost unanimous choice of the people, had he been eligible to the office, the next term. But the 2d Section of the Third Article of the Constitution declared—that, " The First President elected by the people shall hold his office for the term of two years, and shall

9

be ineligible during the next succeeding term." An accident gave the Presidency to Mr. Lamar. Just before the election his rival died !—and no other candidate was brought forward.

XXXV.

It had been said that the President Elect would be the idol of the State, and that Houston's power was gone. The hour of his resignation came, and the largest concourse of people, ever seen in Texas, gathered. An attempt had been made to prevent the retiring President from delivering his Valedictory Address—the arrangements of the Inauguration Committee utterly excluded him. But when the fact was known, a burst of indignation went up from the vast multitude—the Committee and their arrangements were all set aside, and the name of the Hero of San Jacinto was on every tongue.

XXXVI.

When he came forward in the porch of the Capitol, and the people gazed upon his lofty, ample, and heroic form, relieved against the portrait of Washington, suspended behind him, a wild shout of enthusiasm rent the sky. He spoke three hours, and we have been told by those who heard him, that the dense thousands before him swayed to and fro under the impetuous storm of his eloquence, like a forest swayed by a strong wind. He had unrolled the scroll of the history of Texas—he portrayed her future policy, and dwelt upon her great destiny if that policy were pursued. He enjoined most solemnly good faith with all nations—economy in the government and in individuals—the cultivation of peace with the Indians—he warned the people against faction and the rancor of party spirit, and he implored them not to treasure up their hopes in annexation or

treaties, but to rely upon their own public and private virtue—
to be just and magnanimous with all men and with all nations.

And in conclusion, when he took his farewell of the people he
loved, he extended his broad arms, and poured down upon them
from his great heart the benediction of the patriot, and the
soldier, as the tears streamed from his face. When he ceased,
all was still but the deep murmur of subdued feeling, and that
vast multitude of frontiersmen all in tears !

SECTION ELEVENTH.

THE LEGISLATOR.

I.

THE new President began his administration by opposing everything that had been pursued and recommended by Houston. In his Inaugural Address he recommended the extermination of the Indians—pronounced a violent Philippic against Annexation—advocated the establishment of a huge National Bank, and inculcated a *splendid* Government.

II.

The first appropriation for frontier defence was one and a half million of Treasury Notes, and another half million for the civil list—without a dollar to base the issues upon. A regular army of two Regiments was to be raised for exterminating the frontier Tribes. A law was passed to remove the Seat of Government to some point N. W. of the San Antonio Road. Commissioners were appointed by Congress from its own body, contrary to the Constitution, to perform this act. The entire object of the movement was speculation. With land scrip, which they had procured, and certificates of head-rights granted to settlers, they dispatched Surveyors to locate land around the spot where Austin now stands—at the extremest settlement of the Republic even at this day. The expense of removal, with the erection of suitable buildings, caused an additional issue of Promissory Notes. The new Capital was so far from the settlements, that the plank had to be carried thirty miles.

III.

The Republic soon lost confidence in the Administration—the depression of the currency naturally followed. And yet, in this state of embarrassment of the finances, and while Texas was at peace with Mexico, the President caused a proposition to be introduced into both Houses, to conduct an Expedition to Santa Fé, through a wilderness and Prairie more than five hundred miles. The proposition was made in both Houses at the same time, and by both rejected. But the President ordered the Expedition during the recess of Congress in 1840, and upwards of three hundred armed men started on a warlike expedition to a distant country. Its disasters are too well known to need a relation. The President appointed a Governor for Santa Fé—a Custom House Officer and a Military Commandant, and organized a Territorial Government. All his plans subsequently fell into the hands of the enemy, when the men were captured, and were a moving cause for the cruelty with which they were treated. The Expedition flooded the country with another enormous issue of paper "*promises* to pay money," unauthorized by the Constitution or Congress. The horses on that Expedition cost, on an average, a thousand dollars each, the currency of the President had become so depreciated. Costly arms and munitions of war had been abstracted from the public arsenal by Presidential edict—the country was robbed of a large number of its most chivalrous men—the public wagons and means of transportation were laid hold of, and a piece of artillery, with Mirabeau B. Lamar inscribed on its breech, dragged through the Prairies that immense distance, to become the trophy of the enemies of Texas, and afford an illustration of the stupidity of the President, and the degradation of the nation.

IV.

This expedition revived the hostilities between Texas and Mexico, which, but for it, would have slept, perhaps, for ever. Houston had left the two countries really at peace, and the sole cause we have ever been able to ascertain for the renewal of hostilities, was this silly and lamentable Expedition. It is to be remarked, that for some time previous to this Expedition, Mr. Lamar had sent Commissioners to Gen. Arista, and his object is supposed, by his friends, to have been to propose a Union of the Northern Provinces with Texas, forming a great Power, over whose government he was to be placed. The sagacious Arista took advantage of the incompetency of his friend, and returned Commissioners. They were in Austin when the Santa Fé Expedition took up its line of march, and witnessed the foolish display. What passed between " the high contracting parties," is not known with certainty, for the facts have never been officially disclosed. The world knows the result. Arista seems to have given into the plan, for one thing is certain, the Expedition started from Austin with a guide, who had long resided in Mexico, and spoke the language perfectly ; and the commanding officers charged him with their betrayal at San Miguel and Santa Fé. When the guide got them many days in the wilderness, and the miseries of their situation began to press heavily on them, he abandoned them in their calamity, and never was heard of again. The object of Arista doubtless was to have them conducted into the solitudes of the wilderness, and there left to perish—if this should fail, the authorities of San Fé, being duly informed, were to receive, betray and then capture them. The blame of these proceedings is to be cast upon the President.

V.

During his administration, he sent two ministers to Vera Cruz—but neither of them was received ; and they returned, to the disgrace of Texas. There was no method or consistency in anything he did. That he wished to be distinguished and wished well to his adopted country, there is no doubt ; but he was a feeble and puerile statesman. In civil affairs, he was a great schemer. One day, his hobby was a National Bank ; another, it was a great National Road ; a third, it was an alliance with Mexico, by his marrying the daughter of some distinguished public functionary of that country ; for the diplomatist supposed his alliance with some opulent family would be tantamount to an alliance between the two nations. One day, he must make war upon *one* tribe of Indians ; the next day, upon another. His first great exploit, when his administration began, was to attack the Cherokees and drive them from their possessions between the Nueces and Sabine rivers, where they had been settled longer than the Texan colonists themselves. They had been invited by Mexico from the United States, and land had been assigned, and great inducements held out to them. They had settled there, and were quietly and inoffensively pursuing their avocations. In 1835, the Consultation had guaranteed to that tribe undisturbed possession of their territory, by a solemn assurance, signed by each member of the Consultation. A treaty had been subsequently made with the tribe (recognizing the same rights and guarantee) by Houston and other Commissioners, and this treaty had been ratified by the Consultation. The Convention which declared their Independence, had recognized this as well as all other acts of the Consultation as valid. A more solemn ratification of a treaty could not have been made.

VI.

Mr. Lamar began his administration by carrying out that section of his Inaugural Address, in which he had recommended the extermination of the Indians. The Cherokees were a peaceful, industrious, and profitable community. The arts had made considerable progress among them, and they lived nearly as comfortably as white men. During the hostilities with Mexico, they had been prevented by the influence of Houston and Rusk from going over to the enemy, and they had made great advances in civilization during Houston's Presidency. They looked upon the Texans as their friends, and Houston as their "Father." With a force of 700 men, a portion of whom had fought at San Jacinto, Lamar commenced his war of extermina tion against "Houston's *pet* Indians.' His force was some five times superior, and of course he carried ruin to the poor Red men's homes !

This treatment of the Cherokees and other tribes spread scenes of rapine and murder from the Red River to the Rio Grande. Even the President's two regiments of regulars in the field could not secure frontier protection.

VII.

In the disorders of Yucatan, when a separation from Mexico was spoken of, Mr. Lamar entered into a treaty of alliance with a minister sent to him for that purpose, and, without the concurrence of the Senate or the ratification of the treaty, ordered the Texan Navy to sail to the coast of Yucatan. That Province was then an integral part of Mexico, and had not proclaimed revolt or independence.

VIII.

Such were some of the acts of this puerile administration. We should not have glanced at them, even in so brief a manner, had it not been necessary to give the reader an idea of the state of the country when Houston's second term began. Lamar, who had found the Government perfectly organized, succeeded in reducing the country to the very verge of ruin. All the difficulties that had lain in the way of the advancement of Texas, Houston had successfully overcome. Disinterested and sagacious spectators of the progress of affairs beyond the Sabine, have often been heard to say, that in no portion of the world, had civil government ever been established and consolidated in so short a space of time. This was as much the work of Houston, as the victory of San Jacinto had been, although in both instances he was surrounded and aided by brave and true men, or he never could have done it. He left the domestic and foreign relations, the finances and the administration of law, the agriculture and the commerce of Texas, all in a sound, peaceful, flourishing state.

IX.

When Mr. Lamar left the administration, what was the state of the nation? He had committed outrages upon peaceful Indian tribes, and kindled the flames of savage war all along the borders of Texas. He had sent a hostile marauding Expedition into the very heart of the Mexican Provinces, and sent the navy to aid a revolting territory in making war upon Mexico, and now she was rousing all her force for a new invasion of Texas. He had quadrupled the national debt, and squandered the public treasure, till Texan securities depreciated ten to one. The people had lost all respect for the Government, and confidence in its stability. The mail routes had been broken up, profligacy prevailed, and the social compact began to be regarded by the orderly and patriotic everywhere as virtually dissolved.

X.

But Lamar's term had nearly expired, and the eyes of all men, who surveyed with gloomy forebodings the ruin that seemed to threaten the country, were now turned once more anxiously upon Houston. Even the lawless and the desperate began to fear the result of their crimes, and with a united voice, the man, who had already twice saved the country, was called a third time to the helm. Houston was one of the few men who believed that the Nation and the Government could be saved, and he came forward to the rescue. No Conventions were obliged to nominate him. There was an almost universal feeling that no other man could save Texas, and Texas made him her President for the second time, the very first hour the Constitution would allow her to do it.

XI.

During Lamar's Administration, Houston had consented to represent his District in the Congress of 1839–40, and again in 1840–41, and it was well that he had, for he not only arrested the tide of evil—*he prevented a dissolution of the Government.* On a certain occasion, after a stormy debate, Congress was about to adjourn *sine die.* The members publicly proclaimed that all hope of carrying on the Government was gone, and they were determined to end the farce by going home. Houston rose in the midst of the tempest, as the members were leaving their seats, and addressed the Speaker. There never was a time when *that* man could not get a hearing, and the rush to the door stopped. " Let us hear old Sam," was the voice on every side.

XII.

The crowd began to return—members gradually resumed their seats and dropped their hats—they pressed up around him—the House became still, and not ten minutes went by before nothing was heard throughout the hall but the rich, deep voice that had echoed over the field of San Jacinto. No idea of the speech can be given but by telling the result. He closed by reading a resolution, " that the House adjourn till to-morrow morning at the usual hour," and not a member voted against it ! They flocked around him, and so universal was the feeling, that but for him the Government would have gone to pieces, that even his old enemies seized him by the hand, and thanked him " for saving the country."

SECTION TWELFTH.

AGAIN PRESIDENT.

I.

HE was inaugurated the second time, on the 13th of December, 1841. His Message was hardly delivered before the news came of the capture of the Santa Fé Expedition. This was the first greeting he had, in office, of the fatal results of the policy of his predecessor. He, however, began immediately to bethink himself of the redemption of the unfortunate men who had been deluded away into the wilderness—for the lives of Texan soldiers seemed to be as dear to him as they could have been if they had been his own children.

II.

The Government was now in an infinitely worse state than it had been when he took the reins five years before. Then it was a chaos—now it was a *ruin*. The body politic had fallen into premature and inflammatory decay. It was not a disease only, but a *relapse*. The Treasury was not only empty, but millions in debt ; and not another dollar could be borrowed in Christendom. The Promissory Notes and Liabilities of the Government depreciated *ten* to *one*, and they were *postponed*, but not *repudiated*. The money had been squandered, but the debt must be paid. But Texas could at that time have no more paid it than Parliament could pay the Debt of England. But something had to be done. Houston proposed a new currency called the Exchequer System—its entire issues were not to exceed $200,000. He had asked as a guarantee for their redemption, the Customs of the country, and certain tracts of lands, amounting to about three million acres. While in Congress, he had procured an act to be passed, declaring these lands not subject to location. But now the private interests of members were to be interfered with, and although Congress hypothecated the Customs, they would not pledge the lands.

III.

The President was fully aware of the opposition that was combining against him. The same hostile clique which had attempted to ruin him whenever he was in power, and who had come so near ruining the country when they had power themselves, were now determined to control the appointments under the new administration. But all attempts to constrain his policy proved as ineffectual as they had hitherto done. He chose for his cabinet officers men in whom he had unlimited confidence, and they were among the most enlightened and firm statesmen of Texas. Mr. Jones, afterwards President, became Secretary of State ; Col. Hockley, a warm patriot and a devoted friend of Houston in all his struggles, Secretary of War and Marine ; Wm. H. Dangerfield, Secretary of the Treasury, and G. W. Terrell, Attorney-General. During these turbulent times, when prominent men declared openly that they would ruin Houston's administration, even if they had to do it by a revolution, multitudes of broken-down speculators and politicians from the United States were continually flocking into Texas ; and as they found little chance of winning distinction in the new field they had chosen, they joined the ranks of the opposition, and devoted themselves zealously to the ruin of the State.

IV.

But Houston had marked out his policy, and he went calmly and firmly on to its execution. His first measure was to dispatch a minister to Washington, to open negotiations for the annexation of Texas. His first object was annexation—if this failed, his next was the recognition of the independence of Texas by Mexico; and if he failed in both, he was resolved to open negotiations with France and England, and enter into some treaty or alliance which would secure peace to Texas, extend her commerce, and advance her prosperity. His next movement was to recall the Navy, which Mr. Lamar had dispatched to help on a revolt in Yucatan.

V.

In the meantime, the country was absolutely stripped of all her defences. A wide coast and a broad sea were open to the depredations of the enemy; the Santa Fé expedition and the league with Yucatan had given Mexico every provocation for a renewal of hostilities; and the outrages committed upon the Indian tribes, had broken the amity that had subsisted.

VI.

In this exposed situation of the country, when an irruption from the frontiers, or an invasion from Mexico, might be reasonably apprehended, Houston recommended Congress to raise a company of sixty men to protect the archives—for there was then no military force in the field. Congress refused to grant the subsidies necessary, and adjourned the 5th of February. He soon after started for Houston, to bring his family to the seat of government. While he was at Galveston, in the early part of March, the news came of the invasion by Vasquez. The intelligence spread the deepest alarm throughout the country. All along the western border, families were seen flying from their habitations towards the interior. The public mind was stirred by the wildest apprehensions. Everybody knew the provocation that had been given to the enemy—the follies and the disasters of Santa Fé seemed but a prelude to another Goliad or Alamo slaughter—the coast was without protection, and no army concentrated to march on the invader.

VII.

Suddenly all the intrigues and conspiracies against Houston ceased. The very men who had been foremost to threaten the overthrow of his administration in the storm of a revolution, were now the most active in stimulating their neighbors to prepare for approaching disasters. Committees of vigilance and safety were everywhere organized, and all those means resorted to which are called into requisition in revolutionary times. Houston's orders at this time, show that he did not believe the enemy would remain long in the country. The event proved that the Mexicans had already made a precipitate retreat beyond the Rio Grande, after committing outrages upon the citizens of San Antonio.

VIII.

In the meantime, the press throughout the South and West had displayed great sympathy for the cause of Texas, and relying upon the sensation caused in the United States by the news of the reported invasion and the miscarriage of the Santa Fé expedition, Houston made an appeal to the American people. He sent agents to the United States to receive contributions, and procure volunteers. He issued a Proclamation, in which he distinctly required that all troops which came should be perfectly armed and provisioned for a campaign of six months— since Texas had no means of doing it herself. Several hundred volunteers went to Texas, in direct violation of the Proclamation— for they went without arms and without provisions. Contributions were merely nominal. Some generous individuals in Georgia raised something over $500 at a public meeting—but all that was raised besides, throughout the United States, and reported to the government of Texas, in arms, ammunition, provisions, equipments and money, did not amount to five hundred dollars !

IX.

In June, Houston called an extra Session of Congress, to consider the state of the country, and devise means for national defence. They debated and legislated without much formality or delay, for the impression was general, that if anything was to be done, it had better be done quickly. So, too, all wise men would have said, "if 'twere *well* done." But their deliberations ended in passing a bill which invested Houston with dictatorial powers, and appropriated ten million acres of the public domain, to carry on a campaign. But this came no nearer making a provision for war, than a resolution appropriating ten million acres of blue sky, and conferring dictatorial power upon the north wind ! For there was not a dollar of money in the treasury to pay agents to go and dispose of the land, and Houston was the last man to make use of dictatorial powers in resisting the encroachments of a Dictator.

X.

But Congress thought they had acquitted themselves like

men—and their disposition, too, probably, was good enough, but it had no more efficacy than the disposition of the man who willed in his last testament all his debts to be paid, for in neither case could the executor find anything had been left to pay the debts with. Apprehensions had been felt, while the bill was under debate, that Houston would veto it, and the time he could constitutionally keep it had nearly gone by. The excitement was intense ; the Capital was filled with angry and desperate men, and their noisy clamor spread over the country. All sorts of accusations were brought against the Executive, and he was plied with threats from every quarter. He was told that his life would pay the forfeit if he vetoed the bill. His friends, who apprehended his assassination, gathered around him, and besought him not to hazard a veto, for it would end in the ruin of himself and his country. At last the *ebullitions* of excitement began to subside, but they were followed by demonstrations of a deeper and more desperate feeling. For two weeks, few, even of his friends, approached the President's house, and when they did, they stole there under the shadow of night ;—assassins, in the meantime, were lurking around his dwelling. Even his Cabinet officers began to talk about resigning.

XI.

But in the midst of all this storm, which few men could have resisted, Houston was calm and cheerful. He stationed no guard around his house ; he had no spies on the alert ; he did not even inquire what was said in Congress, or done in the streets. The blinds and the windows of his dwelling were wide open, and he was often seen walking across his parlor, conversing cheerfully with his family. His wife, whom he had married in 1840—one of the most accomplished and gifted of women—reposed confidently upon his character, and she calmly and confidingly sustained him by her placid and intellectual conversations. Long after the lights had been extinguished through the town, and sullen, desperate, armed men were gathered in secret meetings to plot, and counterplot, the gay voice of his wife, mingling with the tones of the harp and the piano, which she had carried with her to the wilderness, was heard coming forth from the open windows of Houston's dwelling.

XII.

All this must seem strange to the reader, without doubt, but we shall very soon solve the mystery. It was a fearful crisis ; but Houston was equal to it, and we know of no act of his life in which he gave such indubitable evidence that nature had lavished upon him those rare gifts which make up the really great man. The reader, too, will agree with us.

When the time came, the veto was sent up to Congress. In it he showed that they had utterly and totally failed to accomplish the object for which he had called them together. They had proclaimed war against a powerful and organized foe, but they had made no provision for carrying it on. The President had not the means of buying a pound of powder. If they would provide the means for a campaign, he would head it himself, if necessary ; but without money, no army could be made ready to take the field, and any attempt at hostilities would only bring down upon Texas universal contempt. He also dwelt upon the danger of the precedent they had established, in conferring upon the Chief Magistrate of the country unlimited powers. The prerogatives of a dictator he never would accept, while they were fighting against that same power in a neighboring State.

XIII.

The veto was published,—a universal calm at once succeeded, and the man who had been covered with maledictions, became the idol of the people.

XIV.

In the meantime, General Houston had addressed the following LETTER to SANTA ANNA, his former captive. It should now be carefully read, in justice to both. Thirteen years have since gone by ; but every year has given new significance to this luminous and important Letter. It furnishes a complete confirmation of this History :—

EXECUTIVE DEPARTMENT,
City of Houston, March 21, 1842.

MOST EXCELLENT SIR : Your communications to Mr. Bee and General Hamilton, dated at the Palace of the Government of Mexico, have been recently presented to my notice. At the first convenient leisure, I have not failed to appropriate my attention to the subjects embraced within the scope of your remarks.

They would have met a more ready attention had it not been for a marauding incursion made by a Mexican force on the defenceless town of San Antonio, on the inhabited frontier of Texas. Apprehending that the force had some other character more important than that of bandits and plunderers, commanded as it was by regular officers, it produced a momentary excitement, and claimed the attention of the Executive. But, as the bandits have withdrawn, charaterizing their retreat by pillage and plunder, as has been usual with Mexicans, I am left at leisure to resume in tranquillity the duties of my station.

In reference to your correspondence with Mr. Bee and General Hamilton, I have no remark to offer in relation to the communications which those gentlemen assumed the individual responsibility of making to you. The very nature of the correspondence manifests the fact that it was not done under the sanction of this government, but rests solely upon their action as individuals. Had your response regarded them in the light in which they were presented to you, it would have superseded the necessity of any notice from me. But as you have thought proper to laud my conduct as an individual, and refer to transactions connected with this country, with which I had official identity, and which I also at this time possess, and as you have taken the liberty, to an unwarrantable extent, to animadvert upon circumstances connected with Texas as a nation, I feel myself compelled by a sense of duty to refute a portion of the calumnies which you have presented to the world under the sanction of your official averment.

You appear to have seized upon the flimsy pretext of confidential communications unknown to the officers of this government, and unknown to the world until divulged by you, for the purpose of manufacturing a capital of popularity at home, and which you have submitted to the world as a manifesto in behalf of what you are pleased to term the rights of a great nation, "by so many titles respectable."

Whatever opinions you may have entertained in relation to the difficulties existing between Mexico and Texas cannot materially vary the facts and principles involved, nor will they materially influence the decision of mankind upon the justice of our cause.

Decency and self-respect, at least, should have induced, on your part, the pursuit of a course different from that which you have adopted. The abuse and ribald epithets which you have applied to the citizens of this country, as well as those of the Mississippi valley of the United States, are doubtless characteristic of the individual who gave them utterance. So far as the people of this country are concerned, I shall refer mankind to a history of facts and circumstances connected with the settlement of the country. I shall pass by with slight notice your remarks relative to the people of the United States. So far as our origin is connected with them, and the unity of sympathy exists, we are proud to hail them as our kindred—kindred in blood, kindred in laws, kindred in all the ennobling attributes of humanity. They will hear your taunts of defiance with the same contempt and derision that Texans regard your silly gasconade. If they have heretofore sympathized with us in our struggle for liberty and independence, it was from a knowledge of the fact that we had been deceived and oppressed by Mexico, and that the cause in which we were engaged was that of humanity struggling against usurpation and despotism.

The people of Texas were invited to migrate to this country for the purpose of enjoying equal rights and constitutional liberty. They were promised the shield of the Constitution of 1824, adopted by Mexico. Confiding in this pledge, they removed to the country to encounter all the privations of a wilderness, under the alluring promises of free institutions. Other reasons operated also. Citizens of the United States had engaged in the revolution of Mexico, in 1812. They fought gallantly in the achievement of Mexican independence, and many of them survive, and to this day occupy the soil which their privations and valor assisted in achieving. On their removal here, they brought with them no aspirations or projects but such as were loyal to the Constitution of Mexico. They repelled the Indian savages; they encountered every discomfort; they subdued the wilderness, and converted into cultivated fields the idle waste of this now prolific teritory. Their courage and enterprise achieved that which the imbecility of your countrymen had either neglected, or left for centuries unaccomplished. Their situation, however, was not disregarded by Mexico, though she did not, as might have been expected, extend to them a protecting and fostering care, but viewed them as objects of cupidity, rapacity, and at least jealousy.

The Texans, enduring the annoyances and oppressions inflicted upon them, remained faithful to the Constitution of Mexico. In 1832, when an attempt was made to destroy that Constitution, and when you, sir, threw yourself forward as its avowed champion, you were sustained with all the fidelity and valor that freemen could contribute. On the avowal of your principles, and in accordance with them, the people put down the serviles of despotism at Anahuac, Velasco, and Nacogdoches. They treated the captives of that struggle with humanity, and sent them to Mexico subject to your orders. They regarded you as the friend of liberty and free institutions; they hailed you as a benefactor of mankind; your name and your actions were lauded, and the manifestations you had given in behalf of the nation, were themes of satisfaction and delight to the Texan patriots.

You can well imagine the transition of feeling which ensued on your accession to power. Your subversion of the Constitution of 1824, your establishment of centralism, your conquest of Zacatecas, characterized by every act of voilence, cruelty, and rapine, inflicted upon us the profoundest astonishment. We realized all the uncertainty of men awakening to reality from the unconsciousness of delirium. In succession came your order for the Texans to surrender their private arms. The mask was thrown aside, and the monster of despotism displayed in all the habiliments of loathsome detestation. Then was presented to Texans the alternative of tamely crouching to the tyrant's lash, or exalting themselves to the attributes of freemen. They chose the latter. To chastise them for their presumption induced your advance upon Texas, with your boasted veteran army, mustering a force nearly equal to the whole population of this country at that time. You besieged and took the Alamo ; but under what circumstances ? Not those, surely, which should characterize a general of the nineteenth century. You assailed one hundred and fifty men, destitute of every supply requisite for the defence of that place. Its brave defenders, worn by vigilance and duty beyond the power of human nature to sustain, were at length overwhelmed by a force of nine thousand men, and the place taken. I ask you sir, what scenes followed ? Were they such as should characterize an able general, a magnanimous warrior, and the President of a great nation numbering eight millions of souls? No. Manliness and generosity would sicken at the recital of the scenes incident to your success, and humanity itself would blush to class you among the chivalric spirits of the age of vandalism. This you have been pleased to class in the "succession of your victories ;" and I presume you would next include the massacre at Goliad.

Your triumph there, if such you are pleased to term it, was not the triumph of arms—it was the success of perfidy. Fannin and his brave companions had beaten back and defied your veteran soldiers. Although outnumbered more than seven to one, their valiant, hearty, and indomitable courage, with holy devotion to the cause of freedom, foiled every effort directed by your general to insure his success by arms. He had recourse to a flag of truce ; and when the surrender of the little patriot-band was secured by the most solemn treaty stipulations, what were the tragic scenes that ensued to Mexican perfidy ? The conditions of the surrender were submitted to you ; and, though you have denied the facts, instead of restoring them to liberty, according to the capitulation, you ordered them to be executed contrary to every pledge given them, contrary to the rules of war, and contrary to every principle of humanity. Yet, at this day, you have the effrontery to animadvert upon the conduct of Texans relative to your captivity after the battle of San Jacinto.

You have presumed to arraign the conduct of the then existing Cabinet, and to charge it with bad faith ; and though you are pleased to commend the conduct of the illustrious Stephen F. Austin, the father of Texas, and myself, for acts of generosity exercised towards you, you take much care to insinuate that we only were capable of appreciating your proper merits. That you may no longer be induced to misconstrue acts of generosity and appropriate them to the gratification of your self-complacent disposition, I will inform you that they were acts of magnanimity characteristic of the nation to which we belong. They had nothing to do with your merits or demerits. The perfidy and cruelty which had been exercised towards our companions in arms did not enter into our calculation. Your sacrifice would not restore to our gallant companions their lives, nor to our country their services. Although the laws of war would have justified the retaliation of your execution, yet it would have characterized the acts of a nation by passion and revenge ; and would have evinced to the world that individuals who had an influence on the destinies of a people were subject to the capricious impulses of vengeance, of which you had so recently set an example.

So far as I was concerned in preserving your life and subsequent liberation, I was only influenced by considerations of mercy, humanity, and the establishment of a national character.

Humanity was gratified by your preservation. The magnanimous of all nations would have justified your release, had they known how little its influence was dreaded by the Texans. If, upon your return to Mexico, you should have power, and a disposition to redeem the pledges you had voluntarily made to myself, as well as this Government, of an earnest disposition to see the independence of Texas recognized by Mexico, I believe it would have a tendency to restore peace to the two nations, diminish the aggregate sufferings of their citizens, and promote the prosperity of both countries. In the event that you were not disposed to redeem the pledges thus given, but urge a prosecution of the war by Mexico against us, I wished to evince to mankind that Texans had magnanimity, resources, and confidence sufficient to sustain them against all your influence in favor of their subjugation.

Your liberation was induced by such principles as these ; and though you tendered pledges, doubtless to facilitate and insure your release, they were received, but not accepted, as a condition. I believe that pledges made in duress are not obligatory upon the individual making them ; and, if you intend to exercise the influence which you declared you would, the unconditional liberty extended to you would interpose no obstacle to their fulfillment.

Without adverting to any treaty stipulations which you had made with the Cabinet of Texas, I gave you your entire liberty and safe conduct to the city of Washington.

You have asserted to the world that you have given no pledge to the Texan Government whatever of your disposition in favor of its separation from Mexico. That the tribunal to which you have appealed, may judge of the validity of your assertion, I shall submit with this communication a letter of yours addressed to me at Columbia, dated the 5th November,

1836, after my determination to give you your liberty had been communicated. I shall present it in the original, accompanied with its translation into English. I will also give publicity to a veto which I communicated to the Senate, in consequence of a resolution of that honorable body respecting your detention as a prisoner.

You have spoken of events subsequent to the battle of San Jacinto, and endeavor to convey the idea that promises had been extorted from you "under the rifles of a tumultous soldiery." I am at a loss to comprehend your meaning by this reference. When you were brought into the encampment as a prisoner, the second day after the battle, you were conducted to the presence of the commander-in-chief—not amidst noise and tumult, nor did any exist. When the character of the prisoner became known to the army, much curiosity was excited; but there was no menace used nor violence offered. You were treated with calmness, and every courtesy extended to you that our situation would afford. Had you been a private gentleman and friend, you could have received no greater facilities than those which were extended to you. As you desired, you were placed near my person, and were never sent with the rest of the prisoners. You were informed that you could have your camp-bed and markee brought to my quarters, where I lay confined with my wound. You were permitted to command the services of your attendants. You were informed, also, that your baggage would be selected from the spoils taken by the army on the field; which was accordingly done, and never inspected. These privileges were granted by my order. Your aide-de-camp, Colonel Almonte, and your private secretary, were permitted to remain with you in your markee. A guard was detailed for the purpose of allaying any apprehension you might have for your personal safety, and every liberty extended to you except your absolute release.

You submitted propositions to me embracing the questions of the recognition of the Texan independence, and the termination of our struggle. I unequivocally refused the acceptance of any offer upon the subject of a treaty, alleging as reasons that we had a constitutional government, and that the subject would properly come before the Cabinet of Texas, the members of which would be present in camp within a few days. You urged the further consideration of your propositions upon me, declaring that you would rather enter into stipulations with a general of the army than with the civil authorities of the country. I positively declined taking any action upon them, and they were referred to the Cabinet on its arrival. Declining the consideration of your proposals myself, I required you to issue orders forthwith to the General next in command to evacuate Texas with the troops composing the Mexican army, and to fall back with them to Monterey. Orders to this effect were issued by you to General Filisola, and dispatched by an express, which could not overtake him, however, until he had reached the Colorado on his retreat, conducted in the greatest panic and confusion. Owing to his precipitate flight, and your execution of my orders, the Mexicans were permitted to leave Texas without further molestation.

In the meantime, General Adrian Woll, of the Mexican army, came into the encampment at San Jacinto without my knowledge, and not " upon my word or honor ;" nor was I apprised of his presence until I learned that he, together with his aid, had been traversing our lines. So soon as I was advised of this fact, I ordered them to my presence, and instructed them that such conduct would not be tolerated, and caused them to be placed under vigilance. This reason I deemed sufficient to detain General Woll as a prisoner of war. His subsequent conduct to Captain Dimitt was such as to justify any unfavorable opinion which I had formed of his character. He had rendered himself so obnoxious to the army, that, from a desire for his personal security, I did not permit his release until he could go in perfect safety. In no respect had the prisoners taken on that occasion reason of complaint. Their lives were all forfeited by the laws of war, conformably to the precedent which you had exhibited.

General Cos, who had surrendered in 1835, a prisoner of war at San Antonio, where one hundred and ninety-five Texans stormed and took the Alamo, with the town, when it was defended by seventeen hundred regular troops of Mexico, was again taken prisoner at San Jacinto, after he had violated his parole of honor, by which he had forfeited his life to the law of arms. Yet such was the lenity of Texans that *even he was spared*—thereby interposing mercy to prevent reclamation being made for the brave Texans perfidiously massacred.

From the 5th of May I had no connection with the encampment, nor the treatment which the prisoners received, until the month of October, when I was inducted into the office of Chief Magistrate of the nation. It is true that you were chained to an iron bar, but not until an attempt had been made to release you, with your knowledge and assent. A vessel had arrived at Orizimbo, on the Brazos, where you were confined. In possession of its captain were found wines and other liquors, mixed with poison for the purpose of poisoning the officers and guard in whose charge you were, and thereby insuring your escape. In consequence of the sen-

10

sation produced by this circumstance, you were confined and treated in the manner you have so pathetically portrayed.

Whilst confined by my wounds in San Augustine, I learned that it was the intention of the army to take you to the theatre of Fannin's massacre, and there to have had you executed. Upon the advertisement of this fact, I immediately sent an express to the army, solemnly protesting against any such act, and interposing every obstacle possible against your further molestation, or any action which might not recognize you as a prisoner of war.

Your recent communications have necessarily awakened attention to these facts—otherwise they would have remained unrecited by me. Any part which I bore in the transaction is not related in imitation of the egotistical style of your communication. It is done alone for the purpose of presenting the lights of history. You have sought to darken its shades, and appeal to the sympathies and command the admiration of mankind, and have even invoked " the prismatic tints of romance."

Now the tribunal to which you have appealed, will have an opportunity of contrasting the treatment which you and the prisoners taken at San Jacinto, received, with that of those who have fallen within your power, and particularly those perfidiously betrayed on a recent trading excursion to Santa Fé. You have endeavored to give that expedition the complexion of an invading movement upon the rights of Mexico. To believe you serious in the idle display of words made on this occasion, would be presenting an absurdity to the common sense of the age. Your fears may have given it a character different from that to which it was entitled. Examine the circumstances accompanying it. It was not an act of Texas. Congress had refused to sanction any enterprise of the kind. A number of individuals were anxious to open a lucrative trade (as they believed it would be) with Santa Fé. Such a commerce has been carried on for years by the citizens of the United States from Missouri ; and the preparations, connected with the fact that the citizens took with them a considerable amount of merchandise, show that their enterprise was not one of conquest or invasion. You may allege that it had connection with the Government, from the fact that the President identified himself with it, by furnishing arms to those connected with the project. This may have induced you to characterize the expedition as you have, in your tirade against Texas. Whatever part the President bore in this transaction was contrary to law, and in violation of his duty. A large portion of the people of Texas were apprised of the existence of such an enterprise. You doubtless would insist that it had means of offence against Mexico. So far as their preparation could give character to the undertaking, by carrying with them artillery and other munitions of war, it can be accounted for most readily. They had to pass through a wilderness six hundred miles from the frontier of Texas, before they could reach Santa Fé. It was reasonable to suppose that they would encounter many hostile tribes of Indians, and it was proper and necessary that they should be in a situation to repel any attacks made upon them, and, as their objects were pacific, they were justified in resisting aggression from any quarter. The instructions given to them by the President, did not contemplate hostilities, but that the enterprise would terminate without bloodshed and violence. Scientific gentlemen from Europe and the United States accompanied them, not for warlike purposes, but for the purpose of adding rich stores to the treasury of science. It had likewise been communicated to the people of Texas, that all the inhabitants east of the Rio Grande were anxious to enjoy the benefits of our institutions. You cannot allege that you were not willing to admit the justice of our claims to the Rio Grande, or that you were not anxious to facilitate the object. Your communication to me on that subject is conclusive. Texans were apprised of it from your repeated declarations to that effect while in this country, and on your way to Washington City. At the time the expedition started, no hostilities were carried on between this country and Mexico. Commissioners from General Arista, were at Austin at the time the party started for Santa Fé. They were kindly received, and made the most sincere profession of amity and reconciliation with this Government. They were treated with kindness, and corresponding commissioners appointed to General Arista. To them every facility was extended, and they were permitted to return without molestation. This was the attitude of the two countries at that time. Will you allege that this was not sanctioned by your Government, or will you insist that it was a trick of diplomacy? For myself, I would not have been deluded by any professions which might have been tendered to Texas by Mexico, when a departure from the most solemn pledges would result in injury to the former, and benefit to the latter.

That the ministers of General Arista played their parts with fidelity to their instructions, I have no doubt, and that all the information that could be derived in relation to the trading company was faithfully transmitted to the Government of Mexico. Nor do I doubt but that the population of the northern parts of your country, so soon as the intelligence was received, were thrown into the utmost consternation, and a nation numbering eight millions of people, inhabiting "valleys, mountains, towns, and large cities," "by so many titles respectable," was convulsed at the apprehended approach of three hundred Texan traders! But what has been the sequel of this expedition? On their approach to the settlements of the Rio Grande they obtained supplies from the inhabitants, not as a hostile and marauding party, but they paid a valuable consideration for every supply they obtained. They were met by the Mexican authorities with overtures of peace, assurances of friendship, and pledges of security, provided they would give up their arms for the purpose of tranquilizing the Mexican population. Detached, as the company was, into parties remote from each other, and deluded by pledges, they acquiesced in the wishes of the authorities of the country, thereby evincing to them that they had no disposition to disturb the tranquillity of the inhabitants, and that their objects were pacific. But no sooner were they in the power of the authorities than they were stripped of their clothing, deprived of everything valuable, treated in the most barbarous manner, and marched like convicts to the capital of Mexico. On their route every act of inhumanity, cruelty, and hatred was evinced. When their sick and helpless condition required the assistance of Christian charity and humanity, it was denied them. They were barbarously shot, their bodies mangled, and their corpses left unburied. The butchery of McAllister, Galphin, Yates, and others, appeal to Heaven and this nation for retribution upon the heads of their inhuman murderers. You may allege that you did not authorize the perpetration of these outrages, committed upon men who had violated no rule of law known to this civilized age. This will be no excuse for you. Your sanction to these acts is as culpable as their perpetration was degrading to their authors. Their detention as prisoners by you, may gratify the malignity of little minds; but the just, the chivalric, the brave, and the generous of all nations, may pity, but must despise your conduct. Had it not been for the faithless professions tendered to them, and their too ready belief, they could have maintained their position against all the forces of northern Mexico, and, if necessary, could have made good their retreat to their homes, defying the "generous effort of the people of New Mexico." Your conduct on this occasion will present your humanity and sense of propriety in very awkard contrast with the treatment extended to you and your followers after the victory of San Jacinto, being not, as you suppose, one of the "freaks of fortune," but one of the accompaniments of that destiny which will mark the course of Texas until the difficulties between the two countries shall be satisfactorily adjusted.

But you declare that you will not relax your exertions until you have subjugated Texas; that you "have weighed its possible value," and that you are perfectly aware of the magnitude of the task which you have undertaken; that you "will not permit a Colossus within the limits of Mexico;" that our title is that of "theft and usurpation," and that "the honor of the Mexican nation" demands of you "the reclamation of Texas;" that "if it were an unproductive desert, useless, sterile, yielding nothing desirable, and abounding only in thorns to wound the feet of the traveller, you would not permit it to exist as an independent government, in derision of your national character, your hearths and your individuality." Allow me to assure you that our title to Texas has a high sanction; that of purchase, because we have performed our conditions; that of conquest, because we have been victorious; it is ours because you cannot subdue us; it has been consecrated ours by the blood of martyred patriots; it is ours by the claims of patriotism, superior intelligence, and unsubduable courage. It is not a sterile waste or a desert; it is the home of freemen—it is the land of promise—it is the garden of America. Every citizen of Texas was born a freeman, and he would die a recreant to the principles imbibed from his ancestry, if he would not freely peril his life in defence of his home, his liberty, and his country.

Although you are pleased to characterize our occupation of Texas and defence of our imprescriptible rights as the "most scandalous robbery of the present age," it is not one-fourth of a century since Mexico perpetrated a similar robbery upon the rights of the Crown of Spain. The *magnitude* of the theft may give dignity to the robbery. In *that* you have the advantage. That you should thus have characterized a whole nation I can readily account for. Heretofore you entertained the opinion that Mexico could never conquer Texas, and, if it were possible for her to drive every Texan from the soil, that Mexico could not maintain her position on the Sabine, and the retreat of her army would be the signal for the return of the Anglo-Saxon race, who would re-occupy their homes and pursue the Mexicans as far as the Rio Grande; and that Mexico, in preservation of the integrity of the territory which she then possessed, would gain an advantage by abandoning all hopes of conquering Texas, and direct her attention to the improvement of her internal condition. Your recent opinions, as declared by you, appear to be at variance with these speculations, and are most vehemently avowed. It is an attribute of wisdom to change opinions upon conviction of error, and perhaps for it you are justifiable; at least, I discover that you have one attribute of a new convert : you are quite zealous and wordy in the promulgation of the doctrine which you have espoused.

Sir, from your lenity and power Texans expect nothing—from your humanity less ; and when you invade Texas you will not find " thorns to wound the foot of the traveller," but you will find opposed to Mexican breasts, arms wielded by freemen of unerring certainty, and directed by a purpose not to be eluded. Texans war not for gewgaws and titles ; they battle not to sustain dictators or despots ; they do not march to the field unwillingly, nor are they dragged to the army in chains, with the mock-title of volunteers. For awhile they lay by the implements of husbandry, and seize their rifles ; they rally in defence of their rights ; and, when victory has been achieved, they return to the cultivation of the soil. They have laws to protect their rights. Their property is their own. They do not bow to the will of despots ; but they bow to the majesty of the Constitution and laws. They are freemen indeed. It is not so with your nation. From the alcalde to the dictator, all are tyrants in Mexico ; and the community is held in bondage, subject not to law, but to the will of a superior, and confined in hopeless subjection to usurpation.

In an individual so intelligent as yourself, it does seem to me that you have evinced very bad taste by adverting to the subject of slavery, in the internal affairs of this country. Your opinions, whilst here, on this subject, were fully and freely avowed. You then believed that it would be of great advantage to Mexico to introduce slave labor into that country ; that it would develop her resources, by enabling her to produce cotton, sugar, and coffee, for purposes of exportation ; and that without it she would be seriously retarded in her march to greatness and prosperity. Your sympathy and commiseration at present expressed, are no doubt very sincere, and I only regret that they partake so little of consistency. You boast that Mexico gave the noble and illustrious example of emancipating her slaves. The fact that she has the name of having done so, has enabled you to add another flourish to your rhetoric. But the examination of facts for one moment will disclose the truth. The slaves of Mexico, you say, were emancipated. Did you elevate them to the condition of freemen ? No, you did not : you gave them the name of freedom, but you reduced the common people to the condition of slaves. It is not uncommon in Mexico for one dignitary, upon his hacienda, to control from one hundred to ten thousand human beings, in a state of bondage more abject and intolerable, than the negroes on any cotton plantation in this country. If an individual in Mexico owes but twenty-five cents, by application to an alcalde, the creditor can have him, with his family, decreed to his service, and to remain in that state of slavery until he is able to pay the debt from the wages accruing from his labor, after being compelled to subsist his dependent family. This you call freedom; and graciously bestow your sympathy upon the African race. The Abolitionists of the present day will not feel that they are not indebted to you for your support of their cause. Had some one else than the dictator of Mexico, or the self-styled " Napoleon of the West "—the subverter of the Constitution of 1824, the projector of centralism, and the man who endeavors to reduce a nation to slavery—become their advocate, they might have been more sensible of their obligation. Slavery is an evil; it was entailed upon us by Mexico. So far as its increase can be prevented, our Constitution and laws have presented every obstacle. They will be maintained to the letter : and on account of slavery, Texas, will· incur no reproach.

You tauntingly invite Texas to cover herself anew with the Mexican flag. You certainly intend this as mockery. You denied us the enjoyment of the laws under which we came to the country. Her flag was never raised in our behalf, nor has it been seen in Texas unless when displayed in an attempt at our subjugation. We know your lenity—we know your mercy—we are ready again to test your power. You have threatened to plant your banner on the banks of the Sabine. Is this done to intimidate us? Is it done to alarm us? Or do you deem it the most successful mode of conquest? If the latter, it may do to amuse the people surrounding you. If to alarm us, it will amuse those conversant with the history of your last campaign. If to intimidate us, the threat is idle. We have desired peace. You have annoyed our frontier—you have harassed our citizens—you have incarcerated our traders, after your commissioners had been kindly received, and your citizens allowed the privileges of commerce in Texas without molestation—you continue aggression—you will not accord us peace. *We will have it.* You threaten to conquer Texas—we will war with Mexico. Your pretensions, with ours, you have referred to the social world and to the God of Battles. We refer our cause to the same tribunals. The issue involves the fate of nations. Destiny must determine. Its course is only known to the tribunal of Heaven. If experience of the past will authorize speculations of the future, the attitude of·Mexico is more " problematical " than that of Texas.

In the war which will be conducted by Texas against Mexico, our incentive will not be a love of conquest; it will be to disarm tyranny of its power. We will make no war upon Mexicans, or their religion. Our efforts shall be made in behalf of the liberties of the people, and directed against the authorities of the country, and against *your* principles. We will exalt the condition of the people to representative freedom ; they shall choose their own rulers ; they shall possess their property in peace, and it shall not be taken from them to support an armed soldiery, for the purpose of oppression.

With these principles, we will march across the Rio Grande : and believe me, sir, ere the banner of Mexico shall triumphantly float on the banks of the Sabine, the Texan standard of the single star, borne by the Anglo-Saxon race, shall display its bright folds in liberty's triumph on the Isthmus of Darien.

With the most appropriate consideration, I have the honor to present you my salutation.

SAM HOUSTON.

To His Excellency, ANTONIO LOPEZ DE SANTA ANNA,
President of the Republic of Mexico.

XV.

We are now obliged to cut short our relation of events in detail, to give a brief account of other more important movements. Confidence began to be restored. One open rebellion against the laws of the country Houston put down by going to the scene, and calling out the militia. When desperadoes found there was a man at the head of affairs, who could not be trifled with, they soon disbanded, and the supremacy of law was again restored. A new set of men were in office—justice was efficiently administered—economy was observed, and although Mr. Lamar had saddled an enormous debt upon the country, which could not be discharged for a long time to come, yet public credit was being restored, and men began to feel proud of their Government.

XVI.

Houston had left no resource untried to effect the liberation of the Santa Fé prisoners. He had appealed to all friendly Powers to mediate in their release. The Congress of Texas had adjourned, after the news of their capture had arrived, without doing anything to aid the President in restoring them to their liberty. They had been given up as doomed men ; they had gone to Santa Fé in violation of the law of nations, and with no constitutional authority from their Government. They had been thrown on Houston's hands ; his only reliance was on the terms of their capitulation, for he insisted that, even if they had been outlaws before, this had brought them within the pale of civilized warfare. We have no space to give the history of the negotiations that were carried on for the release of these brave but misguided men. Suffice it to say, that they were liberated. Nor have we space to give the history of the Mier Expedition.

XVII.

Texas had now been repeatedly invaded by predatory Mexican bands, who seemed to have but two objects—to harass the nation they could not subdue, and pay up arrearages due to their soldiers from the treasury of Mexico, with spoils of the robber. Mexico was always talking about a grand campaign, but since the battle of San Jacinto, she had not dared to meet the revolted Province in honorable battle. The people of Mexico knew that the tyranny of her Dictators had lost them for ever that portion of their dominion ; and at no period did they wear the yoke so tamely, that the tyrant in power dared to leave the Capital to head any army of invasion. Whoever that tyrant may have been, he knew that his worst enemies were the Mexicans themselves ; his supremacy rested upon the presence of his troops in the city, and if he succeeded in consolidating his power at home, and turned his face towards Texas, he was sure to be overtaken by a courier from the Capi-

10*

tal with the news, that his dominion was ended, and another dictator had been proclaimed. In the opinion of the Texan President, the time had come when the civilized world should interfere to end this contemptible system of pillage, and robbery of the Republic.

XVIII.

Accordingly, he caused his Secretary of State to address the following high-toned and honorable appeal to the Great Powers, which had acknowledged the Independence of Texas. It shows clearly the condition of Texas, and will correct many false impressions which have gone abroad in reference to the struggles of that nation. It is also proper to add, that this was the paper which proved so powerful in winning the sympathy and respect of Sir Robert Peel, and M. Guizot, who ever after showed the deepest interest in the fortunes of Texas.

XIX.

DEPARTMENT OF STATE, TEXAS,
Washington, October 15th, 1842.

I am instructed by his Excellency, the President, to submit for your consideration and action, a subject of general concern to civilized nations, but of peculiar interest to Texas, viz.: the character of the war at present waged by Mexico against this country. The President is led to believe, from the nature of the facts involved, that this step will be deemed not only admissible, but entirely proper. The civilized and Christian world is interested in the unimpaired preservation of those principles and rules of international intercourse, both in peace and war, which have received the impress of wisdom and humanity, and been strengthened, through a long course of time, by the practice and approval of the most powerful and enlightened of modern States. To these rules, in their application to the pending difficulties between this Republic and Mexico, your attention is respectfully invited.

Whenever a people, separate and sovereign in their political character, are admitted into the great community of nations, they incur responsi-bilities and contract obligations which are reciprocal in their character, and naturally binding upon all the members of the community, the extent and force of which depend upon that code of ethics which prescribes the reciprocal duties and obligations of each sovereign member. Hence arises the right to control the mode of warfare pursued by one nation towards another, and the corresponding duty of providing against the per-petration of acts at variance with the laws of humanity, and the settled usages of civilized nations.

In view of the character of hostilities, at present waged by Mexico against Texas, and of those principles which have been, in the opinion of this government, so frequently and so flagrantly violated by our enemy, the hope is confidently indulged by the President, that the direct inter-ference of nations mutually friendly, will be extended to arrest a species of warfare, unbecoming the age in which we live, and disgraceful to any people professing to be civilized.

The course of conduct uniformly observed by the government and people of Texas towards our enemy, stands in palpable contrast with their manifold enormities and wanton aggression, and will, it is confidently expected, furnish abundant ground for the exercise of the right of inter-ference now invoked.

It has now been nearly seven years since the Declaration and the establishment of the Independence of this Republic. During the whole of this time, Mexico, although uniformly asserting the ability and deter-mination to re-subjugate the country, has never made a formidable effort to do so. Her principal war has consisted of silly taunts and idle threats, of braggadocio bulletins and gasconading proclamations. All her boasted threats of invasion have resulted in nothing more than fitting out and sending into the most exposed portions of our territory, petty marauding parties, for the purpose of pillaging and harassing the weak and isolated settlements on our western border.

Since March last, no less than three incursions of that character have been made, none of which have continued longer than eight days. The *first* party was composed of artillery, infantry, rancheros, and Indian warriors, in all about 700. Their attack was made upon the defenceless town of San Antonio. The second, consisting of about 800, attacked a party of about 200 emigrants at Lipantillan. They were repulsed with loss, and retreated from the country. The last, under Gen. Woll, of about 1300, attacked and took San Antonio the second time, by surprise, during the session of the District Court. His force was composed of regulars, rancheros and Indians. The Indians employed by the Mexicans are fragments of bands originally from the United States, but now located within the limits of Texas. This government has always refused to employ the services of Indians, when tendered against Mexico, and has sought every possible means to mitigate, rather than increase, the calamities of war. Persisting in this effort, the President has had recourse to the present measure, with a hope to subserve the cause of humanity. Should this effort fail, the government must resort to retaliatory measures, growing out of our peculiar situation, which are to be deprecated by every Christian and generous feeling. The rulers of nations are responsible for their preservation, and as a last resort, must adopt a just retaliation. What is most to be deplored in a war of this character, is, that the unoffending and defenceless become victims of the most relentless cruelty. War, in its most generous and noble aspect, is accompanied by great calamities. Nations are not benefited by it, and it must be productive of great individual sufferings. But when individuals and nations are exasperated by repeated wrongs, even cruelty itself may be rendered tolerable, if it be used as retaliation for injuries long endured. The massacres and cruelties which have been inflicted upon Texas, since the commencement of her Revolution, have been responded to by a generous forbearance, but that cannot be expected longer to exist.

The object of Mexico, in her course, cannot be misunderstood. By incursions of the character complained of, the spirits of our husbandmen and farmers are depressed—the cry of invasion is kept up, and the excitement incidental to war prevents emigration, and embarrasses our resources, by deterring men of enterprise and capital from making importations of goods into our country. This, for a time, may avail her something ; but the aggregate of human suffering will be a poor recompense for the advantages she may gain. The origin, genius, and character of the people of Texas, are guarantees for her ultimate success. Nations that contribute to her advancement, will command her gratitude. Never, since 1836, has Mexico attempted anything like a general invasion of the country, or conducted the war upon any plan calculated to test the superiority of the two nations on the field of battle, and bring the war to a close by the arbitration of arms. Her hostile demonstrations, thus far, have consisted, exclusively, in the clandestine approach of small bands of rancheros from the the valley of the Rio Grande, for plunder and theft, but sometimes associated with fragments of the Mexican army, composed for the most part of convict soldiery, fit for nothing either honorable in enterprise or magnanimous in conduct. The people of Texas, being, for most part, agriculturalists, engaged in the tillage of the soil, the consequences of this predatory system of warfare have been to them extremely vexatious and harassing, without in any degree hastening the adjustment of the difficulties existing between the parties. Entirely different is the general character of the Mexican population. They are literally a nation of herdsmen, subsisting, in a great measure, on the proceeds of their flocks and herds. They can move about from place to place, and make their homes wherever inclination or convenience may prompt, without detriment.

Hitherto the conduct and disposition of the Government and people of Mexico have been diametrically opposed to those manifested by the people of Texas. While the one has been depredating upon the property and dwellings of our exposed and defenceless frontier, murdering the inhabitants in cold blood, or forcing them away into loathsome, and too often fatal, captivity ; inciting the murderous tribes of hostile Indians, who reside along our northern border, to plunder our exposed settlements, stimulating to the most cruel and barbarous massacres, and inhuman butcheries, even of our defenceless women and children, and to commit every excess of savage warfare—the other, animated by the hope of a further resort to arms and their attendant calamities, for injuries received, returned forbearance.

The President has sought to abstain from the effusion of blood, and in that aim has uniformly restrained the impetuosity, and calmed the excitement of his countrymen, so often aroused by a course of conduct which violates every right, both private and national, and a cruelty and depravity which would disgrace the darkest ages of feudal barbarism. The popular impulse might have been turned upon the enemy, on their own soil. The result might have proved that a free people, burning with vengeance long restrained, could levy a heavy retaliation.

Such being the character of hostile operations against Texas, on the part of our enemy, which being plainly in violation of every principle of civilized or honorable warfare, and, at the same time, so little calculated to achieve the professed object of the war—the re-conquest of Texas, the President confidently hopes the Government of ———— will feel not only justified, but even called upon, to interpose its high authority and arrest their course of proceedings, and require of Mexico either the recognition of the Independence of Texas, or to make war upon her according to the rights established and universally recognized by civilized nations. If Mexico believes herself able to re-subjugate this country, her right to make the effort to do so is not denied, for, on the contrary, if she choose to invade our territory with that purpose, the President, in the name of the people of all Texas, will bid her welcome. It is not against a war with Mexico that Texas would protest. This she deprecates not. She is willing at any time to stake her existence as a nation upon the issue of a war conducted on Christian principles. It is alone against the unholy, inhuman, and fruitless character it has assumed, and still maintains, which violates every rule of honorable warfare, every precept of religion, and sets at defiance even the common sentiments of humanity, against which she protests, and invokes the interposition of those powerful nations which have recognized her independence.

The Government of this Republic has already given an earnest of its disposition to consult the wishes of other nations, when those wishes do not conflict with the general interests and convenience of the country. Fully appreciating the friendly sentiments of those Powers, which have acknowledged the Independence of Texas, and relying much upon their ability and influence in securing an early and permanent adjustment of our difficulties with Mexico, the President, in compliance with the desire of those Nations, expressed through their Representatives to this Government, revoked the late proclamation of blockade against Mexico, and thus removed every cause of embarrassment to those nations in their intercourse with our enemy. Having thus yielded the opportunity of retaliating upon our enemy the many injuries we have received at her hands, the President feels less reluctance in making this representation, and invoking the interposition of those nations to put an end to a mode of warfare at once disgraceful to the age, so evil in its consequences to civil society, so revolting to every precept of the Christian religion, and shocking to every sentiment of humanity.

G. W. TERRELL,
Attorney-General, and Acting Secretary of State.

SECTION THIRTEENTH.

ANNEXATION—FRENCH, BRITISH, AND AMERICAN CABINETS.

I.

THIS luminous and able paper, unfolded clearly the merits of the Texan struggle, and it received the profound attention of the Cabinets of Washington, London, and Paris. · The leading Journals of England and France, borrowing their prejudices and their *intelligence* about Texan affairs, from powerful and widely circulated American Papers, had hitherto regarded the people of Texas as a band of outlaws. Scarcely a word of encouragement or sympathy had been uttered by their ministers to the agents of Texas in Europe, and beyond a tardy recognition of her independence, they hardly ventured. The American Press groaned under the burden of calumnies against the Texan people and their bold leader.

II.

Consequently, this appeal was received, and read with surprise and mortification. They saw that the same high veneration for justice—the same lofty regard for national honor, and the same (if not a nobler) recognition of the claims of humanity and Christian principle which had characterized the progress and the intercourse of those great kingdoms—inspired the councils of the man who had given freedom to his outraged country.

III.

We have been told, and we do not doubt it, that both of those great ministers, who guided the destinies of England and France, declared, on reading this appeal, that it would have done honor to the bravest nation, and most enlightened statesman. However this may have been, we do know, from the archives of Texas, that immediately afterward, a rivalry began between the French and English Cabinets, for the cultivation of friendly relations with Texas. Instructions were sent to the ministers of those nations accredited to the Texan Government, to allow no opportunity of winning the regard and friendship of the Republic to pass unimproved. We also know, too, that no effort which vigilant ministers could put forth, and no motives which keen-sighted diplomatists could press, were left untried, to gain for their Sovereigns, control over the commerce and the political fortunes of Texas. They saw that, as an independent power, no barriers could be interposed to her ultimate advancement ; and it became a matter of infinite moment to France and England, to prevent the final union of Texas with the United States. Hence, those powers watched with so much vigilance and alarm, the tendency of affairs towards annexation. Hence they brought into requisition all their diplomatic, commercial, and financial machinery, to prevent what they clearly foresaw would prove so detrimental to their ancient supremacy in the New World. We have had facilities for knowing something of these movements, and we venture to say, that had not Houston held the control of these negotiations, and been a man whose policy neither England nor France could constrain or coerce by *any* motives of personal aggrandizement— Texas never would have been a part of our confederacy, and those great powers would have gained a foothold beyond the Sabine, which would not unlikely have transferred to their hands that vast empire which we are now wielding on the shores of the Pacific.

IV.

The very moment the French and British Cabinets saw the tendency of events, they increased their vigilance just in proportion as Texas was spurned from our embraces. But while timidity and apprehensions filled the minds of the friends of Texas in this country, and Congress, blinded by falsehood and prejudice, plied by threats and awed by clamor, still held itself aloof from all legislation on the subject, Mr. Tyler and his cabinet were no idle spectators of the advancing drama. That President—whatever may have been the wisdom of the rest of his course—pursued, in the affair of Texas, a most enlightened, sagacious, and American policy. He saw the vast importance of consummating annexation at the earliest possible moment; and all that vigilance, activity, and a complete understanding of the merits of the question, could accomplish, was done. His efforts were at last successful. And although his reputation as a statesman may have suffered, and he may have paid the penalty of having in some things proved untrue to both parties as well as to himself, yet all this has been in a great measure forgotten, and the time will come when the vast consequences of that great act, whose consummation is so much due to him, will become so apparent to all our people, that his name will be cherished by every American. Throughout his administration, he was true to his policy on this question. Unawed by popular clamor, and unseduced by the minions who pressed around his feet (and who brought the transient eclipse over his fame), he steadily and firmly pursued his noble purpose.

V.

In the meantime, France and England *did* interfere, and brought about an armistice between Mexico and Texas. The friendly offices of our Cabinet were also proffered, but they had little influence with Mexico. The negotiations in London were conducted with consummate ability by Mr. Ashbel Smith.

In a dispatch from the Department of State of Texas, to Mr. Van Zandt, Chargé d' Affaires of the Republic at Washington, dated July 6th, 1843, that functionary was thus instructed : "The United States having taken no definite action in this matter, and there now being an increased prospect of an adjustment of our difficulties with Mexico, the President deems it advisable to take no further action at present in reference to annexation, but has decided to await the issue of events now in progress, and to postpone that subject for future consideration, and for such action as circumstances may hereafter render most expedient for the interests of this country."

VI.

This extract, with others we shall presently give, will unfold what has been a matter of some dispute, viz. :—the policy of Houston on this important subject. Whatever his own private feelings may have been, it was exceedingly doubtful whether our Government would ever consent to annexation on what he considered fair and equal terms ; and he was resolved to maintain with France and England the most friendly relations ; that in the event of Texas being spurned from the embrace of the United States, she might fall back upon a Treaty with a powerful ally, under whose patronage she might claim protection from her foe, and under whose policy (made liberal by interest) she might advance rapidly to power.

VII.

The French and English ministers resident in Texas, had already manifested some little jealousy on the subject of Houston's negotiations with the Washington Cabinet, and seeing little probability of consummating a treaty of annexation, he instructed Mr. Van Zandt to defer all further action for the time being.

Accordingly, instructions were forwarded to Mr. Van Zandt on the 13th of December (1843). The following extracts will clearly unfold the reasons for Houston's policy.

"The interposition of foreign friendly governments, by which an Armistice has been established between Texas and Mexico, and the prospect of a permanent peace with that power given, has been extended by the particular governments mostly influential in obtaining these most desirable results chiefly with a view that, in the event of Mexico's agreeing to acknowledge the independence of Texas, she should continue to exist as a separate and independent nation. The great object and desire of Texas is the establishment of a permanent and satisfactory peace with her enemy, and for this purpose the good offices of these powers have been asked and obtained, and the object sought for, through their intervention, appears now on the eve of being realized.

"This intervention and these good offices have been gratuitously and unconditionally given, and although Texas is entirely free to pursue any course she may please in future, the President thinks that, in the present state of our foreign relations, it would not be politic to abandon the expectations which now exist of a speedy settlement of our difficulties with Mexico through the good offices of other powers, for the very uncertain prospect of annexation to the United States, however desirable that event, if it could be consummated, might be. Were Texas to agree to a treaty of annexation, the good offices of these powers would, it is believed, be immediately withdrawn, and were the treaty then to fail of ratification by the Senate of the United States, Texas would be placed in a much worse situation than she is at present, nor could she again ask or hope for any interposition in her behalf, either by England or France; and with our consequent supposed dependence upon the United States, might again return the apathy and indifference towards us which has always, until now, characterized that government. Texas would then be left in the same situation she was two years since, without a friend, and her difficulties with Mexico unsettled.

"This government is duly sensible of the very friendly feelings evinced by the President of the United States, in the offer to conclude a treaty for the annexation of this country, but from all the information which he has been able to obtain in relation to the views and feelings of the people of the United States, he is induced to believe that its approval by the other branches of that government would be, if not refused, at least, of very uncertain attainment at this particular time—therefore, and until such an expression of their opinion can be obtained as would render this measure certain of success, the President deems it most proper and most advantageous to the interests of this country, to decline the proposition for concluding a treaty. In making a communication of this determination to the government of the United States, it will be proper to inform that government that whenever the Congress or Senate of the United States shall throw wide open the door to annexation, by a resolution authorizing the President of that country to propose a treaty for the purpose, the proposition will be immediately submitted to the representatives of the people of this country, and promptly responded to on the part of its government.

"The present determination of the President on this subject, does not proceed from any change in his views of the general policy of the measure, *but from a change in the relations of this country with other powers.*"

VIII.

These instructions to suspend negotiations on the subject of annexation, with a knowledge that England was pressing her powerful and friendly offices upon the Republic, alarmed the Cabinet at Washington. The facts which were soon after made public, excited the apprehensions also, not only of all the friends of annexation, but of all those Americans, who had the foresight to anticipate the prejudicial consequences that would come upon this country, by allowing England to gain a foothold on our Southern frontier. She had sometimes proved a bad neighbor, as our difficulties growing out of the North-Eastern and Oregon boundaries had abundantly proved—and the deepest anxiety was everywhere manifested for the prompt action of Congress. In the meantime, Mr. Tyler, fearing the result, had instructed his Secretary of State to lose no opportunity of assuring the Texan government of his earnest desire to consummate annexation.

IX.

The President of Texas was placed in a position of extreme delicacy, and any imprudent act or movement would have proved exceedingly hazardous to the interests of his country. He had early manifested his desire for annexation, and done all he could to effect it during his first executive term. Under Mr. Lamar's administration, the question had slept. Houston had pursued a discreet course in regard to it after his re-election, and although he had now been for some time earnestly occupied in securing annexation, he had, like a wise man, kept his own counsels.

X.

On the 20th of January, 1844, however, he sent a secret message to Congress, in which he uses the following language :

"Connected with our present condition, our foreign relations are becoming daily more and more interesting ; and it seems to me that the representatives of the people should anticipate the events which may in all probability occur. 　*　　*　　*　　*　　*　　*

　*　　*　　* "The Executive, therefore, relies upon the deliberative wisdom and decision of the representatives of the people, to give him all the aid in their power to conduct the affairs of Texas to such an issue, as will be promotive of its interests as a community, and at the same time gratifying to the people. Heretofore, he has carefully abstained, during his present administration, from the expression of any opinion in reference to the subject of annexation to the United States. And, in submitting this communication, he does not think it becoming in him now to express any preference.

"It will be perceived by the honorable Congress, that if any effort were made on the part of this Government to effect the object of annexation, which is so desirable, and if it should fail of meeting responsive and corresponding action on the part of the United States, it might have a seriously prejudicial influence upon the course which England and France might otherwise be disposed to take in our favor. And a failure on our part, after a decided expression, could not but be mortifying to us, and to a great extent diminish our claims to the confidence of other nations. It would create distrust on their part towards us ; because the opponents of our interests would allege there was no stability in our purposes, and therefore it would be unsafe in other nations to cultivate very intimate relations with us, or even to maintain those which now exist. They might apprehend that after the lapse of a few more years, Texas, once having acquired increased importance from their friendly aid and good offices, would be induced again, by the agitation of the same question in the United States, to apply for admission into that Union, and that by possibility it might be effected. Hence the utmost caution and secresy on our part, as to the true motives of our policy, should be carefully observed."

XI.

He recommends that in the event of the failure of Texas, she should enter into " a treaty of alliance, defensive at least, if not offensive," with the United States.

" If nothing else," he says, " were effected in a treaty for defence, it would secure to Texas a position that would for ever bid defiance to our Mexican enemy. It would be as important to us, in fact, as the recognition of our independence by Mexico."

He also proposes the appointment of " an additional agent to the Government of the United States, to co-operate with our agent there." He thus concludes :

" If the honorable Congress should think well of these suggestions, they will be aware of the propriety of *immediate* action on the subject. The Congress of the United States have now been in session some time, and there can be but little doubt that if they have not already done so, they will soon indicate their disposition, and course of policy towards this country.

"Believing as the Executive did, at the commencement of the present Session, that the subject of annexation was in the best position in which Texas could place it, he did not allude to it in his general Message—apprehending that any public action taken either by the Executive or the Congress would only have a tendency to embarrass the subject. Action must now be taken by the United States; and we must now watch and meet their disposition towards us.

"If we evince too much anxiety, it will be regarded as importunity, and the voice of supplication seldom commands great respect."

XII.

The spirit of this message inspired all Houston's acts on this great question, and the effect was most salutary. For it is more than probable that our Congress would have turned a deaf ear to "the voice of supplication," had they not discovered that the people of Texas, grown weary of delays and indignant at repeated repulses, would supplicate no longer. The position of parties was suddenly changed—completely reversed. It became clearer than noon-day, that unless Texas was allowed to come into our Union, under auspices the most favorable to her, she would not enter—and in any event, it seemed probable that she was after all to be the sufferer. Her anxiety, therefore, for annexation, was every hour growing less, while ours was increasing.

XIII.

Both parties were aware of the movements of England—and while Texas saw in the extension of that proud shield over her young Republic, the boon of mighty protection, we watched with jealous and anxious interest, the progress of that same imperial emblem. When, therefore, that Republic whose people,

" bone of our bone, and flesh of our flesh," had been pleading on their knees the same admission which had hitherto been cordially tendered by Congress to every other American colony on the continent, was repulsed " like some stranger," she sprung to her feet, and the next moment we saw her youthful figure relieved against the giant form of Old England, whose purple mantle was thrown kindly over her shoulder, and whose flag of St. George was waving over her head. It was a strange, but beautiful spectacle. " Is that," said all, " the suppliant who so lately was kneeling on the steps of our Capitol ?"

XIV.

Texas was now lost to America. The only question was, " Can she be again won ?" and the American Congress was no longer the sole party to answer the inquiry.

The Cabinet at Washington manifested an anxiety to renew negotiations. In his letter to Mr. Van Zandt (29th January, 1844), Houston instructs his Minister to meet the United States half way, and to inform him of any disposition on their part to come to the terms they had rejected. " They must be convinced," says he, " that England has rendered most important service to Texas by her mediatorial influence with Mexico." He then proceeds:

" If the United States really intend to deprive England of connections on this continent, a treaty of alliance, offensive and defensive, formed with this country against Mexico, would enable that government to retain an influence in the affairs of Texas which could be done by no other circumstance. In November, 1842, when Texas protested to the three Great Powers against the course pursued by Mexico in her war with this country. it was understood the three Powers were to act in harmony, so far as any mediation was to be interposed. From some circumstances, England appears to have been most active and efficient in her efforts. The United States, from their contiguity in situation, had greater facilities than

England at their command, and had they been as forward in their efforts at mediation as England, it would have been more grateful to the citizens of Texas. A moment's reflection will present many reasons why it should have been so. When an individual is overwhelmed by misfortune, and that misfortune is lightened or relieved, the beneficiary always feels grateful for the benefits conferred; and in the event of a recurrence, would naturally look to the same source for a renewal of favor. Thus must it be with nations, and it requires no argument to convince the United States, that in submitting the first proposition for a treaty of alliance with them, the authorities of Texas are far from pretermitting any just claims which they may have to the confidence of Texas as a nation, but the reverse.

"It is true that our eyes were directed to the United States, not only as a people but as a government, to which Texas was most willing to feel herself obligated. If we did not realize all our expectations, we are far from concluding that anything left unaccomplished by her arose from hostility to Texas on her part; and for that, among other reasons, we propose an alliance as an earnest of the confidence we are still willing to place upon them and their efforts."

XV.

Negotiations were now once more commenced in earnest, and the two Ministers of Texas (Mr. Van Zandt, and Gen. Henderson, afterwards Governor of Texas), represented their country with great ability, and won for themselves universal respect.

In the dispatch of Houston to Mr. Van Zandt (Feb. 15, 1844), informing him of the investment of Gen. Henderson (just appointed) and himself, "with proper powers to conclude the subject of annexation as far as it can be consummated by the Government of the United States and our Ministers," the President thus speaks of the vast consequences of annexation, if it should be effected.

"It would be useless for me to attempt to portray to you the magnitude of the consequences which are to grow out of these transactions.

11

Millions will realize the benefits; but it is not within the compass of mortal expression to estimate the advantages to mankind. The measures of this Government have not been devised without due consideration of the subject, so far as Texas may be affected by it; and no matter how great the ultimate advantages to the two countries may have been considered, in the event of annexation, it was the manifest duty of this Government to use such precaution as would secure it against any accidental catastrophe. It is now in possession of such assurances from the United States as will hazard the die."

XVI.

In another dispatch, dated the 29th of April, 1844, we find the following language :—

"I have felt, and yet feel, great solicitude for our fate. The crisis to Texas is everything. To the United States it is worth its union. My toil has constantly been for the freedom and happiness of mankind, and if we are annexed, I hope we shall have accomplished much ; but if from any cause we should be rejected, we must redouble our energies, and the accompanying duplicate will express to you decisively what my purposes are. Texas can become sovereign and independent, established upon her own incalculable advantages of situation, and sustained by European influences, without the slightest compromittal of her nationality. If the present measure of annexation should fail entirely, and we are to be thrown back upon our own resources, fix your eye steadily on the salvation of Texas, and pursue the course which I have indicated. I again declare to you, that every day which passes, only convinces me more clearly, that it is the last effort at annexation that Texas will ever make ; nor do I believe that any solicitation or guarantee from the United States would, at any future day, induce her to consent to the measure."

XVII.

But the Mission of General Henderson seemed likely to secure no good results, and in a dispatch of May 17th, 1844, he was advised to return. The President says :—

"Whatever the desires of this Government, or the people, are, or might have been, in relation to Annexation, I am satisfied they are not ambitious, at this time, nor will ever be again, to be seen in the attitude of a bone of contention, to be worried or gnawed by conflicting politicians. The views of the Executive of this country, as well as the views of its citizens, were fairly presented in a willingness to become annexed to the United States, and though the advantages presented to the United States were incalculably greater than those resulting to Texas, she was willing to stand the hazard of the adventure.

" The statesmen of that country appear to be united in opinion adverse to our admission into the Union of the North. We must, therefore, regard ourselves as a nation, to remain *for ever separate*. It would be unpleasant for us to enter into a community, as a member, where we should be regarded ungraciously by either of the political parties. Texas *alone*, can well be sustained, and no matter what sincere desire we may have entertained for a connection with that Government, and the affectionate enthusiasm that has existed in this towards it, we will be compelled to reconcile ourselves to our present condition, or to assume such an attitude towards other countries as will certainly look to our independence. This can be accomplished, if the United States will carry out the pledges which they have already given. The compromittal of our national honor I cannot contemplate, nor would I entertain any proposition which could be averse to our character as an independent nation ; *but Texas can now command interests which will require no such sacrifice.* We must act! ! * * It would seem, from the complexion of matters at Washington, that General Henderson's remaining there longer would be unnecessary. As indicated in my last communication, *negotiations can be very well conducted at this Government,* not designing to cast any reflections upon the representatives of this Government at Washington, in whom the executive has the highest confidence. Moments of leisure could be employed here, and even hours and days commanded, which is not permitted when urgent dispatches arrive. The locality of our seat of Government is such, that the Executive has had no substitute himself in corresponding for the Secretary of State, and dispenses with the services of that valuable officer, for the sake of dispatch. * * The measure of Annexation having been taken up at the instance of the United States, ought to secure Texas, and fortify her against all inconveniences arising from having opened negotiations on that subject. The treaty having been signed and submitted to the Senate, is all that can be performed on the part of Texas. Further solicitation, on her part, would present her as an object of commiseration to the civilized world. If the embarrassments of our condition have presented us in a humiliating posture, it furnishes no excuse to us for voluntary degradation.

" Therefore it is, that my purpose is fixed in relation to the subject of which I have treated. THE DESIRES OF THE PEOPLE OF TEXAS, WITH MY LOVE OF REPOSE (thus far I am selfish), HAD DETERMINED ME IN FAVOR OF ANNEXATION. MY JUDGMENT, THOUGH RENDERED SUBSERVIENT TO THEIR INCLINATIONS AND MY OWN, HAS NEVER FULLY RATIFIED THE COURSE ADOPTED. YET, IN ALL GOOD FAITH, I HAVE LENT AND AFFORDED EVERY AID TO ITS CONSUMMATION."

XVIII

We shall now close our extracts from Houston's Dispatches, by giving a portion of a very important *private* letter to Mr. Murphy, the American Minister to the Texan Government. We have nowhere seen the same views expressed in regard to the future destiny of Texas. The letter shows beyond a question, that the writer was persuaded that Texas, even if she was compelled to stand alone, had no mean destiny awaiting her in the future. The views here given are those of a statesman—of one who knew the history of his nation, and the character of her people—of a patriot, who never despaired for his country, on whose altars he had consecrated himself for ever

* * " The times are big with coming events to Texas and the world. I feel that matters now transacting are, if carried out, to perpetuate the union of the States, by the Annexation of Texas, for centuries. If this great measure fails, the Union will be endangered ; its revenues diminished ; and a European influence will grow up in Texas, from our necessities and interests, that will most effectually prejudice the interests of the United States, so far as they are to look for the sale of their fabrics in the southern section of this continent, and a forfeiture of our sympathies. Mexico, in a short time, by the influences which Texas can com-

mand, will yield everything to the superior energy, activity, and the employment of well-directed capital, which will flow into us from Europe, and render us the beneficiaries of a most important and extensive trade. All our ports will soon become great commercial marts; and places, now scarcely noticed upon our maps, will be built up, and grow into splendid cities.

"These are but few of the advantages which are noticed; but these, to the statesmen of the United States, ought to cause ceaseless efforts to secure so rich a prize.

" The present moment is the only one that the United States will ever enjoy to annex Texas. I am intensely solicitous to see the matter consummated, and my country at rest. 'Tis true that we are not to be great gainers, when compared to the United States, in what they derive. Had I been at Washington, I would, most certainly, not have made a treaty so indefinite as to individual rights which may arise, and be involved in the subject of annexation. We surrender everything, and in reality get nothing but protection—and that at the hazard of being invaded or annoyed by Mexico before any aid could be rendered by the United States. I hope that the precautions taken will be such as to deter Mexico from any attempt upon us.

" The fact, that the United States is one of the rival powers of the world, will render that nation more liable to war than we would be as a minor power. There are a thousand reasons which I could urge, why Texas would be more secure from trouble if she could have present peace—which she can obtain readily if she is not annexed. When we once become a part and parcel of the United States we are subject to all their vicissitudes. Their commercial relations are extensive, which subjects them to jealousy and the rivalry of other powers, who will seek to overreach them, and cramp them by restrictions, or annoy them by interference. They will not be willing to submit to these things, and the consequences will be war. Nor will this danger arise from any one power of the earth, but from various nations. The wealth of European nations depends more upon their labor, than the people of this continent. We look to the soil —they to their manufacturing capacity, for the means of life as well as wealth. These facts are not all ; and, indeed, but a very partial notice of important affairs. The political relations of the United States will increase, and become more complicated and extensive with their increase of power. Not only this, but they, too, will grow arrogant ; and it will not be a half century, if the Union should last, before they will feel a strong inclination to possess, by force, that which they at present would be willing to make a subject of negotiation and treaty.

"In all contingencies, if we are annexed, we have to bear a part of their troubles—no matter of what character. Alone and Independent, Texas would be enabled to stand aloof from all matters unconnected with her existence as a nation ; while the causes of war to the United States would be a source of benefit and prosperity to her. War could grow up between no power and the United States, but what Texas would be the beneficiary. The value of her staples would be enhanced, and that arising from the influence of war upon the United States. Texas, enjoying as she does a situation on the Gulf, and a neutral attitude, would derive the greatest possible benefits. Calamity to other nations, would be wealth and power to Texas. The encouragement given us by the demand for our staples would increase our individual, as well as our national wealth. The fleets of belligerents would be supplied with meats from our natural pastures ; and the sale of our superabundant herds would, when added to the sale of our other commodities, give us more wealth than any other nation, in comparison to our population.

"Apart from this, if we should not be annexed, all the European nations would introduce with alacrity vast numbers of emigrants, because it would enable them to extend their commerce. Those who migrate from the different nations to Texas will retain predilections, for many years, in favor of the partialities which nativity carries with it in after life.

That France and England will pour into our country vast numbers of industrious citizens, there can be no doubt. Belgium, Holland, and other countries, will not be remiss in their duty to ulterior consequences. All these countries have an excess of population, and the common policy and economy of nations are such, that they will have a care to the location of those who leave their native countries. Never, to my apprehension, have all nations evinced the same disposition to commerce as that which is now exercised and entertained. Hence, no time has ever been so propitious for the upbuilding of a nation possessed of our advantages, as that which Texas at this moment enjoys, in the event that the measure of annexation should fail. Its failure can only result from selfishness on the part of the Government or Congress of the United States. If faction, or a regard to present party advantages, should defeat the measure, you may depend upon one thing—and that is, that the glory of the United States has already culminated. A rival power will soon be built up, and the Pacific, as well as the Atlantic, will be component parts of Texas, in thirty years from this date.

The Oregon region, in geographical affinity, will attach to Texas. By this coalition, or union, the barrier of the Rocky Mountains will be dispensed with or obviated. England and France, in anticipation of such an event, would not be so tenacious on the subject of Oregon, as if the United States were to be the sole possessors of it. When such an event would take place, or in anticipation of such result, all the powers, which either envy or fear the United States, would use all reasonable exertions to build us up, as the only rival power which can exist, on this continent, to that of the United States. Considering our origin, these speculations may seem chimerical, and that such things cannot take place. A common origin has its influence so long as a common interest exists, and no longer. Sentiment tells well in love matters or in a speech; but in the affairs and transactions of nations there is no sentiment or feeling but one, and that is essentially selfish.

I regard nations as corporations on a large and sometimes magnificent scale, but no more than this; consequently, they have no soul, and recognize no Mentor but interest.

Texas, once set apart and rejected by the United States, would feel that she was of humble origin ; and if a prospect was once presented to her of becoming a rival to the United States, it would only stimulate her to feelings of emulation ; and it would be her least consideration, that, by her growth to power, she would overcome the humility of her early condition. So the very causes which now operate with Texas, and incline her to annexation, may, at some future period, give origin to the most active and powerful animosity between the two countries. This, too, we must look at, for it will be the case. Whenever difficulties arise between the United States and Texas, if they are to remain two distinct nations, the powers of Europe will not look upon our affairs with indifference ; and no matter what their professions may be of neutrality, they can always find means of evasion. The union of Oregon and Texas will be much more natural and convenient than for either, separately, to belong to the United States. This, too, would place Mexico at the mercy of such a power as Oregon and Texas would form. Such an event may appear fanciful to many, but I assure you there are no Rocky Mountains interposing to such a project. But one thing can prevent its accomplishment, and that is *annexation*.

If you, or any Statesman, will only regard the map of North America, you will perceive that, from the 46th degree of latitude North, there is the commencement of a natural boundary. This will embrace the Oregon, and from thence south on the Pacific coast, to the 29th or 30th degree of south latitude, will be a natural and convenient extent of sea-board.

I am free to admit, that most of the Provinces of Chihuahua, Sonora, and the Upper and Lower Californias, as well as Santa Fé, which we now claim, will have to be brought into the connection of Texas and

Oregon. This, you will see by reference to the map, is no bugbear to those who will reflect upon the achievements of the Anglo-Saxon people. What have they ever attempted, and recoiled from, in submission to defeat? Nothing, I would answer. Population would be all that would be needful, for, with it, resources would be afforded for the accomplishment of any enterprise. As to the proposition, that the Provinces of Mexico would have to be overrun, there is nothing in this; for you may rely upon the fact, that the Mexicans only require kind and humane masters to make them a happy people, and secure them against the savage hordes who harass them constantly, and bear their women and children into bondage. Secure them from these calamities, and they would bless any power that would grant them such a boon.

The Rocky Mountains interposing between Missouri and Oregon will very naturally separate them from the United States, when they see the advantages arising from a connection with another nation of the same language and habits with themselves. The line of Texas running with the Arkansas, and extending to the great desert, would mark a natural boundary between Texas, or a new and vast Republic to the Southwest. If this ever take place, you may rely upon one thing, which is this, that a nation, embracing the advantages of the extent of seventeen degrees on the Pacific, and so extensive a front on the Atlantic as Texas does, will not be less than a rival power to any of the nations now in existence.

You need not estimate the population, which is said, or reputed, to occupy the vast Territory embraced between the 29th and 46th degrees of latitude on the Pacific. They will, like the Indian race, yield to the advance of the North American population. The amalgamation, under the guidance of statesmen, cannot fail to produce the result, in creating a united Government, formed of, and embracing the limits suggested.

It may be urged, that these matters are remote. Be it so. Statesmen are intended by their forecast to regulate and arrange matters in such sort as will give direction to events by which the future is to be benefited or prejudiced.

"You may freely rely, my friend, that future ages will profit by these facts, while we will only contemplate them in perspective. They must come. It is impossible to look upon the map of North America, and not perceive the rationale of the project. Men may laugh at these suggestions; but when we are withdrawn from all the petty influences which now exist, these matters will assume the most grave and solemn national import.

"I do not care to be in any way identified with them. They are the results of destiny, over which I have no control.

"If the Treaty is not ratified, I will require all future negotiations to be transferred to Texas."   *   *   *

It would be difficult in all the annals of history to discover a more striking illustration of far-sighted statesmanship.

SECTION FOURTEENTH.

RETIREMENT—HOUSTON'S CHARACTER.

I.

SUCH was the destiny which, to the keen vision of Houston, awaited Texas if she remained a Sovereign Nation.

The extracts we have given from his dispatches put the question of his policy and his preferences, in regard to annexation, at rest for ever. He was, up to the last moment, in favor of that great measure.

He favored it, because it would secure immediate peace to his fellow citizens, and protection from a perfidious and barbarous foe.

He favored it, because it would settle the affairs and establish the tranquillity of the Republic, and enable him to withdraw from the turbulent scenes of political life, and enjoy the repose of retirement, after his long and ceaseless labors.

He favored it, because it would bind the people of Texas firmly to the great Federal Family of Washington, and link their fortunes to the American Republic.

He favored it, because, like all the true and all the patriotic of his country, he felt an earnest longing to return to the family hearth-stone, where the great Patriarchs of the Revolution had gathered, and unite with twenty millions of his brethern in burning incense to the Genius of Liberty around its holy altars.

He favored it, because he saw that it would narrow the field of many petty ambitious men, whose struggles for power might disturb the tranquillity of Texas, and impede her advancement.

He favored it, because he felt he had himself achieved his work on the field and in the Cabinet, and although he was beloved by the people, and could always have been, in one form or another, their Leader, yet he had no more ambition to gratify. He believed, too, that his beloved country would find under our broad shield, the same repose from her alarms and troubles, that he himself looked forward to in the quiet of his Prairie Home. And yet his dispatches show that he was prepared for any result. He had his eye fixed on the future, and if American Statesmen were resolved Texas never should mingle her fortunes with us, he also was determined to watch over her career and guide her to a nobler destiny.

II.

Up to the very moment the decision was made by the American Senate, he held the question of annexation in the hollow of his hand. And when, at the eleventh hour, we grudgingly opened the doors to let the light of the Lone Star shine into our Temple, there is not a shadow of doubt, that if Houston had resented the tardy offer, it would have been proudly and scornfully hurled back by the people of Texas. He was not then President, actually—but in or out of office, he was still their Leader, the Counsellor of his country. His last term expired just before annexation was passed, and the Constitution would not allow him to be President again. But his own confidential friend, his Secretary of State, his adviser and his supporter, was chosen to succeed him, and it was everywhere understood that Houston's policy was still followed—his feeling still consulted— and his voice still heard.

III.

Great apprehensions were felt by the friends of Texas in this country, about the course Houston would finally pursue—for it was believed that he would carry the people of that Republic with him in his decision. The time at last came—Houston gave his support to Annexation, and by an overwhelming majority Texas became one of the Sovereign States of the American Republic

IV.

The following important Letter of Instructions procured the annexation of Texas.

" City of Houston, April 16th, 1844.

"GENTLEMEN,—Your notes have both reached me, one of the 30th ult., and one of the 1st inst. To-day I forward to the State Department all my dispatches.

"Col. Ashbel Smith, our Chargé d'Affaires, writes from Paris, under date 29th February, this important fact. "The French and British Governments have united in a Protest to the United States against the annexation of Texas to the Union." This is an important fact. Never has the situation of Texas been so interesting since the 21st of April, 1836, as at this moment. You may rely upon it, if the Government of the United States does not act immediately, and consummate the work of annexation, Texas is for ever lost to them.

"In my opinion, England and France will say to Texas, "if you will agree to remain separate for ever from the United States, we will forthwith prevent all further molestation to you from Mexico, and guarantee you independence agreeably to your institutions now established and avowed." You cannot fail to discover what would be the proper course of Texas in such an event. Texas has *done all* that she *could do* to obtain annexation, and you may rely upon this fact, in the event of a failure, that Texas will *do all* that she *should do.*

"If a Treaty is made, it will of course have been done after the pledges given by the United States Chargé d'Affaires have been recognized by his

Government, and then we are secure. If a Treaty has been made, and those pledges exacted by you, and it should be rejected, it will be proper to ascertain if annexation can take place by Congressional action, and this done promptly. Should all fail, you will forthwith call upon Mr. Packenham, and the French Minister, as well as the Government of the United States, and after suitable conversations and explanations, present to them the subject of a Triple guarantee for our Independence, and to prevent all further molestation, or at least an unlimited truce with Mexico. And then, if all prospect of annexation fails with the Government of the United States, and it should refuse to unite upon the basis here laid down, you will then, so far as practicable, arrange the matter with France and England ; and General Henderson, with Mr. Miller, Secretary of the Secret Legation, will make a visit of leave to the Heads of the proper Departments, and return to Texas. Texas ought not, cannot, and will not remain in its present situation.

" The subject of annexation has already embarrassed our relations with Mexico. The Truce will end on the first of May, as I presume, for I did not accede to the terms of the armistice, since Texas was recognized as a " Department of Mexico," in the terms of agreement between the commissioners. Mexico was well disposed to settle matters very amicably, when our Commissioners arrived at Sabinus, but one of the Mexican Commissioners was too unwell to proceed to business. When he recovered, the subject of annexation was mooted in the United States, and the Texan Congress, all of which had reached Mexico. Of these facts, in part, Gen. Henderson was apprised, and the anticipated rupture of our negotiations with Mexico was one reason why I was so careful to require of Gen. Murphy (endorsed by his Government), *such pledges* as would secure us against all contingencies that might arise to us, in consequence of our opening negotiations with the United States, on the subject of annexation.

" This Government has been called on, and requested by her Majesty's Government, to state our relation to the Government of the United States. It was due to England, and her Majesty's Government was informed that an agent, Gen. Henderson, had been sent to Washington City, to negotiate upon the subject of annexation ; but the particulars were not rendered. Since this occurred I had an interview with Capt. Elliot, and I do not think the British Government will withdraw its friendly offices from the subject of Peace between Texas and Mexico.

" It is reported here, that the Government of the United States has refused to sanction the pledges given by General Murphy. This surely cannot be the case. If so, you will have found yourselves in a most awk-ward dilemma. What—disavow such pledges when they were based upon Mr. Upshur's letter ? I cannot believe this, unless the United States de-sired Texas to surrender herself to the uncertainty, or chances of annexa-tion, contingent upon the various political influences which might interpose to the consummation of the object, and subject us to the injurious and annoying action of Mexico, instigated by the adhesion of Texas to the United States. A refusal on the part of. that Government to secure us against consequences, which it has produced by *direct solicitation* of us, would be selfish in the extreme, and indeed I cannot conceive appropriate terms in which to characterize such conduct and policy, in an official dis-patch. It would amount to this only—that if anything could be made out of Texas by the United States, they were prepared and willing to de-rive the advantage, and if that could not be done, they wished to incur no responsibility on the account of Texas, but leave her to all the consequen-ces which might possibly result to her from the course which her generosity and credulity might induce her to pursue. Pitiable would our situation be if we were not annexed, and had required no pledges ; fortunately, *this is not* our situation.

" You have now all the grounds before you, and I hope you will ponder wisely and proceed securely for our safety.

"It is palpable scandal to the nineteenth century, that statesmen should be prating about the emancipation of persons born, and their race held in slavery, by the custom and consent of nations for centuries, while they permit Santa Anna to forge and rivet chains upon eight millions of peo-ple who were born free. Thus will the horrors of slavery be increased, with design to render his success subservient to the subversion of the lib-erties of Texas, and form a new era in the history by degrading to slavery a portion of the Anglo-Saxon race. This ought not, and cannot be. It argues on the part of statesmen a want of perception, as well as self-respect.

" Gentlemen, you will keep the Government advised by every mail, and daily, of important events as they transpire. If you should be thrown for future reliance upon the friendly offices of Great Britain and France, you will, if possible, ascertain from them if they will act promptly, and what conditions they will expect of this Government.

" Mr. Van Zandt has written that the United States were not willing to form any alliance with Texas, as it was contrary to their policy. Hence the necessity, upon the failure of the immediate annexation of this country to the confederacy of the North, and you will, as I have indicated, approach the Governments of England and France.

"It is the first duty of statesmen and patriots to insure the liberty and well-being of their country. This is now our attitude, and every honest man in Texas will justify and approve that policy, which will place us in a situation where our liberties are secured, whether it be by annexation or the establishment of our Independence. France and England will act effectively, if we do not permit ourselves to be trifled with and duped by the United States. But of this subject, as your situation may soon call your attention to it, you will be the best judges.

*   *   *   *   *   *   *   *   *

"This letter does not cancel former instructions from the Department; but it is designed to meet emergencies which may arise, or remedy those which have already arisen. Having awaited the arrival of your dispatches, and there being no time to forward them, and send a reply from the State Department, I have deemed it proper to write to you directly by the return mail; so that you may be ready, in the event of necessity, to take such action as our situation may require, and be prepared for contingencies.   I have the honor to be,

"Your obt. servant,

"SAM HOUSTON.

"To Gen. J. P. Henderson and
"Hon. Isaac Van Zandt, &c. &c., &c."

V.

Henceforth, for weal or woe, her fortunes were to be mingled with the fortunes of the United States. Whether she was to regret it, was yet to be seen. She most certainly would have repented the day she ever sought refuge under our protection, unless she had been allowed to occupy a high and honorable place in our Confederacy. She was no outlaw—no menial—nor was she to be treated as either. With the richest soil and vast natural resources—with a wide territory which stretches from the sea, where it blushes under a tropical sun, to the North where it whitens with the eternal snow of her mountains—with a climate as balmy as the lands which are bathed by the blue waters of the Mediterranean—and, above all, with an ingenious, enterprising, and heroic people, she must become the garden of the New World. Let it be the pride of every man, whose inestimable privilege is to say, " I am an American Citizen," to extend towards Texas and the Texans his generous greeting. They were long misrepresented and traduced ; but the odium has been lifted from their name, for they *are* a brave and a magnanimous people ; and let us be proud everywhere, whether it be by the firesides of our northern homes, or in the courts of foreign princes, to call them brothers. Let us show to them, and the world, that the children of sires who bled at Bunker Hill and Yorktown, know how to prize the heroic men who rang out the Anglo-Saxon battle-cry over the bloody field of San Jacinto.

VI.

But we are admonished that we may have already trespassed too long upon the patience of our readers in these details. Our only excuse is, that, in tracing the fortunes of a brave People and their heroic Leader, we have been beguiled by the pleasant lights and shadows that have fallen over the path where we were roaming.

His predecessor had made war upon the Indians, and carried desolation to their peaceful wigwams. In their forest homes were heard the wailings of women whose chiefs had fallen by the hand of the white man ; and the young Indian boy was sad because his Chieftain Father led him out no more on the path of the forest game. Houston had seen injustice perpetrated upon the Red men, and when his last term began, he at once sent the wampum among the forest tribes, and soon after went himself, in the Indian dress, to the distant woods, and smoked the pipe of peace in the Chieftains' dwellings. He made treaties with twenty-four different Chiefs, and they regarded these treaties sacredly. Among them he felt safe—he wrapped his blanket about him, and laid himself down to sleep by the fires of ferocious savages, near whom other white men did ·not dare to venture. "We have nothing to fear from an Indian," he used to say, "if we only treat him with justice, and he believes us his friends." Peace was again restored along the frontiers, and the green corn was again growing luxuriantly by the side of the primeval forests, where the savage stealthily lurked for his game.

VII.

Houston paid off a large amount of debt incurred by his predecessor, due to other Governments, arising from the prodigality of the administration. He created no new debt—administered the Government on the basis of the revenues, and left the Exchequer Bills issued at the beginning of his term, at par, with a considerable surplus in the Treasury.

He left the country at peace with all the Indian tribes on the frontiers—the Navy was laid up in port, for there was no use for it—the State was blessed with tranquillity at home, the nation was prosperous—emigrants of the better class were rapidly pouring in from the North and from Europe ; and the people were happy. The prisoners in Mexico were all restored to their homes—inland trade with Mexico was brisk and lucrative ; —Texas was respected by all nations, and Annexation was near its consummation.

VIII.

Houston's last term expired. He could never be President again ; and it was with no little sadness that the people saw him lay down the insignia of his office, and take leave of them, to return to private life. He was received back with joy by his family, and they thought that he would part from them no more. His home was on a rolling elevation in the midst of a green prairie, interspersed with islands of trees, and silver lakes, gleaming in the sunlight. His labors, his sorrows, and his struggles were over, and in the bosom of an affectionate family he expected to spend the last peaceful years of his stormy life in the noble pursuits of the husbandman.

IX.

Texas became one of the States of our Confederacy, and she called her old Leader from retirement once more, to represent her—but in the Senate at Washington. It is not strange that he yielded with deep reluctance—for he felt that in his quiet home, he was as happy as the regards of the Nation he had saved, the affection and society of his wife and his child, and the remembrance of sorrows past and victories won, could make him. But he responded to the call of his country, and brought his Republic and laid it on our Federal Altar.

X.

Houston's youth was wild and impetuous ; but it was spotted by no crime, it was not even soiled by indulgence. His early manhood was filled with earnestness and daring, but it was deformed by no act which lost for him the confidence of the virtuous, or the doating love of his mother. We know, too, that just as he was stepping upon the theatre of high and brilliant fame, a cloud came over the sky, and wrapped his heart and his home in sadness and gloom.

There is a sorrow which even the Hero cannot bear. The storms of life may beat against the frail dwelling of man as wildly as they will, and the proud and the generous heart may

still withstand the blast.   But when the poisoned shaft of disappointment strikes the bosom where *all* we love and live for is
treasured, the fruit of this world turns to ashes, and the charm
of life is broken.   Then it is that too often reason and bliss take
their flight together.

XI.

When this dark cloud fell over the path of Houston, he
buried his sorrows in the flowing bowl.   His indulgences began
with the wreck of his hopes, and like many noble and generous
spirits, he gave himself up to the fatal enchantress.   But his
excesses have been exaggerated by his enemies a hundredfold.
We believe no man can say that he ever saw Houston rendered
incompetent, by any indulgence, to perform any of the offices of
private or public life, a single hour.

XII.

But the days of his indulgences have long since passed away.
When the sunlight of domestic happiness again shone through
his dwelling, and he was sustained once more by that great conservative principle of a man's life, a happy home, illumined by
the smile of an affectionate and devoted wife—his good angel came
back again, *and for many years no man has been more exemplary
in all the duties and all the virtues of the citizen, the father and
the husband.*   From that moment he espoused the great cause of
Virtue and Temperance, with all the earnestness of his nature.

XIII.

Whenever an opportunity has been presented, he has eloquently spoken, in public and in private, in favor of that
beneficent movement, which has restored many thousands of

generous but misguided men to the long-abandoned embraces of weeping families, and to the noble duties of citizenship. And who could better tell the horrors and the woes of the poor inebriate's life than the man who had experienced them ? Who could more eloquently and willingly woo back the wanderer to the fold of virtue, than he who had just returned to its hallowed inclosure ? Blessings on the head of the devoted and beautiful wife, whose tender persuasions proved too strong for the clamors of appetite and the allurements of vice ! In winning the stricken wanderer back to the pure charities of home, she saved the State one of its noblest citizens ; and so benign has been the influence of his wonderful example, and so calm, and so holy a light beams ceaselessly around the altars of that distant Prairie Home, that his children will, with the nation he saved, rise up and call him blessed. Houston's indulgences never were carried so far as to give a shock to his constitution. They were only occasional at any period.

XIV.

And now he finds himself standing on the meridian of life, with an erect, well-made form, of perfect health and gigantic strength. His hair has been turned grey by Herculean labors, but his eye is still soft and clear, and it beams with a smile which no man's can wear, whose heart does not overflow with love of country and philanthropy to his race. His countenance is flushed with the glow of health and cheerfulness, which seldom, in a world like ours, lingers after the morning of life is passed. And but for occasional days of suffering from the wound he received in his right shoulder from two rifle-balls at To-ho-pe-ka, forty years ago, he knows no physical ailment. Sometimes these sufferings are intense, and he will never be free from them while he lives, for no surgical skill has ever been able to close up that wound. It has discharged every day for more than thirty years. In a manner almost miraculous, he has entirely recovered from the wound in his ankle received at the battle of San Jacinto.

SECTION FIFTEENTH.

HOUSTON IN THE NATIONAL SENATE.

I.

SUCH was Houston's character, and such had been his achievements ten years ago. On the annexation of Texas to the United States, he and Gen. Rusk were chosen to represent the new State in the National Senate. Our limits preclude us from tracing, as fully as we should desire, his Senatorial career. Abstaining from general or promiscuous debate, he has nevertheless been found punctually in his place and prompt at the discharge of every duty, and whenever great questions have claimed the attention of the Senate, his speeches have shown that he carefully watched the interests of the country, and was always ready to render it his best services. But we must glance over the records of his oratory and services for several years, and come down to the *annus mirabilis* of the Republic.

II.

The year 1850—the middle of the Nineteenth Century— witnessed a sectional convulsion which threatened the union of the American States. The leaders of Parties, and the champions of Section, exulted over the prospect of disunion ; and for a while, the waves of discord ran so high, that the most enlightened and prominent friends of the Union, became deeply alarmed. This exigency called out all the force of Houston's character. He had shed his blood in the Second War with England, where he had learned the science and the practice of warfare, from General Jackson himself. He had been the leader, the father, and the savior of Texas, on whose soil he had again bled in behalf of the independence of a new Republic. When he came into the Senate of the United States, he had no private views or sectional feelings to gratify. He felt jealous indeed, of the interests of his own State, after she had ceased to be an Independent Republic, and its lone star had been added to the National Constellation ; but he went into the Senate *as a national man*, and every act of his, from that day to this, has only stamped his political character as an American statesman, with the broadest impress of nationality.

III.

If our limits would admit, we should be glad to introduce all he said in the midst of that trying crisis of 1850 ; but the whole country well knows the course he took at the time ; while we are compelled to go on to other events of great significance that were fast approaching.

IV.

Before the National Convention of 1852 assembled in Baltimore, a new spirit had gone over the country—the United States of America had become *democratic*, and the new age of the Republic was at hand. General Jackson and his Administration for two terms, had stamped upon the country, deeper than it had ever been stamped before, a National Democratic Policy. Defeated in all their great measures, the Whig party— embracing as it did so large a number of the noblest and best men of the country—had no longer any great common ties to bind it together; and the American people were ready, and willing, to blend themselves together, in a Great National Party that promised to cement the common patriotic feelings of the Nation, and to concentrate the best efforts of all our people, in the inauguration of a New Period of Patriotism and enlightened administration.

V.

Factions raged—Sectionalism had grown furious—Disunion had lifted its serpent head—Abolitionism had inflamed the passions of northern men—and everywhere the political sky was overcast by ominous clouds that foreshadowed a dark future for the great Republic of Washington. But thanks to the God of the Universe, that Republic was too great and glorious to be suddenly destroyed. Heaven watched over our destinies. The great men of all parties in the National Councils, clustered around the Federal Altar, where the Fathers of the Republic had worshiped; and laying aside all sectional feeling, determined to preserve the integrity of that Union which had cost so much blood, and been sanctified by so many years of struggle. Great public meetings were everywhere held, in honor of those men who had, in this moment of danger, struck their hands together in holy love of the Institutions of our Fathers, and sworn to defend them to the last.

VI.

Such was the feeling of the great men of the country; and of the people of the country, when it became necessary to choose a President, in 1852.

VII.

Who should the man be? The Whig Convention met, and
12

three great names came up for their consideration.   First of all, Fillmore—who had by a painful dispensation of Providence been called, unexpectedly, to preside over the affairs of the Nation. He had done well ; and if, at the time, the country could have known how poorly another man would have filled his place, he would doubtless have been nominated for another term of office. And there was Webster, incontestably the mightiest man then living, as the expounder of the Constitution ; and the eloquent, and all but inspired Orator of his age.   But the Convention deemed it necessary to select the name of the hero of Lundy's Lane.   He had rendered great services to the Nation ; but there was a strong suspicion entertained that some of the Catalines of the Republic might control the counsels of his Cabinet, and that suspicion killed him.   And so low had we fallen as a people, at that time, that this great man, who had fought in all the wars of the Republic, except the war of the Revolution—the man who had rendered most signal services to the country, in every position he had held—that on an electioneering tour, he seemed to lose no opportunity, while addressing a mob of foreigners, to announce to them that .he *recognized with enthusiastic delight, their foreign brogue.*   So lately did a popular and a splendid American patriot and hero bend his proud back to the vile herd of foreign paupers that come upon our shores, as the locusts fell upon the garden land of Egypt, eating up every green thing.   And yet but a few years before, he had from the fullness of his patriotic heart, warned his country most fervidly against the dangerous influence of foreigners.

VIII.

Little, or nothing, was known of Frank Pierce—the man who was hit upon by accident, in the Democratic Convention which assembled at Baltimore.   He had been a member of Congress, although he had done nothing there, worthy of recollection, during the time he held his place. When it was announced that he had been a member of the United States Senate, the records of that great body unfolded no further information ; but some wily demagogues, with the aid of deluded but honest men, pitched his name into the Convention at the last moment, when its members had grown tired of strife and struggle, for many days ; and of course, when the Leaders of the Democratic party had all been thrown overboard, "Frank Pierce, of Concord, New Hampshire," was nominated, almost by acclamation. Democracy was satisfied for the moment ; but *nationality went by default.*

IX.

And yet, when Frank Pierce was nominated as a *national American Candidate*, the news was flashed over the country by telegraph ; and the nation lifted its hands in gratitude, that there was the prospect of an administration which would be broad, great, magnanimous, and just. The country clapped its hands with exultation, when Frank Pierce was elected ; for he had, by every pledge, and sign, and promise known to men, sworn fidelity to the great principles of the great Compromise of 1850.

X.

Union Whigs rejoiced in the defeat of General Scott ; and Webster, from his dying bed, sent to Rufus Choate—his personal friend—the message :—"not to mar his future prospects by taking one step in the support of Scott." So dear was the Union of these States, as the Fathers of the Republic had bequeathed it to us, that the mere apprehension that a sectional spirit would guide the councils of the Whig Candidate, turned against him the irresistible tide of Public Opinion. Frank

Pierce was elected by an unprecedented majority ; for he had the votes of twenty-seven States cast in his favor.   There was not a doubt expressed, nor a foreboding entertained through the Republic ; and men everywhere congratulated themselves upon the almost unanimous election of a new man, who it was believed would represent the country, its feelings, and its nationality. Never, since the time of Washington, has a President gone to his inauguration, under auspices which promised more enduring fame.   All that General Pierce had to do, was to fulfill the pledges which he had voluntarily made, and all would have been well with him, and the country.

XI.

He began his administration, by choosing the leaders of factions for his counsellors.   Unlike a general, he deserted the main body of his army, and put into power all the men he could find, who had been guilty of mutiny in the camp.   He denationalized himself on the start.   He did not select a single man for office, at home or abroad, who had signalized himself as a leader in the great cause which he himself was supposed to represent. He started out with the policy that he must *buy his enemies, because his friends were already secured.*

XII.

What were the consequences ?   By the high and magnani. mous policy which had been adopted by the National Democratic Convention at Baltimore, he had been selected as the impersonation of that broad national spirit which was then speaking through all the members of that Convention,—which was then making itself felt through all the leading Journals of America— and through these channels, wise men saw that a new age was dawning upon the country ; and thus near the tomb of Washington, where Frank Pierce swore allegiance to the Constitution, the Compromise Measures, and the nationality of the country; the American people gathered in gratitude to Heaven, and with enthusiasm to their chief, to sustain the Institutions of their Fathers.

XIII.

He had indeed chosen for his counsellors, in the beginning, men who did not command the confidence of the country ; but it was not believed that a man who had been elected under such circumstances, and who had made such pledges to the Nation, could so foully betray his trust as to gather around him public traitors.   But this delusion was soon dispelled, for they turned out to be either mere adventurers, or worn-out and corrupt demagogues, who would buy and sell men, States, principles— and the Republic itself, if by doing it they could make something at the game.

XIV.

This Administration has now been reduced to contempt.   It is unnecessary to say that it has not only violated every pledge it has made—the President has not only refused to do everything he promised, and done everything he was pledged not to do ; but he has disgraced us in the eyes of all foreign nations, by sending incompetent and unacceptable men to represent us abroad.   It will not be denied that, with a very few exceptions, he has chosen the worst set of men he could have found in the United States, to represent us abroad—Red Republicans— German Jews--Filibusters—Factionists—Secessionists—Abolitionists—Loafers—anybody but men born on the soil, breathing the spirit of our Institutions, and comprehending our system of government.

XV.

This will easily account for the fact that the present Administration has not only been reduced to contempt at home, and abroad ; but that even those common measures of necessity which the exigencies of the country have called for, have not been carried through. We have indeed had a bluster about the Koszta affair—we have bullied Spain—and Frank Pierce has bombarded and burned down Greytown. This is all he has achieved :—except—*planting himself in open hostility to the American movement. He* is the man who has lifted his puny and putrid hand, to arrest the avalanche rush of millions of Americans, to secure their birth-right. He does not comprehend the spirit of our Institutions—the spirit of our country— nor the spirit of our times. *He stands* in the way of the People, and he will be crushed. He is peddling out his offices to people who can play the lackey to him in his decadent fortunes, while he has overlooked almost every noble national man in the country, for offices in his gift.

XVI.

He began his Administration by putting a Roman Catholic into his Cabinet, as Post-Master-General—and Roman Catholicism in America, means an attempt to establish " *a monarchy on Republican soil, with a king at Rome*"—and this Post-Master-General has not only control of the transmission of public intelligence to twenty-five millions of people ; but the appointment of one hundred thousand office-holders. He continued it, by bestowing upon thousands of illiterate, bigoted, monarchical subjects of Rome, places of trust and profit in the revenue service, besides making Catholics and Jesuits, District Attorneys, Marshals, &c., &c., &c., throughout the United States ; for this man, and the crew that he has gathered around him, have carried things so far, that no upright American who has any pride in being an American, is left to do him homage. It seems to have been the fate of Frank Pierce to make John Tyler's Administration immortal, by contrasting it with his own. John Tyler was not the worst President we have had.

XVII.

The most dastardly act which this Concord man has perpetrated, was to violate all the pledges he had given, by concocting, with the help of other demagogues, the infamous Nebraska Bill—by which a territory, nine times as large as the State of New York, over whose soil the Missouri Compromise had declared that African slavery, or involuntary servitude should never extend, was freely, and without the asking, dedicated to slavery. It is a fact bad enough in itself, that slavery, through the early wrongs of our monarchial oppressors, should exist in the Republic : but that it should exist at all in the grandest Republic of all the ages, is worse still. We understand the reasons why, and we can explain the thing to ourselves—just as the founders and framers of the Constitution explained it and understood it—for we are a cluster of States that understand each other, and we agreed, in the beginning, that we would not intermeddle with each other's affairs.

XVIII.

This was the spirit in which the Compromise Measures were passed. Upon the maintenance of this state of things, Frank Pierce was elected President.

When he got into power, all his efforts were directed to their overthrow. He is the traitor of all ages ; because he has betrayed more pledges, and deceived more men, than any other man that has lived—and he had been preceded by traitors who had a hundred times his capacity of doing good, although few of them ever attempted to do so much evil.

Reduced at last below the contempt of decent men, he has found himself deserted by all the good who contributed to his elevation, and none even appear to stand by him now, except those he has bought by place, office, or favors.

XIX.

When Frank Pierce found himself in this degraded position, the demagogues who surrounded him, or other demagogues who thought they could play a good card over his political coffin, proposed the Nebraska Bill. In the indignation of his spirit—in the honesty of his political character, and in the might of his genius, Sam Houston rose in the Senate, and pronounced the following words, which added a new seal to the integrity of his political character, and gave new lustre to his patriotism.

XX.

Mr. PRESIDENT : This unusual night sitting is without precedent in the history of any previous Congress at this stage of the session. The extra-ordinary circumstances in which we find ourselves placed, would seem to indicate a crisis in the affairs of the country of no ordinary importance ; a crisis that portends either good or evil to our institutions.

The extraordinary character of the bill before the Senate, as well as the manner in which it is presented to the body, demands the gravest deliber-ation. This, sir, is the anniversary of a protracted session, in which the organization of the Territory of Nebraska was elaborately discussed on the last day of the last session. In that discussion, which, like this, had kept us in our seats to the morning dawn, the prominent points of opposition were such as related to the Indian tribes. Such a bill at the present ses-sion would have met with no insuperable objections ; but what do we now find ? A bill entirely variant, and a bill which involves new and important principles. It has come an unexpected measure without a harbinger, for no agitation was heard of, and the breeze bore no whisper to our ears that the Missouri Compromise was to be repealed.

XXI.

Its presentation has been as sudden as the measure itself is bold ; and the excitement of the public mind is of corresponding intensity. We are told, to be sure, that there is no necessity for agitation, and that soon the public mind will be tranquil, and the country will be in a state of repose and quiet—as it was at the introduction of this measure. The honorable Senator who has just taken his seat (Mr. Douglas), the chairman of the Committee on Territories, in his lecture to the South, exhorted them to stand by the principle of this bill, with the assurance that it will be good for them, and that the country will maintain it. Sir, under proper circumstances, I should recognize the exhortation ; but is the principle such a one as should be adopted by this body, or can it be sanctioned by the nation ? Whether it is expedient and useful at this time I shall take the liberty to examine.

XXII.

Mr. President, I cannot believe that the agitation created by this measure will be confined to the Senate Chamber. I cannot believe, from what we have witnessed here to-night, that this will be the exclusive arena for the exercise of human passions, and the expression of public opinions. *If the Republic be not shaken, I will thank Heaven fo its kindness in maintaining its stability.* To what extent is it proposed to establish the principle of non-intervention ? Are you extending it to a domain inhabited by citizens, or to a barren prairie, a wilderness, or even to forty thousand wild Indians ? Is this the diffusive excellence of non-intervention ? I, sir, am for non-intervention upon the principles which have heretofore been recognized by this Government. Hitherto Territories have been organized —within my recollection Alabama, Missouri, Florida, Arkansas, Mississippi, Wisconsin, and Iowa have been organized—and the principle now proposed was not deemed essential to their well-being ; and is there any infirmity in their constitutions or their growth ? Sir, has any malign influence attached to them from their simple, economical organization ? It

12*

may be that the word "economy" is deemed obsolete in the present condition of our Treasury. Were it otherwise, I am simple enough to confess that the organization of two Territories—when there are not people to constitute an ordinary county in one of the populous States of this Union, and when those who do inhabit the Territories are United States soldiers, who are not entitled to vote at elections in the States or Territories—is not a procedure that can be characterized as economical. If the principle of non-intervention be correct, it is correct where the Territories have been governed by laws of Congress until they are prepared to make application 'or admission as States. Then they have a right to elect their delegates 'o convention, for the purpose of framing State constitutions, which, if accepted by Congress, invest them with all the sovereign rights of States; and then, for the first time, they have the complete power of self-government. A Territory under the tutelage of Congress can form no organic laws, either admitting or excluding slavery. A people without organic laws might alternately enact and repeal all laws, and reënact them without limitation, as they would have no local constitution. Congress has a supervision over the action of all Territories until they become sovereign States. In the formation of State governments, I can say that they have the exclusive right to determine whether they will come into the Union with or without slavery. There, sir, is the application of the principle of non-intervention, and one that I have always maintained.

XXIII.

But gentlemen speak of sovereignty—they say that the people are sovereign, and supreme. Sir, I bow with all deference to that sovereignty; but I do not apply the principle to the Territories in their unorganized and chrysalis condition. Sovereignty implies the power of organization, and a self-acting, self-moving and self-sustaining principle; but the Territories have it not. They only acquire it when they become constituent parts of this Confederacy.

XXIV.

But we are told that the South has stood by the Compromise. I am glad of it. Yet gentlemen have protested against the recognition of North and South. Why, sir, they are recognized every day. The distinction has been recognized by the Statesmen of every day, and every section of the country. Am I to be told that the question has not assumed that character, and that it will not operate to carry sectional influence with it to a certain extent? It is impossible that you can divest it of a sectional character to some extent. Why, we are told, in the very breath that declares there is no such principle recognized, that the North has violated the Missouri Compromise, and the South has maintained it; and yet do you tell me that there is no North and no South? Let us look at the action of the North and South. I am not going back to make a technical, or legal, or constitutional argument upon the facts and circumstances of the Missouri Compromise—its creation, its progress, its recognition, and final decision. I am not going to characterize it a compact as distinguished from a compromise, because I can see no reasonable application of the one that does not belong to the other.

XXV.

The word "compromise" is a more comprehensive and rational term when applied to an amicable adjustment of differences existing between two parties who are reconciled. I well remember that on the organization of Oregon Territory, the South denounced the Missouri Compromise, and did not recognize it. Was not that denunciation subsequent to a joint recognition by both sections of the Union, the North and the South? Had they not united, the South, perhaps, with more unanimity than the North, upon its application to Texas in her annexation? Yes, sir, they had. That was in 1845; and in 1848, three years after, without any intervening act of bad faith on the part of the North, the South repudiated it on the organization of Oregon Territory.

Mr. ATCHISON (Mr. DODGE, of Iowa, in the chair). The Senator says that the southern members of the Senate repudiated the Missouri Compromise on the Oregon bill. Now that, I think, with all due deference to the Senator, is not so. The Senator from Illinois proposed to the Oregon bill the Missouri Compromise, and every southern gentleman, according to my recollection, voted for it—every one in the Senate. The bill went to the House, and the House refused to accede to it.

Mr. DOUGLAS. Yes, sir.

Mr. ATCHISON. The Senator from Texas, and my then colleague, the senior Senator from Missouri (Mr. Benton), alone of all the southern members voted to recede from it.

XXVI.

Mr. HOUSTON. I thank the gentleman for giving me a very pleasing intimation. It reminds me, Mr. President, of what did occur. We voted to recede from it. The other gentlemen did not vote to recede. They had voted in opposition to its organization and admission, or what was tantamount to it. And what was the reason? It was because there was a proposition, and I had introduced resolutions myself, to extend the compromise line to the Pacific ocean. The North did not accept it. I did not believe it would be more than an abstraction. Why did I do it then? I will tell you. But previous to this, and at the time Oregon was organized by the Government, the South went against it, I may say, in a body. The southwestern Senators and myself went for it, under the heaviest denunciations and anathemas that could be applied to any individuals. Was this an abandonment of it by the North? Had it been an abandonment of the application of it by the North, or its non-application by the South, to Texas? Did not the North receive five and a half degrees of slave territory from Texas, and in consideration of that cede to Texas the right of forming four States in addition to the one then formed? Call it a compact or compromise as you please; but then it assumed the character of a compact when applied to Texas, because Texas came in recognizing that as a principle concurred in by the North and the South. They both applied it to Texas, and it was upon it that she came in. And so far, certainly, it was a compact with her. Is not Texas interested in that? Did she not consider the Missouri Compromise practically a compact, so far as she is concerned? Because she predicated her own upon it. And if you deprive her of the benefits resulting from and declared by that compact, when are her four States to come in, if the North has the ascendancy? Cannot they exclude them when they please if the Missouri Compromise be repealed? We hold them by an obligation which it would be dishonorable and infamous to abandon. You cannot repeal that compromise without the consent of Texas. Remember, Texas was an independent nation, a sovereignty, when she came into this Union. She had rights equal to those possessed by this country; institutions quite as good, and a more harmonious structure of her community. Now, will there not be a liability that these four additional States may be denied to Texas? Texas insists upon this right in my person, as one of her representatives. I claim it as no boon bestowed. I ask it as no gift. The State demands it as a *right*, to form four additional States, if she should elect to do so.

XXVII.

But what would the repeal of this Compromise amount to? An abstraction? What would the South be benefited by it? By the amendment of the Senator from North Carolina, the bill is perfectly eviscerated, or, to use a senatorial term, because I think it may be applied with more propriety, *elegantly* emasculated. Yes, sir, it amounts to nothing. It holds a promise to the ear, but breaks it to the hope. If it is ever to be repealed, I want no empty promises. They have not been asked for by the South. They are not desired; and, so far as I am concerned, they will never be accepted. Neither my colleague nor myself have ever been consulted in relation to this subject. On the contrary, we have been sedulously excluded from all consultation. I have never had an intimation that a conference was to take place, a caucus to be held, or stringent measures applied in the passage of this bill. Nothing of the kind. I have been in the dark in relation to it. I feel that Texas has as important an interest as any other section of this Union in the repeal of the Compromise, and would be as vitally affected by it. She must be eventually, if calamities are to fall upon the South, the most unfortunate of all that portion of the Union.

XXVIII.

I will give you my reasons why I think Texas would be in the most deplorable condition of all the Southern States. It is now the terminus of the slave population. It is a country of vast extent and fertile soil, favorable to the culture and growth of those productions which are most important to the necessities of the world—cotton, sugar, and tobacco. An immense slave population must eventually go there. The demand for labor is so great, everything is so inviting to the enterprising and industrious, that labor will be transferred there, because it will be of a most profitable character, and the disproportion of slaves to the white population must be immense. Then, sir, it becomes the gulf of slavery, and there its terrible eddies will whirl, if convulsions take place. I have a right, therefore, to claim some consideration in the Senate for the effect which the repeal of this Compromise will have upon our State. I have a right to demand it, and demand it for other reasons than those which I formerly gave here, that were personal to myself.

XXIX.

It is alleged that the refusal on the part of the North to continue the Missouri Compromise line over the acquisitions of 1847 and 1848 was a repudiation of the Compromise. That may be thought technically true. I grant that a proposition was made, or a Compromise entered into by the North and South, to extend the Missouri Compromise as far as the jurisdiction of the United States extended. That was to the Pacific ocean. When it was, by contract, carried on through Texas on its annexation, then, if I understand it, it was a new line—a continuation of the old line by consent. It was established there by a compact with Texas ; for by the original Missouri Compromise it could only extend as far as the jurisdiction of the United States went. Then the proposition to continue it to the Pacific was a new and substantive proposition. Though it might refer to the original principle of the old, it had no more connection with it than the Atlantic has with the Pacific.

XXX.

I understand, if individuals make a contract, whether they enter into it in writing, or not, if it is to be executed by any given time, and subsequently it is proposed by one of the parties to make another contract, which involves not the first, but is made because it is convenient to extend the first further, the refusal of one of the parties to agree to the second, does not invalidate the former contract. This is a kind of argument I have never heard resorted to, except in favor of the repeal of the Missouri Compromise. I have a great deal of veneration for that Compromise. I recollect the time when I was tried in the Senate Chamber upon its principles. There are Senators here who well remember that I was denounced, more in manner than in words, when I said I planted myself upon the Missouri Compromise line, and that astride of it I would stand, if needs be, and that there I would do battle, and there would I perish in the defence of the rights of the South. That was emphatic language, and I felt all that I uttered. Sir, I have some reverence for it ; and if I should feel such reverence, it is not unreasonable that I should have determinations, too, which will not be changed by all the technical and abstract notions which have been adduced and relied upon to enlighten the public mind, to manufacture public sentiment here, and to give direction to it abroad. Sir, I have no idea that the public sentiment is to be subverted, and I assure you that the North, or West, or South, cannot be willing that this should be done. No one can deprecate more than I do the fearful agitations which, I apprehend, will follow this ; but after the manifestations which we have had here, nothing that I can utter will affect those who are present, or certify to them what must be the inevitable consequence, out of this Hall, when agitation is rife abroad. Do these gentlemen say that I have not made any argument on this point? It is, sir, because I was not sufficiently skilled to meet the refined arguments that were adduced in favor of the repeal. What necessity has grown up for the adoption of this measure since 1850 ? None had resulted at this time last year. None has been heard of.

XXXI.

Three years have passed in tranquillity and peace. Yet the gentleman who urges the measure thinks that he would have been derelict to his duty he had not brought things to their present condition, and presented the matter in the shape in which it now stands. If it was necessary at all, it was necessary last year. No new developments have been made. The great principle of non-intervention existed then. There is no new demand for it now. Is not that a reason why this bill ought not to pass ? Was there any new indication given of its necessity up to the time that the bill was introduced here? None throughout the whole land. How, and where, and why, and when, and with whom this measure originated, Heaven only knows, for I have no cognizance of the facts ; but I well know that persons deeply involved in it, and exercising senatorial privileges here, never received information that such a measure would be brought forward, or would be urged with that pertinacity with which it is now done. Little did we think that it was to be urged upon us as a great healing measure. The honorable Senator from Virginia [Mr. MASON] said last night, that this is to be regarded as a great healing measure for the purpose of preventing agitation. Sir, I heard of no agitation until it arose here, nor would there have been any this day in the United States, if the bill in the form in which it was presented last year, had been brought forward and adopted without any provision either for non-intervention or the repeal of the Missouri compromise.

XXXII.

So far back as 1848, I find that President Polk recognized the Missouri Compromise as of binding force upon this country. He considered it not only binding upon the North in relation to the South, but, as the Chief Magistrate of this Union, he regarded it as binding upon the South, because it accorded certain privileges to the South; for he says, when speaking in relation to his approval of the Oregon bill, that he approved it because it lay north of 36° 30′; but had it lain south of 36° 30′, he would not say what action he would have taken upon it; clearly intimating that he would have vetoed the bill, regarding as he did the Missouri Compromise as obligatory on the two sections of the Union. How has it been repudiated since that time? Was it repudiated and superseded, or rendered null and void, by the Compromise of 1850? No such thing. Do you think that the astute statesmen, the men who managed and controlled the business of that Compromise, as much as any other men versed and skilled in legal lore and in general learning, men of acumen and keen perceptions, would have permitted that matter to go unexplained, if it ever had been contemplated to repeal the Missouri Compromise? Mr. Clay and Mr. Webster would never have done it. Yet no information was given that any such design was entertained by any member of this body I am sure that, for one, I did not entertain it. Other gentlemen, more astute than myself, might have done so, but I am confident that it was not the general understanding that non-intervention was to be applied to these Territories because they lay north of 36° 30′.

XXXIII.

I again ask, what benefit is to result to the South from this measure, if adopted? I have shown, I hope, that if you repeal this Missouri Compromise, Texas has no guarantee left for the multiplication of her States, if she chooses to make them. What are its advantages? Will it secure these Territories to the South? No, sir, not at all. But, the gentleman tells us, it is *the principle* that we want. I can perceive but one principle involved in the measure, and that principle lies at the root of agitation; and from that all the tumult and excitements of the country must arise. That is the only principle I can perceive. We are told by southern, as well as northern gentlemen, those who are for it, and those who are against it, that slavery will never be extended to that territory, that it will never go there ; but it is the principle of non-intervention that it is desired to establish. Sir, we have done well under the *intervention* of the Missouri Compromise, if the gentlemen so call it, in other Territories ; and, I adjure you, wnen there is so much involved, not to press this matter too far. What is to be the consequence ? If it is not in embryo, my suggestion will not make it so. It has been suggested elsewhere, and I may repeat it here, what is to be the effect of this measure if adopted, and you repeal the Missouri Compromise ? The South is to gain nothing by it ; for honorable gentlemen from the South, and especially the junior Senator from Virginia [Mr. HUNTER], characterize it as a miserable, trifling little measure. Then, sir, is the South to be propitiated or benefited by the conferring upon her of a miserable, trifling little measure ? Will that compensate the South for her uneasiness ? Will it allay the agitation of the North ? Will it preserve the union of these States ? Will it sustain the Democratic or the Whig party in their organizations ? No, sir, they all go to the wall. What is to be the effect on this Government ? It is to be most ruinous and fatal to the future harmony and well-being of the country. I think that the measure itself would be useless. If you establish intervention, you make nothing by that. But what will be the consequence in the minds of the people ? They have a veneration for that Compromise. They have a respect and reverence for it, from its antiquity and the associations connected with it, and repeated references to it that seem to suggest that it marked the boundaries of free and slave territory. They have no respect for it as a compact—I do not care what you call it—but as a line, defining certain rights and privileges to the different sections of the Union. The abstractions which you indulge in here can never satisfy the people that there is not something in it. Abrogate it or disannul it, and you exasperate the public mind. It is not necessary that reason should accompany excitement. Feeling is enough to agitate without much reason, and that will be the great prompter on this occasion. My word for it, we shall realize scenes of agitation which are rumbling in the distance now.

XXXIV.

I have heard it said, and may as well remark it now, that the Abolitionists and Free-Soilers, to a certain extent, will affiliate with the weaker political party at the North, the Whigs, and will make a fair contest with the Democrats. If they throw this question in the scale, and the Democrats do not, they will preponderate. Then how are the Democrats to sustain themselves under this pressure? Suppose the repeal of the Fugitive Slave Law, or the repeal of the Compromise of 1850 is proposed, and the Democrats oppose it; they will meet with the objection that it is not more sacred than the Missouri Compromise, and the repeal will be urged before the people; and we shall see our House of Representatives with a preponderating power of Abolitionism, the principles of which will triumph. Every Representative who votes for this measure will be prostrated; he cannot come back, or, if he comes back, he will be pledged to the repeal of a measure fraught with so many blessings of peace to the country. With all the fancied benefits of non-intervention, they cannot overbalance the disastrous consequences that must ensue to our institutions.

XXXV.

This is an eminently perilous measure, and do you expect me to remain here silent, or to shrink from the discharge of my duty in admonishing the South of what I conceive the results will be? I will do it in spite of all the intimidations, or threats, or discountenances that may be thrown upon me. Sir, the charge that I am going with the Abolitionists or Free-Soilers affects not me. The discharge of conscious duty prompts me often to confront the united array of the very section of the country in which I reside; in which my associations are; in which my personal interests have always been, and in which my affections rest. When every look to the setting sun carries me to the bosom of a family dependent upon me, think you I could be alien to them? Never—never. Well, sir, if I am now accidently associated with Abolitionists, in voting against this measure of repeal—if I vote with them, and with individual Senators with whom my relations have always been courteous and polite personally, they well know that I feel no sympathy with their notions—that I think them fanatical—I do not esteem it a greater misfortune attendant upon me than I have witnessed before, in this Chamber, with other Senators from the South. In the passage of the Compromise bill of 1850, I saw associations of extremes quite as extraordinary as on this occasion. I almost thought that the extremes of the Abolitionists and Secession parties had become Siamese twins; they were so intimate that I could not help but remark it.

MR. SEWARD. Who?

XXXVI.

Mr. HOUSTON. I need not mention who ; I merely throw out the suggestion. I do not inquire into the motive which induced the introduction of this bill into the Senate. I cast no reflections on gentlemen either for its introduction or for its support ; but I deprecate the consequences which will flow from it. I have conversed with several Senators, and I have never hear the first who would not admit that it was an unfortunate and ill-advised measure. The venerable and distinguished Senator from Michigan [Mr. CASS], the other day, in his speech, declared, in substance, that he thought it was an unfortunate circumstance that it had ever been introduced into the Senate, although it meets with his approbation when it is here. And now, when he who has been in the councils and transactions of this country for fifty years, who has witnessed all the vicissitudes and mutations through which the country has passed, who has been an actor in the most important scenes of the Union—when he does not recognize it as a healing and welcome measure, I ask Senators if I err in resisting it ? They say it is here. It *is* here, and if I had the power, I would kick it out. What, if a measure unwholesome or unwise is brought into the Senate, and it comes from the party of which I am a member, and its introduction is an error, is it not my duty to correct that error as far as I possibly can ? Sir, I stand here for that general purpose. My constituents send me here for that purpose.

XXXVII.

But I will not admit for a moment that this meets the sanction of the Executive. All his antecedents are in the face of it. Supporting him as I did, I must believe him consistent and truthful. He is upon the record as an opponent to agitation of any kind, whether in the Halls of Congress or anywhere else. He is pledged to keep down and resist agitation, as far as in his power ; and that the institutions of the country shall sustain no " shock " during his Administration. If this bill passes, will there be *no shock?* Depend upon it, Mr. President, there will be a tremendous shock . it will convulse the country from Maine to the Rio Grande. The South has not asked for it. I, as the most Southern Senator upon this floor, do not desire it. If it is a boon that is offered to propitiate the South, I, as a Southern man, repudiate it. I reject it. I will have none of it.

XXXVIII.

Mr. President, not in any spirit of unkindness—not entertaining unfriendly or ungentle feelings,—I will allude here, by way of illustration, to one of the most beautiful and captivating incidents in the Holy Bible —one that shows a forgetting, and kind, and amiable, and forgiving temper, which, even under a sense of deep injuries, was willing to embrace a brother, and forget the past. I need not relate to this intelligent assembly the history of Esau and Jacob. The birthright and the mess of pottage are familiar to all. The two brothers separated in anger, after Jacob had acquired the blessing which should have been given to Esau, and Jacob fled to Laban, his mother's brother, in a distant country, where he greatly prospered. Afterwards, when he separated his flocks from those of his father-in-law, it became necessary for him to journey through the land of of his brother Esau, who was then a man of influence, and power, and wealth. As Jacob approached, he thought it was necessary to propitiate his brother for the wrong which he had done him, and he supposed he could not do that without some atonement, or some gift. He dispatched a portion of his family, some of his handmaidens, and children, and servants, with a drove of cattle, which he intended as an offering to his brother ; and the sacred narrative says that when Esau heard that his brother was journeying towards his land, "Esau ran to meet him ; and they embraced and kissed each other ; and they wept." Now I do not see why the North and South, if they have been separated, might not embrace each other without any feeling of anger. But, after some colloquy had taken place between the brothers, Esau said : "*What meanest thou by this drove which I met ?*" And Jacob said, "These are to find grace in the sight of my Lord." And Esau then made a reply worthy of a generous spirit. He said : "*I have enough, my brother ; keep that thou hast unto thyself.*"

XXXIX.

So, if this is an offering to propitiate the South, the South may say, " I have enough, my brother ; keep that thou hast unto thyself." If this is the only offering tendered to the South, we will not ask it ; we do not want it ; the people will be angry if you give it ; and I never want to make trouble with my friends at home. I would rather you would keep it. If you are indebted in anything to the South, all I have to say is, that you might find some other occasion when it would be more agreeable to cancel the obligation. The South, as a community, only desire their rights under the Constitution and existing compromises.

XL.

But, sir, the people are not going into abstractions to understand this subject. Nor will there be a lawyer at every point, every cross-road, every public meeting, every muster, or every court-house, to give elaborate dissertations upon the unconstitutionality of the Missouri Compromise. I care nothing about its constitutionality or unconstitutionality. Not one straw do I care about it, on account of the circumstances out of which it grew, and the benefits flowing from it. Mr. Jefferson said he could not find constitutional authority for the acquisition of Louisiana. If that was the case, even if the Compromise, based upon an unconstitutional act, to reconcile the different sections of the country, was without authority of the Constitution, it became a legitimate subject of legislation. I say legitimate, because it was an acquisition of territory which must be governed in some manner suited to the exigencies of the occasion. Hence the resort to the principle of compromise, and to legislation. Was the acquisition of Florida constitutional? I think not. Yet we retain it as one of our States. Was the acquisition of Texas constitutional? No, sir, it was not. It was a mere act of legislation on the part of this Government— a compromise—precisely such as the compromise which this bill proposes to repeal. But Texas is in, and you cannot thrust us out ; and that is the whole of it. But it is not constitutional. If it is not, and validity attaches only to *compacts*, in contradistinction to *compromises*, then this is a compact predicated upon the compromise of Missouri.

XLI.

I do not know whether it is constitutional, technically. It is sufficient for me to know that it has stood for more than thirty years, and received the approbation of our wisest and ablest statesmen, from the day of its adoption down to the present, and was never questioned until after the commencement of the present session of Congress. It is strange that an unconstitutional law should have remained so long in force amid all the agitation, and excitement, and bitterness between the North and the South ; and that this is the first proposition ever made to repeal it. Have we to yield to it without any necessity, and without any excuse for it, when we see that discord will run riot in our land?

XLII.

Sir, the occasion to which I have alluded, was not the only one on which I said I was willing to stand on the Missouri Compromise line, in defence of the rights of the South. On another occasion, it will be recollected in this Chamber, when speaking of the obligations the country was under to a distinguished statesman, then in private life, and whose party had postponed his claim, or pretermitted it, or, in common parlance, laid him on the shelf, I said, that when the Missouri agitation was quieted, he was held throughout the land as a great pacificator; and if he had committed a mountain of sins, that single achievement of tranquilizing the great Republic, giving permanency, peace, and growth to its institutions, would have overbalanced them all. I said that Henry Clay deserved a monument of bronze, of marble, or of gold, to be placed in the rotunda of the Capitol, for men in aftertimes-of great excitement to contemplate, and look upon as a man who blessed his country. That was the sentiment I entertained, and it arose from veneration, not only for the man, but for the needed restoration of harmony to our native land. Were I to make such a declaration now, it would be thought that it was an endeavor to bring this bill into discredit. No, sir, nothing is necessary from me to discredit it; for it is its own condemnation under the circumstances in which it is presented here, at this time, in the midst of unity, peace, and harmony, while all is at rest, with not a ripple on the vast ocean of our community. I have seen agitation and bitterness before.

XLII.

I recollect when I ventured to make the first address in this Chamber on the subject of the agitation in 1850, with what discountenance it was received. So little was there a disposition to harmonize, that *when I suggested that six Senators, without regard to party or section, might be selected from the members of this body, who could compose an Address and send it abroad so as to harmonize the country, and hush the fierce waves of political agitation that were then lashing the base of this Capitol, it met with no reponse.* Well, we subsequently obtained peace and harmony. Let us preserve it. And there is no mode by which we can so effectually accomplish that object, as by rejecting the proposed measure. I had fondly hoped, Mr. President, that having attained to my present period of life, I should pass the residue of my days, be they many or few, in peace and tranquillity; that as I found the country growing up rapidly, and have witnessed its immeasurable expansion and development, when I closed my eyes on scenes around me, I would at least have the cherished consolation and hope that I left my children in a peaceful, happy, prosperous, and united community. I had hoped this. Fondly had I cherished the desire and the expectation from 1850 until after the introduction of this bill. My hopes are less sanguine now. My anxieties increase, but my expectation lessens. Sir, if this repeal takes place, I will have seen the commencement of the agitation; but the youngest child now born, I am apprehensive, will not live to witness its termination. Southern gentlemen may stand up and defend this measure. They may accept it from the Northern gentlemen who generously bestow it; but if it were beneficial to the South, it would have been asked for. It was not asked for—nor will it be accepted by the people. It furnishes those in the North, who are enemies of the South, with efficient weapons to contend with.

XLIV.

The Democracy in the North have stood firm to party ties. They have fought gallantly for our rights. If we pass this bill how can they maintain themselves? How can their representatives return to them and say: "We gave it?" Would not the reply be: "You gave it; then you are faithless servants, and we will put you down; you disgraced your party; you have given away a sacred thing, a pledge, a compromise thirty-four years old, which was venerated for its antiquity, and national benefits derived from it?" Depend upon it, they will be held to a strict account. They will have to answer for it. I call upon you to sustain those who stood by you of the South in opposition to those whose fanaticism, and prejudice, and misguided feeling would have wrested your rights from you. If you place them and their party in the predicament which I have mentioned, you will be doing them great injustice.

XLV.

Mr. President, I have very little hope that any appeal which I can make

for the Indians will do any good.   The honorable Senator from Indiana
[Mr. PETTIT], says, in substance, *that God Almighty has condemned
them*, and has made them an *inferior race ;* that there is *no use in doing
anything for them.*   With great deference to that Senator, for whom I
have never cherished any but kind feelings, I must be permitted to dissent
from his opinions.   He says they are not civilized, and they are not homo-
geneous, and cannot be so, with the white race.   They cannot be civilized ;
No!   Sir, it is idle to tell me that.   We have Indians on our western borders whose civilization is not inferior to our own.   It is within the recollection of gentlemen here that, more than twenty years ago, President
Ross, one of them, held a correspondence upon the rights of the Indians
to the Cherokee country, which they possessed east of the Mississippi, and
maintained himself in the controversy with great credit and ability ; and
the triumph of Mr. Adams, if it was one, was much less than he had
obtained over the diplomatist of Spain [Mr. DON ONIS], in relation to the
occupation of Florida by General Jackson.   The Senator from Indiana
says that, in ancient times, Moses received a command to go and drive
the Canaanites and Moabites out of the land of Canaan, and that Joshua
subsequently made the experiment of incorporating one tribe of the heathen with the Israelites, but it finally had to be killed off.   Therefore,
the Senator concludes, the Cherokees cannot be civilized.   There may
have been something statesmanlike in the policy, but I do not discover
the morality of it.   I will say, however, that there is no analogy between
the two cases.   The people of Judea who were killed, or exterminated,
were idolators, and the object was to keep the people of Israel free from
the taint of idols and idolatry, under the command of Providence, and
therefore the extermination in His dispensation became necessary.   But the
Cherokees never have been idolators, neither have the Creeks, nor the
Choctaws, nor the Chickasaws.   They believe in one Great Spirit—in God
—the white man's God.   They believe in his Son Jesus Christ, and his
atonement, and propitiation for the sins of men.   They believe in the
sanctifying efficacy of the Holy Ghost.   They bow at the Christian's altar,
and they believe the Sacred Volume.   Sir, you may drive these people
away, and give their lands to the white man ; but let it not be done upon
the justification of the Scriptures.   They have well-organized societies ;
they have villages and towns ; they have their state-houses and their
capitols ; they have females and men who would grace the drawing-rooms
or saloons of Washington ; they have a well-organized judiciary, a trial
by jury, and the writ of *habeas corpus.*   These are the people for whom I

demand justice in the organization of these Territories. They are men of education. They have more than one hundred native preachers in those tribes, as I have heard. They have their colleges, as I remarked in my former address to the Senate on this subject. They become associated in friendship with our young men in the various institutions in the United States; and they are prepared to be incorporated upon equal terms with us. But even if they were wild Indians, untutored, when you deprive them of what would give them knowledge, and discourage them from making an effort to become civilized and social beings, how can you expect them to be otherwise than savage?

XLVI.

When you undertake to tame wild horses, do you turn them from you and drive them into the desert, or do you take care of them and trea them with humanity? These Indians are not inferior, intellectually white men. John Ridge was not inferior in point of genius to Randolph. His father, in point of native intellect, was not infer¹ any man. Look at their social condition, in the nations to which I alluded. Look at the Chickasaws who remain in the State of Mississi, Even among white men, with all their prejudices against the India with their transcendent genius and accomplishments, they have beel elected to the Legislature. Whenever they have had an opportunity, they have shown that they are not inferior to white men, either in sense or capability.

XLVII.

But the honorable Senator from Iowa [MR. DODGE] characterizes the remarks which I made in reference to the Indians as arising from a feeling of "sickly sentimentality." Sir, it is a sickly sentimentality that was implanted in me when I was young, and it has grown up with me. The Indian has a sense of justice, truth, and honor, that should find a responsive chord in every heart. If the Indians on the frontier are barbarous, or if they are cannibals, and eat each other, who are to blame for it? They are robbed of the means of sustenance; and with hundreds and thousands of them starving on the frontier, hunger may prompt to such acts to prevent their perishing. We shall never become cannibals in connection with the Indians; but we do worse than that. We rob

13

them, first of their native dignity and character; we rob them next of what the Government appropriates for them. If we do not do it in this Hall, men are invested with power and authority, who, officiating as agents or traders, rob them of everything which is designed for them. No less than *one hundred millions of dollars,* I learn from statistics, since the adoption of this Government, have been appropriated by Congress for purposes of justice and benevolence towards the Indians; but I am satisfied that they have never realized *fifteen millions* beneficially. They are too remote from the seat of Government for their real condition to be understood here; and if the Government intends liberality or justice towards them, it is often diverted from the intended object and consumed by speculators.

XLVIII.

I am a friend of the Indian, upon the principle that I am a friend to ᵉtice. We are not bound to make them promises; but if a promise be to an Indian, it ought to be regarded as sacredly as if it were to a white man. If we treat them as tribes, recognize them, send issioners to form treaties and exchange ratifications with them, the treaties are negotiated, accepted, ratified, and exchanged— ing met with the approval of the Senate—I think they may be called ompacts; and how are those compacts regarded? Just as we choose to construe them at the time, without any reference to the wishes of the Indians, or whether we do them kindness or justice in the operation, or not. We are often prompted to their ratification by persons interested; and we lend ourselves unintentionally to an unjust act of oppression upon the Indians by men who go and get their signatures to a treaty. The Indian's mark is made; the employees of the Government certify or witness it; and the Indians do not under stand it, for they do not know what is written. These are some of the circumstances connected with the Indians. Gentlemen have spoken here of voting millions to build ships, and placing the Army and Navy at the disposition of the President in the event that England act inconsistently with treaty stipulations. This is done because, if England violates a treaty with us, our national honor is injured. Now, I should like to know if it becomes us to violate a treaty made with the ·Indians when we please, regardless of every principle of truth and of honor. We should be careful if it were with a power able to war with us; and it argues a degree of infinite meanness and indescribable degradation on our part to act differently with the Indians, who confide in our honor and justice, and who call the President their Great Father, and confide in him. Mr. President, it is in the power of the Congress of the United States to do some justice to the Indians by giving them a government of their own, and encouraging them in their organization and improvement by inviting their delegates to a place on the floor of the Senate and house of Representatives. If you will not do it, the sin will lie at your door, and Providence, in His own way, mysterious and incomprehensible to us though it is, will accomplish all His purposes, and may at some day avenge the wrongs of the Indians upon our nation. As a people we can save them ; and the sooner the great work is begun, the sooner will humanity have cause to rejoice in its accomplishment.

XLIX.

Mr. President, I shall say but little more. My address may have been desultory. It embraces many subjects which it would be very hard to keep in entire order. We have, in the first place, the extensive territory ; then we have the considerations due to the Indians ; and then we have the proposed repeal of the Missouri Compromise, which seems to require the most explanation, and to be the main point in the controversy. The great principle involved in that repeal is non-intervention, which, we are told, is to be of no practical benefit, if the Compromise is repealed. It can have no effect but to keep up agitation.

L.

Sir, the friends who have survived the distinguished men who took prominent parts in the drama of the compromise of 1850, ought to feel gratified that those men are not capable of participating in the events of to-day, but that they were permitted, after they had accomplished their labors, and seen their country in peace, to leave the world, as Simeon did, with the exclamation : " Lord, now lettest thou thy servant depart in peace, for mine eyes have seen thy salvation." They departed in peace, and they left their country in peace. They felt, as they were about to be gathered to the tombs of their fathers, that the country they had loved so well, and which had honored them—that country upon whose fame and name their doings had shed a bright lustre which shines abroad throughout all Christendom—was reposing in peace and happiness. What would their emotions be if they could now be present and see an effort made, if not so designed, to undo all their work, and to tear asunder the cords that they had bound around the hearts of their countrymen? They have departed. The nation felt the wound : and we see the memorials of woe still in this Chamber. The proud symbol (the eagle) above your head remains enshrouded in black, as if deploring the misfortune which has fallen upon us, or as a fearful omen of future calamities which await our nation, in the event this bill should become a law. Above it I behold the majestic figure of WASHINGTON, whose presence must ever inspire patriotic emotions, and command the admiration and love of every American heart. By these associations I adjure you to regard the contract once made to harmonize and preserve this Union. *Maintain the Missouri Compromise!* Stir not up *agitation!* Give us peace!

LI.

This much I was bound to declare—in behalf of my country, as I believe, and I know in behalf of my constituents. In the discharge of my duty I have acted fearlessly. The events of the future are left in the hands of a wise Providence.

LII.

Frank Pierce's Nebraska and Kansas Bill, had long been under discussion, and as his partisans in the Senate were numerous enough to pass it when they pleased, General Houston rose in his place late on Friday night, March 3d, 1854, and delivered the following great argument. It was the last and most powerful remonstrance that fell on the ears of that Senate, until the vote was taken. Let men read it at the North and the South—for it speaks the truth to America—our common country. Its prophecies have already become history.

LIII.

Such were the noble words, which late that night fell from

the lips of Houston. His speech, although pronounced in the fervor of his native and impetuous eloquence, is already by the march of events conserted into history. It seems at the first blush as though it must have been changed since its delivery— so perfect a transcript is it now of what has since taken place. But we copy it from the official Congressional Report.

LIV.

The prospect of the overthrow of the Missouri Compromise, by the Congress of the United States, spread general alarm throughout the country. Petitioners by tens of thousands sent in their remonstrances and memorials, praying that the Bill might not pass. But the memorial which attracted most attention, was " from upwards of three thousand ministers of the Gospel of all denominations and sects, in the different States of New England, remonstrating against the passage of the Nebraska Bill. Demagogues had affected indifference or contempt towards this petition; and even Senators who were looking to the Presidency, allowed themselves, in the heat of debate, to treat 3,000 New England clergymen with contempt. These Senators forgot, that these 3,000 ministers had been put into the pulpits of New England, by the *people* of New England; just as really, legitimately (and without political corruption), as Senators at Washington had been placed in their seats. They should have remembered moreover, that these clergymen more faithfully reflected the opinions of their congregations, on this subject, than Senators represented the opinions of their constituents.

It was expected, in this crisis, that Mr. Everett—who then filled Daniel Webster's place in the Senate—would, as a Massachusetts man, rise and rebuke the demagogues, for their unprovoked assault upon 3,000 of the Protestant clergymen of New England. But Mr. Everett was silent; and Sam rose and did the work which WEBSTER would have done, had he not left the Senate and the world for ever. Mr. Houston said :—

LV.

Mr. PRESIDENT : I think that a petition of this kind ought to be received, and that it is not subject to the charge brought against it by the Senator from Illinois [Mr. DOUGLAS]. It does not arraign our action by being drawn up after that action was had. The Nebraska Bill passed this body on the night of the 3d, or rather, on the morning of the 4th instant. The memorial appears to be dated on the 1st of March. I cannot think that it meant any indignity to the Senate. There is nothing expressive of any such feeling in it. It is a right that all individuals in the community have, if their terms are respectful, to memorialize the Senate of the United States upon any subject. Whether there is any ulterior object in this I know not ; but from the date of the memorial, and from the number of signers, I am induced to believe that that memoralists thought there was something wrong in that bill ; and if they believe that its passage would be a breach of faith on the part of the Government, they had a right to say so. I took the liberty of making the same charge here. There were more questions than that of non-intervention involved in that bill. It involved an infraction of faith with the Indians, of pledges given to them under all the solemn forms, yet mockery, of treaties. That was one point involved ; and I charged that the passage of the bill would be a violation of plighted faith in that particular. Was it a violation of faith to disregard the Missouri Compromise, which was of so much antiquity and utility to the country ? That is a matter of discussion. I have not arraigned the action of any gentleman since the passage of the bill, but anterior to it I gave my opinions in relation to its character as a disregard of treaties, and as a flagrant violation of the plighted faith of the nation towards the Indians.

LVI.

With respect to the Missouri Compromise, I believe its repeal to be as flagrant a breach of faith as the violation of treaties made with the Indians. I have not charged Senators with corrupt motives, nor have I charged them with anything selfish ; but I certainly can see no more impropriety in ministers of the Gospel, in their vocation, memorializing Congress, than politicians, or other individuals. I do not believe that these ministers have sent this memorial here to manufacture political capital, to have it entered on the records of the Senate, so that it might be taken back and disseminated through the country. Sir, it comes from the country. I told you that there would be agitation ; but it was denied upon this floor. Is not this agitation ? Three thousand ministers of the living God upon earth—his vicegerents—send a memorial here upon this subject ; and yet you tell me that there is no excitement in the country ! Sir, you realize what I anticipated. The country has to bear the infliction. Sir, the *coup d'état* was not successful. The bill did not pass before the community was awakened to it. The community was awakened to it not alone in New England, for I have seen letters from the South and West stating that it was there regarded as a breach of faith ; and I can see no wrong in ministers expressing their opinion in regard to it. This protest does not attack the reputation of Senators. It does not displace them from their positions here. It does not impair their capabilities for the discharge of the high functions which the Constitution has devolved upon them. I see nothing wrong in all this.

LVII.

Ministers have a right to remonstrate. They are like other men. Because they are ministers of the Gospel they are not disfranchised of political rights and privileges ; and, if their language is respectful to the Senate, in anticipation of the passage of a bill which is obnoxious to them, they have a right to spread their opinions on the records of the nation. The great national heart throbs under this measure ; its pulse beats high ; and is it surprising that we should observe the effects of it ? I trust, sir, that the nation may yet again see the blessed tranquillity that prevailed over the whole country when this " healing measure " was introduced into the Senate. The position of the nation was enviable. It was unagitated. There was not, in my recollection, a time so tranquil, nor a community more happy. A nation more prosperous existed not upon the earth. Sir, I trust that there will be no continuance of agitation ; but the way to end it is not to make war upon memorialists. Let them memorialize if they think it necessary. If they state what is incorrect, let the subject be referred to committees, and let the committees give an exposition of the truth, and lay it, in reports, before the public, and then the intelligence of the nation will determine as to what is right, and what consideration ought to be given to it. I would not take away the liberty to indulge in the freest expression of opinion, or the exercise of the rights and privileges which belong to any portion of this country ; yet I would discourage agitation. I may hold the contents of this protest, to some extent, heretical ; yet they are not expressed in such offensive language as would justify a denial of their right to memorialize. If it had been intended to impugn our motives or our actions, either as corrupt or immoral, we could bear it. The people surely have a right to think and speak upon our action. We are not placed in a position so high that we are elevated above the questioning power of the people. They have the right to look into our action, and investigate our conduct ; and, if they do not approve of it, to express their opinions in relation to it. I shall never make war upon them on that account ; yet, I trust, that whatever disposition may be made of the bill which we have passed, the agitation has already reached its acme ; and that, from this point it may decline, until the country is again restored to peace and happiness.

LVIII.

Mr. President, I have the misfortune to differ from my friends in relation to this measure, but that difference is not sufficient to induce me to enter anew into the discussion of it. I will, however, discuss the propriety of this memorial. The gentlemen misapprehend its character entirely. I understood the honorable Senator from Virginia—but I may have been mistaken—to say that it invoked the vengeance of the Almighty God upon the Senate.

[Mr. MASON. In substance it does, as I understand.]

Mr. HOUSTON. There is no invocation contained in the memorial. It is a respectful protest, stating their appreciation of the measure then pending before the Senate of the United States, and not one word is contained in it derogatory to the Senate at the time it was drawn, and there is no invocation of wrath or vengeance upon the members of this body. It is a respectful protest, in the name of the Almighty God.

By the expression which I used, that these ministers were the vicegerents of the Almighty, I merely intended to say that they were harbingers of peace to their fellow-men ; and if it was a *lapsus linguæ*, or improper expression, it does not change the intention that I then entertained in my mind, of expressing a belief, that it was nothing else than an extraordinary emergency that diverted men from their ordinary pursuits in the ministry of the Gospel, to engage at all in, or to step even to the verge of, the political arena.

LIX.

We are told, Mr. President, that this was intended for the purpose of agitation. It is certainly a manifestation of agitation ; but it could not have been intended to create agitation, for the thing was done, and here is one of its developments and consequences. Yet, sir, I can see nothing wrong in the memorial, so far as I am concerned. If ministers of the Gospel are not recognized by the Constitution of the United States, they are recognized by the moral and social constitution of society. They are recognized in the constitution of man's salvation. The great Redeemer of the World enjoined duties upon mankind ; and there is a Moral Constitution from which we have derived all the excellent principles of our Political Constitution—the great principles upon which our Government, morally, socially, and religiously, is founded.

LX.

Sir, I do not think there is anything very derogatory to our institutions in the ministers of the Gospel expressing their opinions. They have a right to do it. No man can be a minister without first being a man. He has political rights : he has also the rights of a missionary of the Saviour, and he is not disfranchised by his vocation. Certain political restrictions may be laid upon him : he may be disqualified from serving in the Legislatures of the States, but that does not discharge him from political and civil obligations to his country. He has a right to contribute as far as he thinks necessary, to the sustentation of its institutions. He has a right to interpose his voice as one of its citizens, against the adoption of any measure which he believe will injure the nation. These individuals have done no more. They have not denounced the Senate, but they have protested, in the capacity of ministers, against what I and other Senators on this floor protested. They have the right to do it, and we cannot take that right from them. They will exercise it. The people have the right to think, and they will exercise that right. They have the right of memo-

13*

rializing, and they will exercise that right. They have the right to express their opinions, and they will exercise that right. They will exercise their rights in reprobation or commendation at the ballot-box, too; and preachers, I believe, vote. They have the right to do so. They are not very formidable numerically, but they have the right to do this as ministers of the Gospel, as well as we Senators have a right to vote for the adoption of a measure; and if it is not in accordance with their opinions, they have a right to condemn it. They have the right to think it is morally wrong, politically wrong, civilly wrong, and socially wrong, if they do not interfere with the vested rights of others in the entertainment of those opinions.

LXI.

I understood my honorable friend from Mississippi to say, that the South had been groaning for a long time under this oppressive measure. The South, sir, are a spirited people, and how they could have submitted, for more than a third of a century, to this indignity, this wrong, this act of oppression, which has ground them down in their prosperity and development, and never have said a word about it until this auspicious moment arrived, and that, too, when political subjects have been agitated at the North and South—that it should have been reserved for the action of the present Congress, after all others had glided by without complaint, rebuke, remonstrance, or suggestion of appeal, is a most extraordinary thing. My friend does not apprehend it; but there was no excitement out of this Capitol, or out of the city of Washington. It originated here. This was the grand laboratory of political action and political machinery. The object was to mature the measure here, and inflict it, by a *coup d'état*, upon the nation, and then radiate it to every point of the country. The potion does not react pleasantly. There is a response, but how does it go down? Not well. The physic works; it works badly; it works upward.

LXII.

I am willing to receive any memorials that are presented to this body which are respectable in terms, whether they come from preachers, politicians, civilians, or from the beggars that congregate about your cities, and I will treat them with respect and kindness. As long as they are respectful in terms to this body, though they express their apprehension of a calamity about to fall on the country, it brands no man; and if they denounce a measure in advance, it is what they have a right to do. We have a more eligible position here to advocate our opinions than individuals have in social life to maintain their positions. We have all the panoply of power and State sovereignty thrown around the members of this body to guard and shield them against attacks; but they are thrown in the midst of the community without any shield, except it is the shield of morality and propriety of conduct which gives protection to their persons. While they express themselves respectfully I shall never treat with disrespect preachers, or any other individuals who come before this body to give us their opinions upon political subjects.

LXIII.

In reply to some remarks of Mr. Douglas—

Mr. HOUSTON said: Mr. President, as the honorable Senator from Illinois, the chairman of the Committee on Territories, seemed in a most emphatic manner to address his remarks to me, I think him fully entitled to the respect of my attention. He has dwelt upon the Abolition character of this document. So far as any such character may be embodied in it, I have nothing to say. There are various opinions entertained here and elsewhere upon various subjects with which I have nothing to do, and with which I have no affiliation; but with this subject, as it is presented to the Senate now, I have some connection. With the controversy which exists between the honorable chairman of the Committee on Territories and the gentleman from Ohio (Mr. Chase), and the gentleman from Massachusetts, (Mr. Sumner), I have nothing to do. I was not here when the controversy originated, nor when it was first introduced into the Senate. I have not participated in it since; and however unpleasant such altercations or controversies may be, and however I may regard them as impeding the transaction of business in this body, I have forborne either public or private expressions of opinion upon that matter.

Mr. DOUGLAS. Mr. President, I will say to the Senator that the only allusion which I had to him was the simple quotation which I made from his remarks when he spoke of these ministers being the vicegerents of the Almighty. My other remarks were intended for another quarter, so far as they had an application anywhere. If he is under the misapprehension of supposing that they referred to him, I wish to correct him; that is all. I do not want to interrupt him.

LXIV.

Mr. HOUSTON. I am very glad to hear the disclaimer, for the gentleman's remarks appeared to be directed so unequivocally towards me, that I was led into the misapprehension of supposing that they were intended perhaps to apply to me, in a manner in which it was not the purpose of the gentleman to apply them. But, sir, I explained, when I was up before, the misapplication of the term 'vicegerent,' and I expressed my opinion to be that the ministers of the Gospel were the heralds of the Almighty God, or his ministers of peace upon earth. I thought the gentleman would not have carped upon that expression, unless with reference to some particular influence which my views might have upon the auditory. It was a mere misapplication of a term, and I so explained it. But, Mr. President, I think the object of this memorial is misapprehended. I find no fault with its introduction either before or after the passage of the bill to which it refers, for that bill may be returned to the Senate with amendments. Such things very frequently occur. At all events, as the memorial has been prepared with great care, and as the gentlemen who have signed it have been anxious that their views should be laid before the Senate of the United States, lest other measures embracing similar principles should be introduced, I can see nothing improper in allowing them to lay their views respectfully before the Senate. I do not think there is any evidence that the gentlemen who have signed the memorial have any disposition to establish theocracy in our country, or that they wish to take the Government into their own hands, and exercise a controlling influence over it. We find that those who have signed this document are of different sects and various denominations. I think there is no danger that such an amalgamation of interests and opinions will take place as to embody a force sufficient to make any great impression on the institutions of this country, or to endanger our liberties.

LXV.

Mr. President, this memorial is regarded as a substantive and independent matter, as intended to produce agitation, and to insult the Senate ; but it is really the effect of a measure which I predicted would have this influence upon the community. The cause exists in the Senate. It exists in the amendment inserted into the Nebraska Bill proposing the repeal of the Missouri Compromise, and this is but responsive action to that. The cause is not in the clergymen who have signed this memorial. The memorial is the effect of a cause brought forward and presented in the Senate. The memorial impugns the action of no one. It is true the memorialists speak of the measure as immoral. Surely that ought not to insult Senators. They are not such paragons of morality that they cannot bear to have their moral character questioned, if they should happen to do anything which would not be strictly moral, according to some standards, but which I should not think to be very immoral. But is their morality of such a delicate texture as to be affected by a memorial coming from " the land of steady habits ?

LXVI.

We are told that there is a great principle involved in the bill to which this memorial refers. This is a very formidable and very visible response to that great principle which it is said has lain dormant. Sir, I need not name the number of years that it has lain dormant. No bright genius ever elicited it ; no brilliant conception ever discovered it until this session had progressed for some time, when the great principle of non-intervention at once sprang up to illumine the world, to be regarded as one which, at some future day, would be a universally-recognized principle. Sir, I recognize the principles of self-government, but I do it in sovereignty. A people in tutelage cannot exercise sovereignty, but States can. A people who are in a territorial existence, which is fitting them to become States, exercise what may be called a *quasi* sovereignty. They are never really sovereign until they are recognized by Congress as such, and are received into the Union as sovereign States. Then is the time for the operation of self-government, but it grows out of sovereignty. Is it to be in five squatters? They may pass a law to-day and repeal it to-morrow, and the next day they may pass another law, and so on successively from day to day, and from year to year, they may pass and repeal laws. The Territories have no power to pass organic laws until the attributes of sovereignty are about to attach, or have actually attached to them. That is what I call non-intervention. That is what I call sovereignty and self-government. This is the great principle which it is said is involved in the bill which we have passed ; and now we are receiving the response to it. I hope we may never have any more responses of this description. I pray Heaven that we may never have another such protest in this body. I pray that there may never exist any necessity for it. But for the necessity or cause, which originated in this body, this memorial would never have been laid upon your table. This is but the effect; the cause was anterior to it. If we wish to avert calamitous effects, we should prevent pernicious causes.

LXVII.

This calm and noble appeal, to the just judgment of the high Tribunal which heard it was impotent there. But it was heard and cherished by many thousand hearts among the hills and valleys of New England. The Protestant Clergy of the United States, are the best exponents of the enlightened moral feeling of the American People. From the foundation of the country, they have been the enemies of a union of Church and State. They have always been foremost in the cause of civil and Religious Liberty. They have—as a class—abstained from an improper interference in public affairs. They have shown even too much delicacy in this regard. If they had been bolder, and rebuked Demagogism in all its forms, we should not have witnessed what we have now seen—politicians of Protestant origin, bowing to court the vote of ignorant, bigoted paupers, who in consequence of the laxity of our Naturalization Laws, are allowed to vote in masses almost as soon as they land on our shores, and before they understand even our language— much less our system of Government. No reply was made to this able speech of Houston on the RIGHT OF PETITION—and none could be.

LXVIII.

It is refreshing, in the midst of modern political competition, to hear such a tribute to unostentatious virtue and patriotism. If we turn back in the Records of Congress, we shall find that in 1836, not long after the Battle of San Jacinto, Hon. Thos. H. Benton thus spoke of Houston in his place in the United States Senate :—

" Of the individuals who have purchased lasting renown in this young war, it would be impossible, in this place, to speak in detail, and invidious to discriminate. But there is one among them, whose position forms an exception ; and whose early association with myself, justifies and claims the tribute of a particular notice. I speak of him whose romantic victory has given to the Jacinto* that immortality in grave and serious history, which the diskos of Apollo had given to it in the fabulous pages of the heathen Mythology. General Houston was born in the State of Virginia, County of Rockbridge : he was appointed an ensign in the army of the United States, during the late war with Great Britain, and served in the Creek campaign under the banners of Jackson. I was the lieutenant colonel of the regiment to which he belonged, and the first field officer to whom he reported. I then marked in him the same soldierly and gentlemanly qualities which have since distinguished his eventful career : frank, generous, brave ; ready to do, or to suffer, whatever the obligations of civil or military duty imposed ; and always prompt to answer the call of honor, patriotism, and friendship. Sincerely do I rejoice in his victory. It is a victory without alloy, and without parallel, except at New Orleans. It is a victory which the civilization of the age, and the honor of the human race, required him to gain : for the nineteenth century is not an age in which a repetition of the Goliad matins could be endured. Nobly has he answered the requisition ; fresh and luxuriant are the laurels which adorn his brow.

" It is not within the scope of my present purpose, to speak of military events, and to celebrate the exploits of that vanguard

---

* Hyacinth ; hyacinthus ; huakinthus ; water flower.

of the Anglo-Saxons who are now on the confines of the ancient empire of Montezuma ; but that combat of San Jacinto ! it must for ever remain in the catalogue of military miracles. Seven hundred and fifty citizens, miscellaneously armed with rifles, muskets, belt pistols, and knives, under a leader who had never seen service, except as a subaltern, march to attack near double their numbers—march in open day across a clear prairie, to attack upwards of twelve hundred veterans, the *élite* of an invading army of seven thousand, posted in a wood, their flanks secured, front intrenched ; and commanded by a general trained in civil wars ; victorious in numberless battles ; and chief of an empire of which no man becomes chief except as conqueror. In twenty minutes the position is forced. The combat becomes a carnage. The flowery prairie is stained with blood ; the hyacinth is no longer blue, but scarlet. Six hundred Mexicans are dead ; six hundred more are prisoners, half wounded, the President General himself is a prisoner ; the camp and baggage all taken ; and the loss of the victors, six killed and twenty wounded. Such are the results, and which no European can believe, but those who saw Jackson at New Orleans. Houston is the pupil of Jackson ; and he is the first self-made-general, since the time of Mark Antony, and the King Antigonus, who has taken the general of the army and the head of the government captive in battle. Different from Antony, he has spared the life of his captive though forfeited by every law, human and divine."

SECTION SIXTEENTH.

HOUSTON'S STATESMANSHIP.

I.

An estimate of the qualities which distinguish Houston as a Statesman, must place his character in an elevated and brilliant light. Many men are good soldiers, but add not to skill in the arts of war, the graces of judgment which make valuable and trustworthy legislators. It is no man of ordinary gifts who combines in himself the warrior of renown, and the profound lawgiver, and the just civilian. Wellington, the hero of Waterloo, was one of the modern heroes of this stamp, though falling far behind our own Washington in the prudence of his counsels, and in his clear foresight of the probable effects of causes set in motion. The latter was devoted to broad principles of right and justice, and had no artificial forms of power, or barriers for privileged classes to consolidate or to protect. The former was always busy in wresting principles from the inevitable conflict with the machinery of the British government—which, however wonderful in its construction, must ever be subject to modifications suited to that enlarged freedom, the growth of which has been steadily increasing since Milton—Cromwell's great Secretary of State—and the mighty master of Protestant republicanism, poured forth his great anthems of thought at the consecration of human liberty.

II.

Houston's career as a statesman, has been briefly sketched in the preceding pages ; but the analysis of his qualities as a ruler and as a legislator, will distinguish him more and more, the closer the microscope reveals the motives of his conduct through the trying and stormy period that he presided over the destinies of Texas.   The world will not readily forget, and will be more ready to admire, the man who, at the peril of popularity, and even of life itself, dared to stand between the lawless elements of passion and the fixed code of his race, and stay the former from being swept upon by a flood of dangerous experiments, which would have resulted in multifarious embarrassments for the country, or hurried it on to the verge of ruin, or plunged it into a chaos.

III.

The numerous instances in which Houston exercised the veto power, however much they may have subjected him, during the Texas Presidency, to the temporary censure of the politicians of the hour, will be remembered in the future as the substantial evidences of lofty, manly courage, elevated and sincere patriotism, and of uncommon political sagacity and foresight.   The original veto of Andrew Jackson was one of the monuments of that illustrious man's political fame—but in the scores of instances in which Houston exercised a similar prerogative, the builders of new republics will read a series of lessons in the sublime principles of law, which will sink deep into the heart of the political philosopher, while the spirit of them will be felt and enforced, in that silent embodiment of action, with which political virtue noiselessly erects the homes of men, for the happiness of the human family.   To be a popular ruler, regardless of the

ultimate effects to a people or to mankind, is not a difficult task
—but to be so well acquainted with the history of nations, and
with those interior powers of legislative enactments, as intuitive-
ly to feel " the future in the instant," and to foresee the long
train of unhappy consequences which would spring from a
disruption of the laws of probity and right, while the moral
force and the noble courage are equal and ready to check the
impetuosity of political passion, and the hasty impulses of
suddenly acquired power—is the gift of few men in these days
of intrigue and corruption.

IV.

Houston was a brave man—brave in a moral as well as a
physical sense. Early in the month of June, 1837, there were
public journals in New York, in Richmond, and at Washington,
which did not hesitate to propel the slander, that this bold
soldier, and braver governor, had played the part of a coward,
and retreated before the Mexicans, till he was compelled to
fight ! Such is public detraction !

V.

That Houston should be branded as a coward, by the enemies
of Andrew Jackson, was not stranger than that Jackson was
branded as a coward, even in the same breath that would have
consigned the man of San Jacinto to infamy. History, however, when it speaks of battle-fields, will not hesitate to avow
who it was that, with a handful of troops, gave battle to Santa
Anna on the 21st of April, 1836, and brought the Mexican
President and his suite the next day captives into the camp of
the Forlorn Hope. But history will not require to cite this
physical triumph as a proof of the courage of a noble nature.

The knowledge men possess of the human heart will never let them find a cranny in the imagination, where the breath of suspicion can sough against the bravery of Houston. He who stood by Texas in her hour of attempt—in her day of triumph —and in her night of starless gloom and pitch darkness, when even her own star seemed to be seeking its last fate—a Pleiad among nations—who breasted every danger, and, single and alone, stood forth an embodiment of personal, political, and moral courage, while the popular will muttered and rebuked, and the midnight assassin would have murdered Texas through its President, but that the form of the modern pioneer of republics, moving calmly before the open window of his own delightful home, awed the abashed malcontent into impotency— he it is, that History will never have occasion to defend from the attack of any reputable man, on the charge of cowardice. The President of Texas, who accomplished all that has been cited in these pages, is not one whose name can be tarnished by the breath of captious or ignorant slanderers.   If ever a states- man, in the annals of modern governments, has earned the regard of men, or the gratitude of nations, for self-sacrificing heroism of the mind, surely Houston may claim the highest meed of honor in this respect. Without indulging the spirit of a dictator, his deliberations were crowned by wisdom, and he shrank not from the conscientious discharge of his duties to the State, rather than to gain the temporary applause of those, who, inflamed more by the successes of a popular leader, than animated by carefully weighed principles of patriotism and public policy, were zealous without wisdom, and powerful without judgment.

VI.

It is deeply interesting to contemplate the opinions of Houston's statesmanship which were entertained by those who knew the man best, at that moment, when the whole of the United States, and of Texas, was excited by the news of Texan success against the arts and arms of Mexico. Notwithstanding, there were calumnious reports in circulation, on the arrival of General Houston at New Orleans, after the battle of San Jacinto, attributing his departure from Texas to a quarrel with the civil authorities of the infant Republic, yet there were capable minds watchful of the history of that period, and hopeful for the future of Texas, and its distinguished hero

VII.

The fact that Andrew Jackson was the friend of Houston was well known everywhere throughout the land—but the deep personal interest that he took in Houston's career was not so publicly known. It can well be imagined how painful to him must have been the series of attacks on Houston's character, which were made in 1836, not so much for any effect that they may have been intended to accomplish on Houston's destiny, as on the mind of the friend of the hero of San Jacinto. It is well known that President Jackson viewed these attacks with indignation and abhorrence.

VIII.

The libels upon the character of General Houston's statesmanship, were scattered broadcast over the United States. The most influential presses opposed to President Jackson's administration, were active in sowing the seeds of discontent and slander, and in preparing the public mind to oppose the introduction of Texas into the Union—a measure which, had it been successful, would have produced untold trouble for our country, and have weakened its borders beyond the power of man to estimate.

Although these slanders were eventually eaten by those who had planted and cultivated them, yet they were not without their temporary effect upon the public mind, ever ready to catch the speediest solution to any problem, the character of which is not fully comprehended.

IX.

Among the efforts made to repel the slanders upon General Houston's fair fame, was one so marked and important that it carried uncommon weight to every candid judgment. Though it was not penned by President Andrew Jackson himself, it is reasonable to assert that it was published either at his suggestion, or under his own immediate sanction,—the allusion to Jackson himself being only made by the writer from prudential motives. It appeared, immediately after the cruel statements and insinuations which were made against General Houston by the opposition press, in the editorial columns of the official organ of the Administration.

X.

After stating the nature of the libels published against General Houston, the vindication proceeds in the annexed language : " We sincerely hope that General Houston's future conduct as *the first man in Texas,* may correspond with the wisdom and vigor, and patriotism of the past. If he follows the disinterested, honest, unambitious course, which distinguished the great men of the State in which he was born (Virginia), or that of the great man under whose auspices he became first distinguished himself, *he will leave a noble name behind him.* If he fulfills in *good faith* the will of the people of Texas, without thinking of Sam Houston—if he contributes to raise a free government, and to secure its stability by all the means he can command, unswerved by the lust of power or wealth, or the poor vanity of strutting about in the ostentation which once made up the happiness of the men he has vanquished—then *his name will go down to future ages with those of the benefactors of this continent*, who have considered true glory to consist in building up free and safe institutions."

XI.

Such language as this is seldom or never applied to a common mind.   Had Houston written it in his "heart of hearts," and conned it unceasingly, he could not have lived up to its precepts more completely and thoroughly than he has done.   In no single point has his character travelled out of this record for his government as a statesman.   In the history of his public career in Texas, as has been seen, there is nothing to be pointed at which is derogatory to the proud name thus promised.   By those who have weighed, or who will weigh, the public services of the man, in rescuing a vast territory from tyranny, for future blessings to the innumerable sons of liberty, his character as a statesman must stand second to none who are now living in the lustre of their laurels.

XII.

It is not alone, however, to the thoughts and acts which distinguished Houston in Texas as a statesman that the historian is obliged to refer.   The councils of the Confederacy have been made illustrious by his practical good sense, by his prompt and determined action, by his sincerity of purpose, by his frank avowal of opinion, and by an enlarged and liberal American feeling, earnest for the welfare of every man worthy of bearing the American name.   No sectional prejudice has blinded his mental perceptions. The fountains of Eternal Justice are the sources whence such men derive inspiration and safety. With no personal ends to gain—with a strong love of country—with patient toil for the right, and its gradual rescue from the jaws of error—his public deliberations have rebuked lawless power, and have been always devoted to the "greatest happiness of the greatest number."

XIII.

Before concluding this section, let us glance at the character of Houston's statesmanship, as displayed in the general policy of his government of Texas, during the terms of his office— filled, as has been seen, to the full measure and limit permitted by the Constitution of that State. On being inducted to his place of trust and power, the affairs of the government were in the utmost confusion. Public credit was at a low ebb, and something of the distressing experiences of a Washington seemed necessary to nerve a man to meet the terrible troubles of that period. Houston did not flinch from his task. An honest and a brave man knows no fear. With him all possible things are probable. In this spirit, Houston examined every department of the State, with a view to reform. History will never do justice to his labors in this field of inquiry. The very founder of the Republic had seen it tortured and twisted into every shape that expediency could suggest, to give it a temporary existence—but in the eyes of nations, and of men, it was a dead Republic. He looked upon it, however, not with dismay, or alarm. The warm glow of sympathy animated his bosom— the stricken child of men's hearts and hopes was before him, prostrate—and, with a will, exalted till it awakened all his energies, and vitalized every fibre of his being, he breathed upon empire, and bade it "Arise!" Texas started to its feet, in all the glow of youthful beauty and vigor. She took her place in the midst of nations. Millions looked upon her with earnest eyes and hopeful hearts. Monarchs stood ready to pay her homage, as one of the daughters of the earth.

XIV.

What produced this reaction—this resurrection from the deep sleep of death ? It was the policy of Houston—that policy which was based upon broad principles of honor and of justice. " Honesty is the best policy " for nations as well as for men, and this was the grand basis for his action, after being made President of Texas. Under his enlightened administration all that was weak, and subject to distrust and contumely, was made strong, and commanded the attention of men. It was not a policy of expediencies, but it was one that held the pledged faith of the nation to be a sacred thing—whether that pledged faith had been given in so many words of congressional resolution, or under the tacit recognition of the comity of civilized nations. Conduct of this kind could not fail to secure public respect for Texas—and eventually his administration showed how much better he had calculated in behalf of his country, than all other men who had endeavored to sustain her in the days of her infancy and weakness.

XV.

In his policy, Houston was simple, and, therefore, he was effective. He may be esteemed *the only primitive statesman of our day.* Contrasted with the Founders of States and Empires, his name shines with no diminished lustre. Like William Penn and Captain John Smith, he went into the wilderness as one of the great pioneers of civilization. He saw an empire in the

14

solitude, and he dashed through the tangled way, till he brought it out into the full blaze of day, for the admiration and enjoyment of mankind.   It was no mean, grovelling policy that accomplished all this.   It was the policy of the Christian soldier —the policy of a man understanding the great universal springs of human affection and confidence—which no diplomacy, however cunningly devised, can rival, and which alone can prove successful in the best sense of that term.   Penn in Pennsylvania, and Smith in Virginia, and Miles Standish, in the colony of Massachusetts Bay, at an earlier period, accomplished, by similar means, precisely what Houston effected on the wilds of our southern frontiers, even though assisted by a less orderly set of comrades than distinguished the bold pioneers of this continent.

XVI.

We have said Houston was a primitive man.   In his temper and spirit, as well as in his policy, this is true.   There is no place on the face of the earth where the mind of a man, who has a will to that end, can expand and ripen into value and power more rapidly than in the wilderness, or on the extreme borders of civilization.   Houston had the advantage of an education of self-culture in the solitudes of the Southwest.   Here, it is evident to us, he gratified himself not solely with the contemplation of the ways of men, but with the mysterious yet certain workings of that inscrutable Providence that overrules alike the fall of a sparrow and the fall of nations.   From the Sacred Volume he appears to have drawn largely those precepts of good-will to men, and those ancient maxims of charity, which, above all others, grace the scholar, the soldier, and the civilian. There is a distrust in many minds of their fitness for a public profession of faith in that hope which all Christians find to be a consolation in their last moments, and it may be that on this very account Houston did not associate himself with any denomination of Christians at an early period. Yet the man of piety and of humanity was seen in the enlarged Christian charities which he exhibited from the first moment of his distinction. His generosity to Santa Anna—his protection to his Mexican captive, when threatened with assassination, even at the peril of his own person and popularity—show that he was animated by Christian precepts, not less than by a determination to save Texas from the unfading infamy which would have gathered over her name had this vacillating Mexican perished by the hands of an enraged soldiery while he was a prisoner of war.

XVII.

The dispatch, dated at Head Quarters of the Army, San Jacinto, April 25th, 1836—a model of style in its modest expression after a great victory—is concluded by General Houston in these significant words, which follow his tributes of praise to those who shared with himself the glory of the action : " Nor should we withhold the tribute of our grateful thanks from *that Being who rules the destinies of nations,* and has, *in the time of greatest need, enabled us* to arrest a powerful invader, whilst devastating our country." The intelligent reader will not fail to notice that the whole success of the most brilliant capture on the field of recent warfare, is unhesitatingly ascribed to the agency of that Divine Power that guides men by laws as certain to promote His will, as they are unseen and uncomprehended by His erring children ; who, nevertheless, as their studies increase, will never fail to recognize God in history.

XVIII.

Of the statesmanship of Houston we may, then, say with

truth, and with the concurrent assent of mankind, that the rapid progress of Texas, until its admission into our National Confederacy, is his most enduring and noble monument. The progress of time will only increase the curiosity of men to know the means by which order was eliminated out of chaos, while the examination of the policy of this statesman will lend renewed brilliancy to his name as an able expounder of the great principles of law, a thorough student in the history of men and empires, a just and noble governor, and every way fitted to hold the highest position in the gift of a people, especially in periods of storm and turbulence. Men who desire to rule, with the sacred form of justice ever enshrined in the sanctuary of their hearts, are seldom raised to power, but such men are too valuable to the cause of freedom and humanity to be overlooked, when it is necessary to meet an important crisis.

SECTION SEVENTEENTH.

HOUSTON AND THE INDIANS.

I.

In new countries the standard of commercial morality is always low. Indeed, it may be said, there is no such thing, except as it is defined by the public statutes. There are in our Atlantic cities large buildings, erected by *millionaires,* from the marble and granite drawn from the original hunting-grounds of the North American Indians, every block of which has been cemented with the Red Man's blood. For many years the butchery of the Indian was considered scarcely more criminal than the slaughter of the wild buffalo—and great companies of traders went to the far West, and with impunity, fortified by the general negligence on the subject, sacrificed at the altar of Mammon, thousands of noble hearts. This history of slaughters, innumerable and disgraceful, has not been published, though it has more than once been written. Fire-water has not been the sole exterminator of the Red Man. His bones have whitened on the plains, the prairies, and the hills, as he has been shot down by the unerring rifle of the trapper and hunter, acting under the authority of men of commercial enterprise.

II.

Philanthropy and justice shrink from the recital of those traditions, which tell the story of the Red Man's wrongs and the

White Man's perfidy.   Happily, however, within the last thirty years, a new and more generous feeling in favor of the Indian and his rights has dignified the public mind.   The daily massacre of Indians is at an end—and minds, sympathizing with the first owners of the soil, have exerted their eloquence in favor of the Aborigines.   This better state of public feeling has had its effect even on the frontiers, for the morality of true civilization, like the sun's beams, sheds its genial light wherever it has once been felt, to bless and to invigorate.   As the Indian character has been more and more studied, there has been a more enlightened appreciation of the condition and desires of the native tribes.   The government has been paternal from the first, and has done much to atone for injuries, and to smooth the path of the Red Man's apprehended annihilation—but much more might have been done by our government, had its agents been men of noble character—of the army, for instance—instead of scheming traders, not sensitively alive to those high principles of duty which should incite all men clothed with power by the government.   The hundred millions of dollars appropriated by Congress for the benefit of the Indian tribes, at various times, have been diverted from their true destination and purpose, and squandered, while the condition of the Red Man has been deteriorated rather than improved by the generosity or justice of the country, thus expressed in its bounties. This has been caused by the mode of distribution, which has been a careless, if not criminal negligence, and has proved more beneficial to speculators than to those whom it was intended to benefit.

III.

Evils of this kind have long been subjects of indignant remonstrance and discussion, and on the frontier are many noble men who know and love the Indian, who have partaken of his rude hospitality, or who have married in his wigwam, who raise the despairing cry for justice in the future. No men more thoroughly understand this subject in all its details—no men are more conversant with the wrongs endured by our Indian tribes than those spirits, who, from love of adventure, or to gratify their own tastes, have penetrated beyond the borders of civilization, and made their abiding-place with the children of nature. Houston was one of these. The story of his exit from the pleasures and amenities of civilization into the wilds of nature's wide domain has been told. He there learned to sympathize with the Indian, and to feel with him, because he knew his situation in the day of his decadence from power. In this way he became his defender. That hearty love of justice and mercy which so ennobles man, and which has marked his every step, could not shut the Indian out from his exertions and his hopes.

IV.

Accordingly, we find him second to no one, in the National Congress, in watching with lynx-eyed vigilance the cause of the Indians. While he would protect them from imposition, he would have no community imposed upon by them. It is averred that Indians, through Mexico, are now sold to Cuba as slaves. Time will decide if this allegation be true. If it is, surely every good man will desire that so atrocious a system should be terminated at once.

V.

The views of Houston with respect to the Indians, though somewhat mingled with opinions upon other topic, are to be found in what he said in the Senate of the United States, on the last day of 1854. They are all-important at this period of our survey of his life and character, and we should look to the public report of his speech on that occasion. Though many more brilliant speeches have fallen from his lips on the subject of Indian rights, and the necessity of being true to our Indian treaties, yet in the subjoined frank and noble avowal of opinions, all men will learn to honor the man, even more than the orator.

VI.

Mr. HOUSTON—Mr. President, I hardly know what to say in reply to the senator from Iowa, for I hardly know what to think of his speech. (Laughter.) If I were to characterize his remarks in any way, I should say that they were, at least, very remarkable. In the first place, let me say to that honorable senator, and to the honorable senator from Florida, that they were talking about things of which I knew very little, for I was not in the United States when the occurrences to which they alluded took place, and I was not, therefore, familiar with the history of those wars. If I am not mistaken, however, it was an outrage *of a very delicate character which brought on the Florida war.*

Mr. MALLORY—That is a mistake, sir.

VII.

Mr. HOUSTON—Well, sir that was the report which was brought to Texas. Whether it was true or not, I do not know; but that was the information which I received from people from that section of the country. As for the Black Hawk war, I know little or nothing about it; for, in Texas at that time, we had no mail communication with the United States, and we got but few papers from the States, so that I remained uninformed in relation to those matters; but, no doubt, they were very exciting. The senator from Iowa said the Black Hawk war was brought on by a council of the nation; but I have heard that an examination of the circumstances will show that the first outrage was committed by an individual, not by the concurrence of the nation, though they afterwards became involved in the general war. In that statement, I believe, I am sustained by the history of the times.

VIII.

I have already stated that occasions occur where outlaws among the Indians commit acts of aggression on the whites, and the whites immediately retaliate on the Indian nations, and these nations, in self-defence, become involved in war ; but I *never knew a case where a treaty, which was made and carried out in good faith, was violated by the Indians.* In Florida the Indians complained that they had been deceived in the treaty, and that the boundaries assigned were not as they understood them ; and they killed their own chiefs. It was charged that some of the agents were involved in speculations to a great extent dependent on the treaty. I recollect it was so stated at the time.

IX.

I think, sir, the senator's speech was of a remarkable character in relation to politics and other matters, which I am sorry that he has introduced. He has undertaken to admonish me, and for this admonition I am much obliged to him. His experience, his superior opportunities, may entitle him, in the opinion of others, to the right of admonishing me ; and I am perfectly willing, on that point, to yield my own opinion to what may be the general impression of the body. I did not provoke his remark by any allusion to any one, predicated upon my own disposition to arraign the conduct of others ; nor have I asserted anything in regard to the officers of the army, but what are matters of fact, taken from the official documents. When I made suggestions of a speculative character, I gave them as such.

X.

But, Mr. President, the senator from Iowa has said that he would not have been astonished if the rankest abolitionist had made such a speech, and had avowed such sentiments as I did. He says that, if a man in western New York had presented such views, he would not have been surprised. Now, I wish to know what connection my remarks had with abolition ? What connection they had with any one in western New York ? In what respect have I catered to any prejudice or morbid sensibility ? I have stood here alone in this body, against a powerful array of talent and

14*

influence, contending for what I conceived to be a great principle, and which must obtain, or the Indian race be exterminated.

XI

In regard to that principle, I have the concurrence of the senator from Tennessee (Mr. Bell), who was once Secretary of War, and, as such, had control of the Indian Department, and who has, since that period, been a prominent member of the Committee on Indian Affairs of the Senate. I believe that my opinions are also concurred in by the senator from Arkansas (Mr. Sebastian), who is the head of the Committee on Indian Affairs. I can inform the senator from Iowa that I will sustain him to the extent of my humble abilities in any measure he may introduce in favor of the Indians, and for the establishment of a policy which will ultimately benefit them, and reflect credit upon the government of the United States.

XII.

I have not been regardless of what I considered the honor of the United States, and the interest of the Indians. In no instance have I been remiss in these particulars. I could not cater to any passion or prejudice on this subject, *because I know of no societies in the North, or in the South, or in any section of this Union, for the advancement of the civilization of the Indians. If such societies exist, I am not in correspondence with them,* nor am I aware of the existence of any such associations. Then, for what ulterior purposes could I advocate the rights of the Indians, or invoke the justice of this government towards them? Could it be any expectation of political benefits? None upon earth.

XIII.

I presume the abolitionists are perfectly absorbed in the subject of abolition. For myself, I would rather see them turn their attention to the amelioration of the condition of the Indians on our western wilds, or to the reclamation of those whom they hold in slavery. There are not less than two thousand prisoners in the hands of the Camanches; four hundred in one band, in my own State. The prisoners can be reclaimed from those

Indians, who are coming down to settle upon their reservations. They take no prisoners but women and boys. The boys they treat with a degree of barbarity unprecedented ; and their cruelties towards the females are nameless and atrocious. Our government is silent in relation to them. Has humanity no claims upon us in this respect ? Has justice no demand unanswered ?

XIV.

Sir, we have not seen the facts to which I have just alluded impressed on a page of our official communications from the War Department. The officers stationed near the places where those transactions have taken place have not reported them. No effort has been made to obtain appropriations for the reclamation and redemption of those prisoners. This is a subject which calls aloud for the humane influence of the senator. There is no sickly sentimentality in this, but a manly upheaving of soul, that, in consideration of suffering humanity, demands that the government shall rescue them from the most cruel and unrelenting bondage.

XV.

I have been accused of catering to a morbid, sickly sentimentality. Sir, I never yielded anything of my own conscientious convictions to consult the opinions of others. I never stooped to solicit office ; but I have received and accepted it to my own disadvantage. I might have hated the Indians, if I had a soul no bigger than a shell-bark. [Laughter.]

XVI.

In my boyish days, before manhood had hardened my thews and muscles, I received balls and arrows in this body, in defence of suffering humanity, particularly women and children, against the Indians ; and I aided in reclaiming the brightest spot of the South—Alabama. When I remember that, in those early days, I assisted in rescuing females and children from the relentless tomahawk and scalping knife, it seems to me that the charge that I have stooped to court favor by the expression of my sentiments on this question, is one which falls harmless at my feet.

XVII.

So far as the subject of our relations with the Indians is concerned, this, the most recent speech of Houston, stands creditably by the side of his other efforts in the same field. We learn something from it, too, of his own early history, which will be read with no ordinary interest. The remainder of his speech on the occasion will be suitable for the next section of this work, as it is connected with a topic that is becoming the ruling theme in every State in the Union—and not without reason, for if our institutions were worthy to be gained, most assuredly it is worthy of us to endeavor to preserve them from the corruption that is stealthily impairing our nationality. Yet, ere the subject of our Indian relations is dismissed, it should not be forgotten that though Senator Houston does not conceive that any political value can accrue to him from an advocacy of the Indian's cause, the public will view the subject differently. There is in the American heart, a deeply-seated and ineradicable sense of justice, that will not submit to any outrages upon the Indian nations. Besides they are valuable to our coast on the Pacific, and will eventually blend with the natives of Eastern Asia, producing results of vast importance to the growth and prosperity of the continent. On this point, therefore, the views of Houston cannot be deemed either trivial or unimportant in a political or national point of view.

SECTION EIGHTEENTH.

HOUSTON AND FOREIGN EMIGRATION.

I.

It was in the same speech, on the last day of 1854, that Houston was called upon by a senator, to *answer* questions so pointed as to demand replies without either reservation or prevarication. The plain, blunt manner in which the answers were given, will not be without their effect upon every sincere lover of this country, who has determined to find here a home for himself, or for his children—for there is no man worthy of the name of American citizen who is not alive to the danger to be apprehended from the present inroads made upon the political power of our States, by the immense influx of foreigners unprepared to feel and know the value, much less to comprehend the importance of preserving our institutions as nearly as possible as they were transmitted to us by our political fathers. The apprehension that Houston will prove the most powerful candidate in the field for the next Presidential campaign was the cause of the attempt on the part of Mr. Mallory, to obtain something like a platform for the politicians to understand, probably with a view to that ultimate defeat which is more easily desired than safely prophesied. Let us not detain the reader, however, from studying the replies of the hero of San Jacinto.

II.

I hardly know what to think of the gentleman's remarks as to catering for the Presidency. I hardly know what to say about the extraneous subjects which he has introduced. I suppose the shortest way of naming what he intended to allude to, is by the term "Know-Nothing." *Now, of the Know-Nothings I know nothing* (laughter) ; *and of them I care nothing.* But if the principles which I see charged to them in many instances are the principles which they seek to carry out, I can say to gentlemen that I concur in many of them. If their object is to resist the encroachments of one religion or sect upon another, I am with them. I say resist all such encroachments, and leave all religion uncontaminated by the perversion of power that might accidentally result in proscription and the inquisition. "I'll none of it ;" I am opposed to and would prevent such a result.

III.

I admit that we are all descended from foreigners, because, originally, there were no natives here who were white men. Many of those foreigners who originally came here, were baptized in the blood of the Revolution ; but they were not such men as are now coming to our shores, and should not be named in connection with those who are spewed loathingly from the prisons of England, and from the pauper houses of Europe. Such men are not to be compared to our ancestry, or to the immigration which, until recently, has come to our shores from foreign countries. *If the object of those to whom the Senator from Iowa has referred, is to prevent men of infamous character and paupers from coming here, I agree with them. I would say, establish a law, requiring every person from abroad, before being received here, to bring an endorsement from one of our consuls abroad,* and produce evidence of good character from the place whence he emigrates, so that when he comes here, we may receive him into full communion with all the rights guaranteed to him by the laws which may exist at the time of his emigration.

IV.

But, sir, to say that a felon, who left his prison the day he sailed for this country, or, perhaps, was brought in chains to the vessel which bore him here, is, in five years, to stand an equal with the proudest man who walks on our soil, the man who has shed his blood to consecrate liberty and his country, is not the kind of arrangement that I go for.

Mr. MALLORY—Will the Senator from Texas allow me to ask him one question ?

Mr. HOUSTON—With pleasure.

Mr. MALLORY—As the subject of Know-Nothingism, as it is called, has been brought here——

Mr. HOUSTON—I have not introduced it, and I am not going to comment on it.

V.

Mr. MALLORY—Precisely so ; the senator has not introduced the subject, and perhaps he is not responsible for its introduction ; but he is undertaking to say what he himself thinks upon it. Now, as he is speaking on the subject, I should like to understand distinctly, whether he *approves or does not approve of so much of the creed attributed to the Know-Nothings, as would make those who profess the Roman Catholic religion ineligible to office ?*

Mr. HOUSTON—I would vote for no such law.

Mr. MALLORY—I asked the gentleman whether he approved that or not—not whether he would vote for it.

VI.

Mr. HOUSTON—No, sir ; *I could not approve of such a law.* But the proscription which is charged on those to whom allusion has been made, is no more than formerly existed between whigs and democrats. When party discipline was kept up, if a whig voted for a democratic candidate, he was ruled out of his party, and branded as a deserter ; and if a democrat voted for a whig, he was disowned by his party. That species of political proscription will exist everywhere, according to the notions of people. I do not set up my opinion as the doctrine by which other people are to be governed. I am governed by my own principles, and my own sentiments, and I have a right to vindicate them, and I am responsible for them to the world. When the Senator from Iowa supposes that I would cater for the Presidency of the United States, he does me great injustice. I would not cater for any office beneath heaven. (*Pause.*) *But, sir, I know one thing : if it were to be thrust upon me, I should make a great many changes in some small matters.* [Laughter.]

VII.

Mr. DODGE, of Iowa—Mr. President, I have no desire to prolong this controversy with the senator from Texas. No man understands better than I do, how much I must suffer in any intellectual contest with one so skilled and renowned in debate, almost as much as he is in arms. I know his ability to say as much on one side as on the other, a manifestation of which we have had, in the conclusion of his remarks. (Laughter.) Sir, I charged, and I repeat the charge, that the speech of the senator from Texas, would have done well if delivered by a Massachusetts federalist, or for a man from western New York—that region in which all the *isms*, from anti-masonry down, have originated. I have read the speeches of these eastern gentlemen, and I am aware of the manner in which this Indian question has been dragged into politics in times past ; and I know the purpose to which it is to be again prostituted in the approaching Presidential canvass ; I see attempted, in connection with the Kansas and Nebraska law, the appeal that is to be made to couple with that measure this one, which is to provide for the defence of the country. I repeat, so far as I am concerned, that so long as I have a voice or a vote, I will remember those who refuse to give us protection

VIII.

Unquestionably, should the popular will in behalf of Houston be expressed with the same warmth that it has been for some considerable term now gone by, these views will have no weight except to carry the balance in his favor. However, it is our province to record, rather than to conjecture. We have to do with the man as he has been—not as he may be. The struggle to satisfy the demands of the country, when the candidates for the next Presidential term are selected, will be great. Doubtless, it will be impossible to leave out of the list the man who, above all others, tried or untried in holding the reins of power, stands conspicuous for qualities of head and heart inherent by nature and chastened by cultivation, which stamp him as signally fitted for the position to which the wants of the country, as well as the popular voice, should raise him. In the next contest, if we err not in our estimate of the motives which will rule the popular vote, conventions will be obliged to surrender the old machinery of party to those general expressions of the public voice, which will grow more and more loud as the hour approaches for determining who shall be the Chief Magistrate of the United States.

SECTION NINETEENTH.

THE ANNEXATION OF TEXAS.

I.

THE struggle made in the Congress of the United States to bring Texas into the Union, was so important that some further reference to the subject should be here made. While Texas was yet a Republic, and as early as 1838, an application was made by Houston to place it under the jurisdiction of our Federal Government. It was his first official act as President of Texas, to send an agent to Washington to make known his wishes and his hopes. Soon after, he dispatched another envoy with extraordinary powers, but to these applications there was no satisfactory result. In 1841, another trial was made through Mr. Riley. This was followed up by Mr. Van Zandt. Nothing, however, was accomplished—and Texas was forced to stand alone.

II.

Wearied with these vain attempts to gain admission into the Confederacy, a policy was adopted that hastened the destiny of the young Republic. England was coquetted with, till apprehensions were entertained by men in the United States, and by its Government, that there was a possibility of losing Texas for ever. This feeling increased even to alarm: for even at that period it was well understood that the British Government would gladly interpose barriers to our growth in national wealth, dominion, and power, for the sake of checking the progress of republican liberty, by which European governments have been so much menaced during the present century. At that time it was contemplated, even by the British Government, to gain California, and thus to place a monarchical colony on our most important border. The action of Texas, therefore, in seeking the good will of Great Britain was more than diplomatic. It was sagacious ; and, as events have proved, was vastly important in its results.

III.

At the beginning of President Polk's administration, and while the Northwestern Boundary Question was agitating the whole country, and wearing a warlike aspect, the Texas dispute was at its height. On the one hand, the country was threatened with a war with Great Britain ; and, on the other hand, with Mexico. The Oregon boundary was settled by negotiation —but the Texas controversy ended in a war with the Mexican power. In August, 1845, General Zachary Taylor encamped at Corpus Christi, on the Gulf of Mexico, and remained there until the ensuing month of March. Annexation had taken place by a Joint Resolution of Congress, passed in February ; and in obedience to instructions, General Taylor, on the 11th of March, went towards the Rio Grande, and commenced a correspondence with the Mexican Dictator, Paredes, on the true boundary of the new State.

IV.

On the first of May, the Mexican General, Arista, marched a force to the Texan bank of the Rio Grande, and this was the commencement of the war with Mexico, in which, it may be said, with truth, that the American people displayed but little of that spirit of nationality which distinguishes all other nations. A large portion of the people were opposed to the war, and did not cast aside their prejudices in one common feeling against the enemy. This state of affairs was caused by the passions which had been inflamed by tne introduction of Texas into the Union—a measure that was opposed, as was alleged, on the ground that it was "unconstitutional to admit her without the intervention and sanction of the people, and, also, because there was a strong apprehension of dangers from increasing the area of slavery."

V.

The debate upon the proposition to admit Texas into the Union had been warm in both houses of Congress, and the excitement attending the final action on tne subject was intense. Men were more engaged in magnifying the dangers to be apprehended from a possible extension of the slavery system, than in contemplating the grave importance, in every aspect of public economy and of national aggrandizement, of possessing so grand a territory for future improvement and use as the soil of Texas. Its commercial value was lost sight of. Its command of the Gulf trade, or the most western ports of the Atlantic, was overlooked, and only a few men dared to maintain that the wants of posterity would render the new State an invaluable possession. "The great, and vast, and illimitable Texas," as Webster styled it, was deemed of little importance compared with the turbulent expressions of sincere, or pretended dread, that the extension of territory liable to slave labor, necessarily involves the perpetuation of African servitude—a problem still unsolved, but not without solution, when the subject is left to the wisdom and to the commercial sagacity of those most interested in the question.

VI.

It is not our purpose to enter upon the political history of the time in which Texas and its admission to the Union became a vexed question. It is our object to glance at some prominent facts connected with the subject, before we proceed to show the value of the State of Texas to the Confederacy. And we cannot better commence this part of our work, in order to show the claims of Houston to the distinction which has been awarded to his exertions, than by quoting from a Mexican newspaper, of 1845, a prophecy which has passed on to its fulfillment. The writer says : " Texas is gone—gone for ever, and beyond redemption—to our natural enemies, the Anglo-Americans, who know but too well how to estimate us at our just value. Let us not be deceived by the promised vindication of our rights, so pompously paraded in public speeches, and official documents. Our threats are paper threats, as was justly observed by one of the boldest statesmen in the neighboring Republic. Texas, we repeat it, is lost to Mexico ! And here we are forced to a confession—a bitter one, indeed. That Department, wrested from us by an act of usurpation and perfidy never before equalled, will at once start on a new career of improvement and prosperity—safe from savage inroads, arbitrary exactions, and unjust prohibitions and monopolies. A fertile soil will plentifully reward the honest labor of the husbandman, the mechanic arts will flourish, each citizen will be free to arm himself for his own and his country's defence, and each will have the right to practice, unmolested, the religion which his conscience sanctions and dictates. Texas, by renouncing her separate sovereignty, will cease to be, as heretofore, a country of outlaws, and become a part of a powerful nation, whose growing prosperity will shed its beneficial influence over the new territory.   Such is the destiny of that Department severed from us, and now forming part of the American Union.   The tendency of an example so pernicious, is clear to all."

VII.

There was occasion for alarm on the part of Mexico, at this position of Texas, for there were Departments in her domain which, at the time, were ripening for political revolution and change.   On this point we need not dwell.   Let us notice, rather, the very important improvement which took place in Texas, immediately after she became one of our States, in respect to her social character.   Law and order soon softened and harmonized the crude elements which marked her population ; and villages, towns, and cities, arose on every hand, busy with the industry, skill, and vigor of a thriving and worthy people. The school-house was built by the way-side.   Churches dotted the lawns and the hill-sides.   The courts of law administered justice to all—and, on every side, there were indications of prosperity and security.   The Mexican prophecy was more than fulfilled ; and the wisdom of the man who had patiently sought, calmly waited, and confidingly persevered, to rescue a vast domain from lawlessness, and to place it as a star in our constellation of republics, was shown in the culture of the soil and in all the external symbols of refinement and civilization. At the present time, no State in the Union is more inviting to those who would seek a home in a new country, as will be evident to those who endeavor to learn the nature of her social character—the extent of her industrial resources, and the opportunities which may be secured for advancement in all the learned professions, and in the walks of commercial and agricultual life.

VIII.

When Texas was first a debated question, little was known of her vast and multiform resources. Time has made the world wiser. The soil and climate are such that the State is now looked upon as the Garden of the World. For the cultivation either of tobacco, or cotton, corn, wheat, or hemp, her soil is not surpassed by the most generous lands of other States. The peculiarity of her soil renders the wheat grown within her borders the most profitable yet known to our country, and with but little labor the ground produces abundantly, giving its crops as early as June. Tobacco and cotton are seen growing on the field where corn is a neighbor. Nature is everywhere bountiful. With further exploration, her mines will be found, it is thought, second in importance to none in the other States. As a grazing country she is without a rival, and the animals slaughtered for their hides and for provisions, furnish afterwards thousands of tons of bones annually, which are shipped to New York, where they are converted into phosphate of lime, and sold to our farmers for the improvement of the wasted or sterile soils of the North. Thus the benefit of Texas to the North is witnessed in many States which were originally opposed to her introduction into the Union. This is not all. The trade of the Atlantic States with Texas is every day becoming more and more important. Every year increases it—and, as the climate is salubrious, the population is rapidly increasing, and the State will eventually become the most important in the Southern country.

IX.

There is another point not to be forgotten. Texas is the great Commercial Isthmus, by which the nations of the earth will pass ere long to the Pacific Ocean. Geographically, this does not appear so ; but the surveys made for railroads to our Western shores conclusively demonstrate that when a road is built to connect the Atlantic and Pacific oceans, it will run through Texas. Such a road will not be obstructed by the snows and ice incident to more northern latitudes. Besides, this road, if constructed to San Diego, in California, will bring Australia fifteen hundred miles nearer than it would be from any other point that could be designated. These considerations will increase in importance as the necessity for the construction of a national road is felt by the public. A military road to California, is now needed by the government for purposes which prudent statesmen can easily comprehend as possible—and a wise policy will not neglect, till the force of circumstances incite to action, an application to a subject so important to us as a commercial people, and as a nation. The money expended by the country in building and keeping in repair forts and fortifications on the western frontiers, might be disbursed more judiciously in the construction of military roads, which would be safe highways for the great tide of emigration sweeping Westward. The question of the province of Congress with respect to Internal Improvements does not trench upon this species of enterprise—for the wants of the people and the demands of humanity alike suggest, that the Federal Government should make some provision for opening ways across the country to our Western shores. This is not the place, however, to enlarge upon this interesting subject. Our design is to show that Texas is the ground over which *the great national road to the Pacific must pass*—and so well assured are we of this, that we advert to it as another proof of the great importance of the annexation of Texas to the Union. The conformation of continents and oceans, must make Texas the highway from New York to San Francisco.

X.

There are other reasons for estimating the acquisition of Texas as a national blessing. When we reflect upon what she might have become, had we refused her admission to the Union, we cannot look upon the past but with mingled feelings of dread and thankfulness. Had the sectional animosity that opposed the admission of Texas prevailed, the most serious consequences might have ensued. Happily the luxuriant and swelling prairies, the fertile hills, and the beautifully irrigated valleys of that delightful country are our own—happily, that coast which stretches along the Gulf of Mexico is ours for the enlargement of commerce, and for the protection of our Southern borders—happily, the jurisdiction of the United States, though it has no power over her domain, as in some other territories, can be exerted to extend the benefits of legislation to her people, and to those who hereafter may desire to become residents of that State, or sojourners in it on their way to the extreme West. Whenever the road to California is completed, then, over this Commercial Isthmus of the Continent, the American people will appreciate how far superior to all minor questions are those great national ones which involve the happiness of millions upon millions of men, and which tend to perpetuate the security of the nation ; at any time liable to temporary aggression from nations desirous to check our advancing prosperity, between the two oceans which gird our shores.

XI.

A fatal political mistake would have been made, had the councils of party prevailed over the stern necessity of circumstances with respect to the admission of Texas to the Union. In 1802, Georgia was induced to cede that part of her territory

15

now known as Alabama and Mississippi. In 1803, Louisiana was purchased from France—and from this we have the States of Louisiana, Arkansas, and Missouri. In 1819, the cession of Florida was made by Spain. What more natural and inevitable destiny was there for Texas, from its geographical and political position, than to yield to the embrace of the Confederacy ? It is in vain for men, when circumstances of every kind point to a result so manifestly necessary, to array the league of abstract morals and sectional jealousies against it. Thus it proved in the case of Texas ; and, whatever may be the particular scruples of conscience in individual minds as to the means employed to secure such a benefit as Texas has proved to be to the United States, all will agree that we have been enriched by this acquisition of territory, great as has been the cost, beyond any possible human estimate. Of the issues which have grown out of it, the future will declare more than prophecy itself could foresee. With an efficient Chief Magistrate to stay the inflammatory fever raised during the last year so needlessly, and in opposition to all the desires of the nation at large, both at the North and South, we may expect to live through the " trouble," and not even regret that Texas was a proximate cause of so gratuitous an agitation of the public mind. Should the people be alive to the interests of the country as a confederated nationality, we need not fear that any regret will attend our recollections of the annexation of a State of which Houston was the political father.

XII.

From present appearances, we may then conclude, that the beautiful country given to the Union by the man whose services to the public we are considering—is destined to be second in importance to no other, when the public mind becomes acquainted with the almost boundless extent of her resources, with the remarkable geographical position she occupies in reference to our Pacific coast, and with the delicious mildness of her climate. Already thousands of persons have emigrated to that State, where all the enjoyments and privileges of refinement and civilization are rapidly increasing, to open an inviting way, by an overland route, to California, and thus to secure to the United States the full measure of prosperity promised by the discovery and acquisition of the gold regions on the Pacific. Health and its preservation are not subjects of trivial importance, and emigrants will select the road through Texas in preference to any other, when it is built, because it will offer the greatest number of facilities for a speedy and safe passage to the Pacific coast. Should, then, the future establish Texas as the great gate and highway to California, how much reason have we to congratulate ourselves on the annexation of Texas, once deemed so disastrous, and how pitiably insignificant in comparison is the slavery question as a barrier to the march of all nations towards increased happiness and prosperity. On the whole, then, we may rejoice that we have Texas in the Union—and learn, also, from the outcry made against her admission, how unimportant it is to believe that the North is to be the sufferer by what is said to be the extension of the "peculiar institutions" of the South. May the day come when the agitation on this subject shall cease, that involuntary servitude may perish from natural causes, and not be made stronger by the very means employed to destroy its existence!

XIII.

Lest the reader may suppose that Texas was acquired for the purpose of extending slavery, as party politicians averred before she came into the Union, we may cite from a speech made in the Senate of the United States, to show by facts that this was not the case. It was said by Mr. Benton, in 1836 : "Heartless is the calumny invented and propagated, not from this floor, but elsewhere, on the cause of the Texan revolt. It is said to be a war for the extension of slavery. It had as well been said that our own Revolution was a war for the extension of slavery. So far from it, that no revolt, not even our own, ever had a more just and a more sacred origin. The settlers in Texas went to live under the form of government which they had left behind in the United States—a government which extends so many guarantees for life, liberty, property, and the pursuit of happiness, and which their American and English ancestors had vindicated for so many hundred years. A succession of violent changes in government, and the rapid overthrow of rulers, annoyed and distressed them ; but they remained tranquil under every violence which did not immediately bear on themselves. In 1822 the republic of 1821 was superseded by the imperial diadem of Iturbide. In 1823 he was deposed and banished, returned, and was shot, and Victoria made President. Mentuno and Bravo disputed the presidency with Victoria ; and found, in banishment, the mildest issue known among Mexicans to unsuccessful civil war. Pedraza was elected in 1828 ; Guerrero overthrew him the next year. Then Bustamente overthrew Guerrero ; and, quickly, Santa Anna overthrew Bustamente, and, with him, all the forms of the constitution, and the whole frame of the federative government. By his own will, and by force, Santa Anna dissolved the existing Congress, convened another, formed the two Houses into one, called it a Convention —and made it the instrument for deposing, without trial, the constitutional Vice President, Gomez Fatias, putting Barragan into his place, annihilating the State government, and establishing a consolidated government, of which he was monarch, under the retained republican title of President. Still, the Texans did not take up arms : they did not acquiesce, but they did not revolt.· They retained their State government in operation, and looked to the other States, older and more powerful than Texas, to vindicate the general cause, and to re-establish the federal constitution of 1824. In September, 1835, this was still her position. In that month, a Mexican armed vessel appeared off the coast of Texas, and declared her ports blockaded. At the same time, General Cos appeared in the West, with an army of fifteen hundred men, with orders to arrest the State authorities, to disarm the inhabitants, leaving one gun to every five hundred souls ; and to reduce the State to unconditional submission. Gonzales was the selected point for the commencement of the execution of these orders ; and the first thing was the arms, those trusty rifles which the settlers had brought with them from the United States, which were their defence against savages, their resource for game, and the guard which converted their houses into castles stronger than those ' which the king cannot enter.' A detachment of General Cos's army appeared at the village of Gonzales, on the 28th of September, and demanded the arms of the inhabitants ; it was the same demand, made for the same purpose, which the British detachment, under Major Pitcairn, had made at Lexington, on the 16th of April, 1775. It was the same demand ! And the same answer was given—resistance—battle—victory ! The American blood was at Gonzales what it had been at Lexington ; and between using their arms, and surrendering their arms, that blood can never hesitate. Then followed the rapid succession of brilliant events, which in two months left Texas without an armed enemy in her borders, and the strong forts of Goliad and the Alamo, with their garrisons and cannon, the almost bloodless prizes of a few hundred Texan rifles. This was the origin of the revolt ; and a calumny more heartless can never be imagined than that which would convert this rich and holy defence of life, liberty, and property, into an aggression for the extension of slavery. Just in its origin, valiant and humane in its conduct, the Texan revolt has illustrated the Anglo-Saxon character, and given it new titles to the respect and admiration of the world. It shows that liberty, justice, valor—moral, physical, and intellectual power— characterise that race wherever it goes. Let our America rejoice, let old England rejoice, that the Brasos and Colerado, new and strange names—streams far beyond the western bank of the Father of Floods—have felt the impress, and witnessed the exploits of a people sprung from their loins, and carrying their language, laws, and customs, their *magna charta* and its glorious privileges, into new regions and far distant climes."

XIV.

It may not be less a calumny for men to avow that the early population of Texas was composed of outlaws. Every new country offers fields for the honorable efforts of those who would retrieve the errors by which they may have purchased experience. While Texas was no exception to the general rule of all new colonial countries, the defence of its character from too much stress upon this point was thus given before the Senate of the United States. With it we will conclude this section of our work : " Great is the mistake which has prevailed in Mexico, and in some parts of the United States, on the character of the population which has gone to Texas. It has been common to disparage and to stigmatize them. Nothing could be more unjust ; and speaking from knowledge, either personally or well acquired (for it falls to my lot to know, either from actual acquaintance, or good information, the mass of its inhabitants), I can vindicate them from erroneous imputations, and place their conduct and character on the honorable ground which they deserve to occupy. The founder of the

Texan colony was Mr. Moses Austin, a respectable and enterprising native of Connecticut, and largely engaged in the lead
mines of Upper Louisiana, in 1815. The present head of the
colony, his son, Mr. Stephen F. Austin, then a very young
man, was a member of the Territorial Legislature, distinguished
for his intelligence, business habits, and gentlemanly conduct.
Among the grantees we distinguish the name of Robertson, son
of the patriarchal founder, and the first settler of West Tennessee. Of the body of emigrants, most of them are heads of
families or enterprising young men, gone to better their condition by receiving grants of fine lands in a fine climate, and to
continue to live under the republican form of government to which
they had been accustomed. There sits one of them, [pointing to
Mr. Carson, member of Congress, from North Carolina, and then,
1836, Secretary of State for Texas.] We all know him ; our
greetings on his appearance in this chamber attest our respect ;
and such as we know him to be, so do I know the multitude
to be who have gone to Texas. They have gone, not as
intruders, but as grantees ; and to become a barrier between
the Mexicans and the marauding Indians who infested their
borders."

XV.

Surely a population, originating in such a primitive stock as
this has been described to have been, though bold rather than
wise spirits were her counsellors at first, cannot be other than
suitable for the association of those enterprising men of other
States, who see in the wilderness fields worthy of cultivation, and
which more rapidly than those of older States give speedy rewards
to industry. The means used by party newspapers to strengthen
the public animosity towards Texas, included, for several years,
exaggerated and abusive misrepresentations of the people of the

new Republic.   " G. T. T.," or " Gone to Texas," was the favorite mode of accounting for the absence of any person who had
forfeited, by design, or through misfortune, his claim to be considered a good citizen.   In this way Texas became a name for
reproach.   Time has changed all this ; and now the State is a
favorite one for emigrants from every part of our country and
from Europe, and she is, therefore, becoming rapidly rich in the
great increase of her population.

XVI.

Before leaving this important branch of our subject, and for
the purpose of showing the extent of that political foresight
that distinguished Houston in associating his fortunes with
those of Texas, it will be profitable to look at the very valuable
moral for States and people which is found in the still earlier history of Texas, and in the causes which shut her out from the
position, which, happily for the United States, she now occupies.
Had she come into her proper place at an earlier period, and
not been kept in obscurity by considerations which seemed
important to individuals, rather than to the aggrandizement of
the nation at large, we should have been spared the long train
of evils which terminated in the expensive and disastrous, though
successful and brilliant, war with Mexico.   Such has been the
fruit of the agitation of the slavery question !   Similar will be
the results in all cases while men persist in making that subject
a party question, instead of leaving the institution to the manifest and inevitable destiny to which it must hasten, when left
free to compete with the general freedom in commerce and
trade which animates our prairies, and extends itself to the most
tangled regions of the Western wilds.

XVII.

In 1819, in acquiring Florida, the government of the United States abandoned Texas. The new boundaries made by the negotiator of the treaty, John Quincy Adams, at the suggestion of a majority of President Monroe's cabinet, not only cut away Texas, but surrendered a portion of the Mississippi valley. This was a popular measure ; and, though the Spanish government had offered the country more than it had accepted, yet the policy of our government was so weak as to deprive us of that which has since cost us so much blood and treasure to regain. In 1820, Mr. Monroe, in endeavoring to justify his action with respect to the treaty, stated that the "difficulties" were not with Spain alone—they were "internal, proceeding from various causes which certain men are prompt to seize and turn to the account of their own ambitious views."

XVIII.

These "difficulties" were the fear that the slavery extension question would become a test in the Presidential election, and the repugnance in the Northeast to territorial aggrandizement in the Southwest—the folly of which is clearly demonstrated by every step in our country's history, though the agitation of this subject, in some shape, still afflicts the public mind, and hinders our progress as a united nation.

XIX.

Three times did the treaty come before the Senate of the

15*

United States for ratification. This was caused by the state of affairs between Mexico and Spain, which rendered it necessary to establish the boundary with the government of the former, instead of that of the latter. Three times did the American press congratulate the people on this action of our government—one of the gravest political blunders of the nation.

XX.

As our pages have already shown, a few years only elapsed, before there was a general desire on the part of the American people to possess this very Texas, which we would not receive from Spain originally, because by so doing the "ambitious views" of men might have been disturbed. The moral thus far is important enough—but it can be extended, because, strangely enough, all that had been accomplished was the work of Southern men, with the sanction of the South—men who were candidates for the Presidency, or who hoped to advance to high offices of trust and power. No wonder that the question is so frequently asked, if there is such a thing as American nationality —when the people will permit trivial political topics to interfere with the natural growth of the nation. Texas, however, is now a part of our political unit, and that it is so every honest American will rejoice—and, while doing so, will render due praise to him whose exertions saved her from the grasp of a foreign nation, and gave her to us, even at the sacrifice of all the allurements which excite ambitious men. That his proposal to declare her a part of Louisiana, under the treaty of 1803, was disregarded, should excite our regrets, but for the valuable lessons the nation has gained in its political experience.

SECTION TWENTIETH.

THE PRESENT AND THE FUTURE OF TEXAS.

I.

A RAPID survey of the Present of Texas will not be uninteresting, as it will prepare the reader to form an estimate of its probable Future. Let us not forget that only a few years ago this State was repulsed by hundreds of thousands of American citizens, as a useless and dangerous addition to the Union—and thereby learn, when contemplating any great official act of the country, to cast aside prejudice, and the sinister judgments of others, as of little value compared with the lessons of experience which every few years furnish an enlightened people, who strive to understand for themselves the political problems of the time.

II.

Texas is divided into eighty counties, containing about twelve million acres of land, of which about one-twelfth is improved. The value of this land in money has been estimated to be eighteen millions of dollars. Probably not less than twenty-eight thousand farmers are at work, at the present hour, to enrich this State, employing farming implements and machinery, valued at nearly three million dollars. In 1850 there were over seventy-five thousand horses, twelve thousand mules, two

hundred and fifteen thousand milch cows, and fifty thousand working oxen, in the State, the free population of which was not far
from one hundred and fifty-five thousand persons. The slave
population was about fifty-eight thousand. The population has
increased rapidly within the last five years, and when the
returns are made under the next census, the increase in all that
makes a State valuable to itself and mankind, will be such as
to gratify every one who delights in the prosperity of his
country.

III.

We have before alluded to the productions of Texas ; but to
show her commercial value more clearly, we may cite from
public documents a few important facts.   In 1850 the value of
the live stock was upwards of ten millions of dollars, and of
slaughtered animals upwards of one million of dollars.   In the
same year, the following were the principal products—forty-two
thousand bushels of wheat ; three thousand bushels of rye ; six
millions of bushels of Indian corn ; two hundred thousand bushels
of oats ; eighty-eight thousand pounds of rice ; sixty-seven
thousand pounds of tobacco ; fifty-eight thousand bales, four
hundred pounds each, of ginned cotton ; one hundred and thirty
one thousand pounds of wool; one hundred and seventy-nine
thousand bushels of peas and beans ; ninety-three thousand
bushels of Irish potatoes ; upwards of one million bushels of
sweet potatoes ; five thousand bushels of barley ; twelve thousand dollars' worth of orchard products ; the same amount of
kitchen garden products ; two millions four hundred pounds of
butter ; ninety-five thousand pounds of cheese ; eight thousand
tons of hay ; one thousand pounds of flax ; twenty-two
pounds of silk cocoons ; seven thousand three hundred and fifty
hogsheads of sugar ; five hundred thousand gallons of molasses ;
and four hundred thousand pounds of beeswax and honey.

IV.

Such are the staple products of this once proscribed State, and the variety of them will most clearly indicate the character of that soil and climate which is destined to be known to thousands of emigrants within a few years, and by the world generally. There is no new State in the Union that holds out greater inducements to the mechanic and the agriculturist, than Houston's Own, as it has been styled by one of our public writers. Education is not neglected in this State. There were in 1850 two colleges, with seven teachers, and one hundred and sixty-five students, three hundred and fifty public schools, and ninety-seven academies and other schools. The number of pupils at school returned in the census of 1850 amounts to upwards of nineteen thousand, thus assuring the country that the elements of a future race of usefulness and prosperity are at work in the heart of Texas, which will yet distinguish it among the older and more highly favored sovereignties.

V.

With such a Present, what may not reasonably be expected as a Future? There has been growing in the public mind, for some time past, a feeling of political compensation amounting almost to a national instinct, by which, in the selection of candidates for the Presidential Chair, each section of the country, in its turn, shall be honorably remembered. Our new States have not yet been complimented by the American people in this way, and now seems to be the period when the attempt can be made. Should the merits of Houston bring him forward, and place him at the head of the nation, the influence upon the State of Texas would be very great, when combined with the power she possesses in her own remarkable and varied resources.

Besides, there is almost a certainty that the State will become the great and popular *dépôt* of commerce between the whole world and California, before the lapse of many years, when the construction of a railroad to the Pacific will bring within her domain an amount of population, enterprise, capital, industry, and energy, that will have a vast effect upon her wealth, and the individual prosperity of her people—vitalizing her rich and prolific soil, and bringing to her coast the ships of every nation, till history shall look back with wonder at the strange fact, that a territory so recently recovered from barbarism, even amidst the sneers and opposition of a large portion of a civilized nation, should become, in so short a time, second in importance to no other State washed by the waters of the Atlantic.

VI.

The Future, then, of Texas, as one of the States of the Union, promises to be of the gravest interest to our commerce ; and it is not necessary to invoke the forecast of the Prophet to declare that she will shine second in brightness to no other star in our political firmament.

SECTION TWENTY-FIRST.

HOUSTON'S EDUCATION AND ELOQUENCE.

I.

THOUGH specimens of the literary capacity and intellectual cultivation of Houston have been given in this work, yet to afford a more complete insight into his moral and political character, further extracts from his speeches may be cited. The reader will be gratified to find that this man, under circumstances quite unfavorable to the cultivation of letters, has acquired a power of expression, and facility in illustrating his subject, which only could have been gained by a persistent study of the literature of the world. In his military dispatches, he shows an admirable style—a wholesome, though not barren brevity—and a precision such as becomes an able general, in correspondence with the State. In various parts of this book, we have placed some of these before the reader, not less for the value of their contents, than for the beautiful perspicuity and directness of their style. In themselves, they furnish the very highest compliment to the innate taste and scholastic facility of their author, and we cannot but admire the man, who, under the most discouraging obstacles, and with powerful incentives to other accomplishments and deeds, has been able to distinguish himself in the literature of his native language, as well as in the active duties of public life.

II.

In his speeches, Senator Houston displays a native earnestness and force far more effective than the studied graces of the schools. His clear mind is not burdened with the sophistries of logic or the casuistry of politics. He speaks right on —animated with his subject, and as if certain that the orator never need to fear the result of unfolding the strong feelings of the heart, when the promptings of conscience, and not the dictates of self-interest, inspire the tongue. This species of appeal to the sensibilities and judgment, can never fail to have its due weight upon deliberative assemblies, or upon the people. The charms of rhetoric, like the purple and jewels on the shoulders and breast of the tyrant, may dazzle with gaudy brilliancy for a moment, and make men overlook their danger from the triumph of errors and oppression ; but the plain heart-spoken words of a true, patriotic man, are like the Apostolic apothegms—so in consonance with the conscience, as to proclaim the divinity of their origin. Senator Houston is not a great orator, but he is an effective one. His power is in his simplicity of expression, and in the familiar manner in which he speaks the native feelings of his heart, and the unselfish convictions of his judgment.

III.

The extracts from his speeches which we shall give in this chapter, will convey to the intelligent reader, not only Houston's opinions on many subjects of vast interest to the public, but may be deemed as average specimens of his style. On the subject of "Intervention" he remarked that our government ought to abstain from entangling alliances with foreign nations, and confine its policy to the full development of its resources. He said—

IV.

" The House has been told that this is a subject of vast importance. In this light he regarded it, as far as he had been able to view it. He thought it a subject of no common importance, because it was about to take a direction perfectly novel. It is proposed to meet different nations, or their representatives, in a deliberative body, to establish certain regulations which are to govern our relation to foreign powers, and in our immediate relations. He concurred with the gentleman from South Carolina that it was quite new, because its effect would be to introduce a new era in the annals of this country. Hitherto we have evinced a disinclination to entangle ourselves with alliances. We have exalted ourselves by persisting in a system that has been extremely beneficial to us, so long as this system in which we persist, proves beneficial to us, either as a nation, or as individuals, so long ought it be retained. We stand unshackled from all connection with the nations of the earth. We have our relations of amity and commerce with them, not treaties of alliance, offensive and defensive. Such relations the United States had hitherto sustained, and he hoped ever would sustain.

V.

" But are we to be benefited in our institutions by our associations with these other powers? So far as any advantage was to be obtained by it, so far he was in favor of it; but he was not willing that we should be embarrassed by a connection with them. The benefits of our institutions are free to all. Let them come here and receive them. If there were any good purpose to be answered by associating ourselves with them (Mr H. said), he would cheerfully coincide in so doing; but he could not perceive the necessity of immediately dispatching ministers to meet in this assembly at Panama. We are not aware of what call they may make on us, nor could we see any probable benefits to the United States by this general meeting which would not result with our treaties with them in their individual national capacities. Hitherto we have been pursuing a rational policy. We have exalted ourselves by it. We stand *alone*, and we are well able to sustain ourselves. Twice have we been tested, and twice have our principles triumphed; and they ever will triumph as long as we remain untrammelled and unburdened by foreign alliances. There are no dangers to impede us in our progress but such as can be guarded against.

Whilst we are in this situation we have no serious dangers to apprehend, but such as, in the progress of nations, will result, and which the good sense and wisdom of counsellors are always able to remedy before they became ruinous."

VI.

In February, 1850, Houston spoke on the Compromise Mea sures. There is so much of earnest love of the Union—so much spontaneous patriotism in the few words before us, that we must place them in this work, as further illustrative of his character.

VII.

" I call on the friends of the Union from every quarter to come forward like men, and to sacrifice their differences upon the common altar of their country's good, and to form a bulwark around the Constitution that cannot be shaken. It will require manly efforts, sir, and they must expect to meet with prejudices growing up, that will assail them from every quarter. They must stand firm to the Union, regardless of all personal consequences. Time alone can recompense them for their sacrifice and their labors ; for devotion to country can never be forgotten when it is offered freely, and without expectation of reward. The incense of self-sacrifice, when thus offered on their country, will be acceptable to the people. I have no doubt that this question might be easily adjusted, if gentlemen would encourage such disposition and feeling, as doubless actuate a large portion, if not all, of this body, if they would come up to the work. I have no doubt six senators could here be designated, without reference to party (you may if you please disregard the portion of the country from which they come), who would act as a Committee of Conference, and sit down together as wayfaring men, and produce satisfactory reconciliation, thereby diffusing universal peace, and calming the agitated waves that are lashing at the base of our capitol, and speak comfort and solace to millions of freemen.

VIII.

" Do not the American people love this Union ? Are they not devoted to it ? Is not every reminiscence of the past associated with its glories, and are they not calculated to inspire prayers for its prosperity and its perpetuity ? If this were not the case, you might think lightly of our noble confederacy ; but so it is—it stands connected with every fibre of the national heart, and is interwoven with every glorious recollection of the past, which affection or reverence can inspire in the minds of the American people. It is not, Mr. President, that twenty-three millions of souls are involved in the perpetuity of this Union ; it is not that every consideration of happiness connected with country appertains to it ; but it is because it is the great moral, social and political lever that has moved, is moving, and will continue to move the world. Look abroad at foreign nations, and behold the influence of our example upon them—not ours, for I feel a sense of humiliation when I contrast the efforts of any man now living with the illustrious achievements of the departed sages and heroes who performed this mighty work.''

IX.

On the subject of Disunion — that subject which Andrew Jackson had to deal with boldly, as he did effectively, in the course of his Administration, we find a passage or two of great strength and significance.

X.

" Mr. President—Twenty-seven years ago I had the honor to occupy a seat in the House of Representatives from the State of Tennessee. I recollect that in the discussion of the Tariff Act of 1824, for the first time in my life I heard the idea suggested, that there might be secession, disunion, or resistance to the constitutional authorities of the land. It produced deep and intense meditation on my part. I did believe, then, that an example ought to be made of it ; but there was no way to touch it. I have heard principles of disunion boldly avowed in this hall, and have heard Senators avow what was treason, not technically, but which was not stripped of one particle of the moral turpitude of treason. *Disunion* has been proclaimed in this hall. What a delightful commentary on the freedom of our institutions, and the forbearance of the public mind, when a man is permitted to go unscathed and unscourged, who, in a deliberative body like this, has made such a declaration! Sir, no higher assurance can be given of the freedom of our institutions, and of the forbearance of the American people, and their reliance upon the reason, and the intelligence of the community. The intelligent mind is left free to combat error. Such sentiments, with their authors, will descend to the obscurity and the tomb of oblivion. I have only to say, in conclusion, that those who proclaim disunion, no matter of what name, politically—that those who, for the sake of disunion, conspire against the Union and the Constitution, are very beautifully described in Holy Writ. They are 'raging waves of the sea, foaming out their own shame ; wandering stars, to whom is reserved the blackness of darkness for ever.' "

XI.

In reference to the policy of following the advice of Kossuth, with respect to the affairs of Hungary, and thereby embarrassing our system of foreign relations, Houston took a manly position. He said—

XII.

" We had not escaped from these difficulties (the attempt to invade Cuba), when the advent of the illustrious stranger, Kossuth, was announced. I was not captivated by his advent, Mr. President. A portion of my life had been spent among the Indians. They are a cautious and considerate people, and I had learned to reconnoitre character a little when it comes about me, and I am liable to come in contact with it. I played the Indian, and was wary. I received him, sir, in concurrence with the other senators. I wished his country liberty, as I wished the world liberty ; but I did not wish to disregard our relations and obligations to other countries. He was hailed, he was greeted, he was welcomed, on some occasions, more triumphantly than even Lafayette, the friend of Washington. Compare the men, compare their feelings, their impulses, and their actions, and—

—·' That was, to this, Hyperion to a satyr.'

What claims had he upon us? He had claims of sympathy. If he ever flashed his sword for Liberty, he had a claim on our admiration and our fraternal feelings. But he had not done it. He had left Hungary, he had denounced Görgey, and had thrown upon him the responsibility of the government. He disregarded his colleagues in office when he was at the head of affairs in Hungary. He threw all the responsibility upon Görgey when Görgey was helpless, and he himself had retreated with five thousand men. A beautiful army for liberty! Five thousand men alone, would strike for liberty against thousands on thousands. Yet he retreated with a body-guard of five thousand. And after he had negotiated for a succedaneum, for a resting-place, he went away, leaving 'poor Hungary' downtrodden and bleeding. Sir, much as I admire the patriots who strike for liberty—much as I admire the noble people whom Kossuth purported to represent—much as I admire all men who have struggled, even unfortunately or misguidedly, for liberty, no matter where—much as I admire the promptings which actuated them, and love the cause in which they have been engaged, yet when a man proves recreant to a noble cause, forgets his people, lives in comfort, splendor, and display, when they have to bite the dust, or gnaw the file in agony, I have no sympathy for that man."

* * * * * * * *

XIII.

" Was there then (in the Texan Revolution) a voice heard in this chamber advocating or introducing a resolution in vindication of the rights of Texas? Not one voice was heard at that time. Those gallant spirits who fell in hecatombs, with their footsteps almost on American soil, were hardly washed out or obliterated ; yet this nation was not convulsed. We heard of no sympathetic throb issuing from these chambers, no indignant voice raised in denunciation of the barbarities committed towards Texas. Did Texas ever complain to this government? From 1836 to 1843, did she ever remonstrate to this government? In 1843, when she did remonstrate, what was it? She said to the three great powers of the earth, to France, England, and the United States :— ' We ask no assistance, we invoke the invasion of our enemies, and upon a well-arranged and well-fought field, we will stake our liberty ; but compel our adversary to the rules of civilized warfare.' That was all we asked. The government of the United States, acting upon its wise, and prudent, and proper policy, did not interfere.

" I contend that while we maintain our national faith, it is not right to extend our jurisdiction beyond our own hemisphere. Let us be staid, quiet, industrious, and reflective. When subjects are presented requiring action, let us act. Sir, this nation is destined to fill a vast space among the nations of the earth. Already, in its youth, it is great and mighty; majestic is its renown, and most infinite are its resources; but those resources must be husbanded, and they must be cared for, for a while. It is in vain to extend speculations beyond the necessity of the times, and involve ourselves in fruitless troubles by anticipation.

"Sir, we have much to do for ourselves to give us that iron hoop of which General Jackson spoke, which should be thrown around our continent. Sir, let us make an iron hoop binding California to the Atlantic. It is worth all the resolutions that could be introduced here in a thousand years on international law, foreshadowing our policy. That is a matter which enters into the very vitals of our national existence, and one that must be cared for, looked to, and by some means executed. It is a vast and eminently national work. Without it we are two nations. With it we should be one ; and we should command the trade of the world."

XIV.

On a resolution offered by Mr. Foote, declaring that the celebrated Compromise Measures " Are, in the judgment of this body, a final settlement of the dangerous and exciting subjects which they embrace, and ought to be adhered to," Houston made a speech on the 22d of December, 1851, which has many points of great interest and force. Let us present some of them.

XV.

" I understand that the democratic party is tolerant in its principles ; that they are not proscriptive ; that they are not for applying the Procrustean rule to every member of the party. Harmonious, as they generally are, some gentlemen of the same party differ essentially upon the subject of internal improvements. That has been evinced on former occasions here, within my recollection, and I believe it extends much further than my familiarity with the proceedings of this body. And not only that, for I have heard discussions here by the members of the same political party on the tariff, in regard to which there was a wide difference of opinion; yet it was not a ground for proscribing the members of the party, or excluding them from participating in all the rights pertaining to it.

XVI.

"It is a boast of the democratic party, I believe, that it is the true conservative party of this country, though, at the same time, *this* is the boast of every political party. I will not deprive either of them of the agreeable assurance. But, sir, if the democratic party is truly conservative, I think the platform on which it now stands, is wide enough, broad enough, to embrace the whole Union. If it is not, I am not a member of it. I know that I have been arraigned for having been too latitudinarian in my feelings; but I must confess that my country seems not too large to love, to cherish, and support. Then, sir, if the object of the party is conservatism, and to preserve what we believe the true constitutional principles of government, whoever loves and supports that constitution strictly, is my fellow. I know how the Constitution was formed. It was by concessions made by the several States, or by grants of certain powers that were to remain in the Federal Government; but these delegated functions were to be exercised by it for the benefit of the whole. So far the Federal Government has rights, but no further. The States were free, sovereign, and independent, until these concessions were made. The Federal Government became the repository of delegated powers, and there they remain for the benefit of the several States. The States in the full enjoyment of the powers reserved, are independent within their sphere, and subject to no control from the Federal Government. These are my opinions, and I believe they agree with the democratic faith. Incidentally various subjects have arisen in this body since I have been a member of it, and upon all these I have recorded my opinions. I know they have been at variance, on some occasions, with my party, or rather the party with which I act. I will not call it mine: I belong to *it*. I had hoped that the agitation on this question (slavery) was fast dying away. And it might ere this have been forgotten, had it not been for the introduction of this unfortunate resolution, which has renewed all the agitation of former times, and produced crimination and recrimination, and scenes not less violent in their character than those exhibited upon the adoption of the Compromise itself. It is unfortunate; and if in the inception of a resolution of this kind, such are the fruits, and if such are in a green tree, what must they be in a dry? I apprehend that no earthly good can grow out of the adoption of the resolution. The usurpation of the people's rights will be manifest. If a modification is to take place in the democratic platform, let it take place in a convention of the delegates of the people sent there for a political purpose, not for the purpose of legislation, but for the formation of certain creeds and embodiments of opinions, by which the party is to be regulated in its actions. There is where I wish to see such action take place. But further than this I am not prepared to go.

XVII.

"The Compromise, sir, was the work of able, patriotic, and renowned statesmen. Some of them are no longer in this body. It is with regret, sir, that I witness the absence of one who bore an important and conspicuous part in the accomplishment of that Compromise. I allude to the venerable senator from Kentucky (Mr. Clay), who is detained from this chamber by sickness, with which he is deeply afflicted. I trust he will again resume his place in the Senate. The wisdom of his counsels, the brilliancy of his genius, the strength of his will, and the patriotism of his heart, never shone brighter than during their manifestation in this body in the achievement of that Compromise. But my State has been arraigned by a portion of the Union, and of the democratic party, too, for making a disposition of a portion of her territory to the detriment of Southern interests; and *that* I felt. It was not that she was disposed to abridge or impair any of the rights of the South. Texas, no doubt, had a right to dispose of it. Did not Georgia dispose of her territory to the Federal Government? Did she not sell enough to make the States of Alabama and Mississippi? And have any complaints been made against her for it? And had Texas, who came into this Union as free and as independent as Georgia did, no right to dispose of her domain to the Federal Government? She did it, sir; and I have this to remark, that had it been any obstacle to the compromise to the jarring interests of this country, and to their reconcilement, I would have been willing that every foot of the territory which she claimed, should become a lake of fire and brimstone rather than it should have thrown an impediment in the way of the peace and the harmony of this Union.

XVIII.

"I voted also for the admission of California. I did it on the acknowledged and avowed principle of the South : 'Let us alone ; let the people regulate their municipal and domestic institutions; let them alone.' And I put it to the candor of honorable Senators from the South, no matter how ardent their feelings may have been, whether, if California had made application for admission into the Union, with a constitution declaring that Slavery should exist, they would not have disregarded all the irregularities which may have been connected with it, and readily have voted for her admission as a slave State? The same rule which would induce me to vote for it in one situation, would constrain me to do so in another. I did it. What advantage would have resulted from a delay? Was there any hope for a change in her institutions? Was there any probability of it? No. She came in ; and whatever reproaches are attached to the vote I gave, I derive my consolation from the general prosperity and happiness of my country."

XIX.

In this same speech, Houston replied to the charge made by Mr. Foote, that the Senator from Texas was given to demagogism, and to wire-pulling for the Presidency. As the replication has something in it of an auto-biographical significance, the reader will be gratified by recurring to·what he said on the occasion.

XX.

"I was very much edified, and I might say amused, by remarks of the honorable gentleman from Mississippi. I cannot but be astonished at the temper of the gentleman. I had not intended to say anything to excite his ire, because I flatter myself that I am a prudent man, and do not like to provoke assaults. I am exceedingly gratified at one thing. In the course of his entire tirade, I believe the gentleman did not state a single *fact*. He has indulged in many conjectures in relation to Freesoilism, and catering for the Presidency. Why, I should feel that I was not only degrading myself, but degrading the nation and the body in which

16

I stand, if I would cater to the passions of men, or compromise my principles, for the Presidency. What I have, I have. I wish to make no new voyages. I am satisfied with the position which I occupy. What I might adventure might be lost. Therefore, I have *no petty hankerings after office* to gratify. Nor have I any *party intrigues* to enter into. I have no correspondence on the subject of the Presidency. The world is acquainted with what I have said.

XXI.

" What I do, they make it a point to know. I should be sorry to suppose that there could be the least ground for applying to me the term 'demagogue.' What demagogism was there when I gave unpopular votes in this body, when there was no prospect for advancement in popularity, for I was denounced far and near. What intrigue could I then have had, with a party unimportant in the country, when I could have gone with the whole South, if I had chosen to sacrifice my own opinions on the Oregon question ? Was I playing the 'demagogue' when I refused to sign the Southern Address ? Did I not vote for every one of the Compromise measures ? Mr. President, I assure you, I assure the Senate, I assure the country, that every insinuation against me of indirect plotting, by myself or by my friends, within my knowledge, with one party or another—every insinuation that imparts to me any other design than that of preserving the government in its purity, and the democratic party in its own faith, without an extension of platform, is altogether unfounded. Whoever insinuates that I have any intrigue, or any understanding, or any correspondence upon the subject of free-soil, abolition, disunion, or secession, insinuates what is utterly unfounded, and without the slightest countenance of truth."

XXII.

When Kossuth was introduced to the Senate of the United States, it may be mentioned that as the martial form of Gen. Houston approached Kossuth, there appeared to be a personal attraction in the person of the hero of San Jacinto. The introduction having been made, a brief but expressive dialogue ensued.

XXIII.

" Mr. HOUSTON—Sir, you are welcome to the Senate of the United States."

" M. KOSSUTH—I can only wish that I had been as successful as you, sir."

" HOUSTON—God grant that you may yet be so."

XXIV.

On the twenty-ninth of January, 1855, the United States Senate having resumed, as in Committee of the Whole, the consideration of the bill from the House of Representatives, making appropriations for the support of the Army for the year ending the 30th of June, 1856, the pending question being on the amendment of Mr. Shields to the amendment of Mr. Hunter (which was to provide for two additional Regiments of Regular Cavalry and five hundred Rangers), to substitute for that provision two Regiments of Infantry, and two of Cavalry, Houston spoke upon an increase of the army, and on the Indian policy of the government. The chief portions of these speeches are worthy of preservation—and will be acceptable to every American reader.

XXV.

" Before the Senate proceeds to vote upon the adoption of the new policy now proposed, I think it would be well to examine the causes which have led to the present condition of affairs, and then to inquire into the best means for the restoration of peace upon our Indian frontier. An examination of this sort will inform us whether there is any necessity for an increase of the military force of the country. I am aware, sir, that in discussing subjects which relate to the Indians, or to their rights, I shall command but little sympathy from the Senate, and not much from the country. They are a people isolated in their interests, and solely dependent for protection and justice upon the government of the United States.

How far justice has been accorded to them in the past, or how far it is, in all probability, to be awarded to them in the future, is a matter beyond speculation. If we are to judge from the past experience of our times, we should infer that there is but very little hope of anything being done for the Red man ; and we should infer that, in the opinion of his white brethren, his doom has already been written and recorded. Mr. President, the Indians have been charged with an aggressive and hostile spirit towards the whites ; but we find, upon inquiry, that every instance of that sort which has been imputed to them, has been induced and provoked by the white man, either by acts of direct aggression upon the Indians, or by his own incaution, alluring them to a violation of the security of the whites. They have tempted the cupidity of the Indians. If a lawless fellow happens to prove vagrant to his band, and throws off all the rules and restrictions imposed by the chiefs on their warriors, and chooses to involve his nation in a difficulty by taking the life of a white man, if he can do so, as he supposes, with impunity, his action is charged to his tribe ; but they should not be held responsible. Sir, we have seen thrilling accounts of sanguinary massacres, which alarm us at the first blush ; and if we are to believe the paragraphs disseminated through the medium of the press, we should suppose, in reality, that the Indian is as barbarous as he had ever been, and that all the assaults or massacres, as they are termed, are unprovoked and wantonly inflicted on the defenceless white man. As an instance of this, let me mention the massacre at Fort Laramie, and from that instance you can pretty accurately deduce the true condition of other acts of a similar character. What were the circumstances in connection with that case?

XXVI.

" During the last summer, some bands of the Sioux nation of Indians were encamped within six miles of Fort Laramie. They were in amity with the United States, and on terms of good friendship and good feeling with the officers of the neighboring fort. A man from a neighboring tribe, whose relatives had, a year before, been slaughtered by the troops at Fort Laramie, happened to be among these bands of Sioux. Some Mormon emigrants passed by the camp of the Indians, and a cow escaped from them, made towards the village, and the Mormons pursued her, but unsuccessfully. The Indian to whom I have referred, by way of revenge

for the loss of his relative, slaughtered the animal. Complaint was made
at Fort Laramie. The chiefs instantly said that they would see that repa-
ration was made for the injury which had been done. Was this satisfactory to the commanding officer? No, sir; but he detailed a brevet lieutenant, with a company, for the purpose of arresting the Indian. The
company arrived at the encampment of the Indians with two pieces of
artillery. Demand was made of the chiefs, but this Indian said to them,
'I have taken a lodge here; I am willing to die; you have nothing to
do with this matter; you have no concern with it; the responsibility is
not upon your people, but it is upon me alone.' So soon as this reply was
given to the lieutenant, he fired and crippled one of the principal chiefs,
and killed a man. The delinquent still refused to give up. After that
the chiefs rallied and exhorted the men to commit no outrage; their influence controlled the action of the Indians; but a drunken interpreter, who
was calculated to incite the lieutenant to action, caused him, no doubt, to
fire his cannon. The next thing was that the war-whoop was sounded,
and the lieutenant and part of his men were killed. The others, dispersed, were pursued by the Indians in hot blood, and every man was
slaughtered.

XXVII.

" This is a succinct narrative of that event. Were the Indians to blame?
He who violates a law is the man who is responsible for the consequences
of that violation. The Indian intercourse laws of the United States, have
pointed out the manner in which to proceed in such a case. If a citizen
sustains injury from any tribe, or from an individual of a tribe, information is to be given to the Indian agent for that tribe. He is immediately
to make a demand upon the chiefs of the nation. If they do not surrender the individual, which, in all probability they would do immediately,
if they were treated in good faith, deduction is made from their annuities
for the amount of the injury, and there the matter stops. If no annuities are due to them, rather than bring on war, the United States Treasury is responsible to the individual who has sustained loss. These are
the provisions of the intercourse laws. In this case, did either of the officers make a demand on the chiefs? The chiefs sent an assurance that
justice would be done, and the individual given up, though he did not
belong to their band. The officers, unwilling to receive that assurance,
dispatched a handful of men against several lodges of Indians, and among

whom there had been some ground of complaint. The consequences which I have narrated, resulted from this indiscretion and violation of law. It was a violation of law, for no demand was made upon the chiefs for indemnity, and no response was received from them. These gallant gentlemen thought they should go there and make war. They are paid for it ; 'it is their vocation.' Are such men entiled to sympathy ? Are they entitled to respect ? But their conduct alarmed the Sioux ; and because that tribe proposed to confederate with other tribes, we are asked to increase the military force of the country ; forsooth, we are to wage war upon the winds, for you might as well do it, as upon the prairie Indians.

XXVIII.

"But this is not all that grew out of that transaction. A clamor is raised about the mail party who were destroyed subsequently to that. It was very natural to expect that it would be done. The Sioux chief, who was wounded on the occasion to which I have referred, was taken to Arkansas, and there he expired in consequence of the injury he had received. His kindred resolved to revenge his death. The Indian appreciates the ties of kindred far beyond any white man. They may have less intelligence ; but the chords of nature are stronger, the sensibilities of the heart more lively, than those which stimulate our Christian enlightened action. It is well known that the grief which resounds through the Indian camp, when a warrior or chief expires, or when a relative dies, is like the wailing of Egypt. When this chief expired, his friends sought for a white man, that they might take vengeance on him—not for those who had inflicted the wrong, but whomever they might happen to find among the whites. They came first upon the mail party. One, who was not a relative of the chief, said to one of his kindred, ' there is a white man, you can now take vengeance on him ; you are a coward if you do not do so.' He said, ' I am no coward ; but if you say it, I will kill him.' Then he went and killed two out of the three composing the mail party.

XXIX.

" Now, sir, what had been the condition of the Indian country previous to these occurrences ? I have been assured by gentlemen who have passed from California to Fort Laramie, a distance of one thousand four hundred or one thousand five hundred miles, that they met individuals travelling alone through that vast region. They passed through a wilderness of one thousand four hundred, or one thousand five hundred miles, unassailed, and without injury from any one. Did this look like a desperate feeling on the part of the Indians, when they allowed unprotected individuals, sometimes singly, occasionally in small companies of three or four persons, to pass through their country unmolested? No, sir. It is some sudden act of wrong and outrage which stimulates the Indian to aggression. He has no inducement to it, unless he expects great plunder, because he is well aware that if he cultivates kind and friendly relations with the whites, he can receive from them supplies that he cannot obtain in any other way—things which gratify his taste for dress, and supply his wants and appetites. For this reason, the Indian is always disposed to be in peace and friendship with his white neighbors if he can.

"I have given some illustrations of the so-called Indian outrages. I may refer to another one, which, not long since, took place in Oregon, and which is given, in some quarters, as a reason why an increase of the army is required. I refer to a recent massacre of the Indians at a ferry-house in Oregon, as described by the agents and superintendents of that territory. A number of miners to the amount of forty, associated together to attack a village of seventy Indians, men, women, and children, without any means of defence, with only five pieces of fire-arms, pistols, and guns, and two of them entirely useless. The officer, who reports the action, describes in a most military and elegant style, the manner in which he assaulted the village in three divisions. They were entirely successful; killed some sixteen men, killed one squaw, and wounded a couple, and no children—that was merciful! But, sir, they scattered the warriors, who were there defenceless, and applied the torch to their wigwams. We are told by the gallant gentleman who reported the matter, that the next day the Indians were there hovering about the mouldering ashes of their wigwams. This gallant and chivalrous man, wonderful to relate, says he did not loose a man in the attack. Was he not lucky? [Laughter.] That fellow must look out for a brevet; though I hope he will hardly come here claiming bounty land. [Laughter.]

XXX.

"This act is denounced by the agent and superintendent as most cruel and barbarous. The poor creatures were willing to do anything and everything which was asked of them. They denied every charge that their malicious enemies had wantonly brought against them; and the truth of the narrative is endorsed by the agent, a man of intelligence. I do not know him; but his report bears the impress of intelligence and integrity.

XXXI.

"Well, sir, these circumstances, it is said, call for an army of three regiments, or three thousand men. What are they to cost? Five millions of dollars is the amount which it is proposed to appropriate by the bill which was reported by the Senator from Illinois. We are to appropriate $5,000,000 to bring on a great Sioux war, to meet a most wonderful confederacy, which, it is said, is forming among the Indians. Why, sir, they cannot keep together, because they are starving in little bands, even in those parts of the country where they can command the most game. How could they remain embodied for any length of time without supplies, without animals, and without food, when their women and children are starving? How could they, under such circumstances, remain a mighty confederation, to sweep our frontier? Why, sir, from the display that is made, by the terrible cry of alarm, one would think that New Orleans itself could hardly be safe, but that the Indians would sweep down the Missouri and Mississippi, and carry death, destruction, and devastation in their course! Are these causes calculated to produce such mighty effects? Is it proper that the nation should be involved in a general Indian war at this time? Is it proper that $5,000,000 should be expended from the Treasury to begin this war? If this be done, what will be the consequence? The Indians will not be embodied to meet you. Your troops will hear that in some direction there is a Camanche, or a Kioway, or an Osage camp, and they will advance upon it with " all the pomp and circumstance of glorious war.' A morning gun will be fired as a signal to rise and prepare for the march. On such an occasion, with the bugle sounding in advance, how beautiful must be the reflection from the arms and banners floating in the prairie! That is to be the spectacle which is to amuse or drive the Indians ahead. They are to meet the Indians on a trackless waste. You might as well pursue the course of a ship's keel on the ocean, as to pursue the Indians of the prairies. They would disperse, and your army would be left there ; and they, perhaps, surrounding you, in the distance, and laughing at the glorious pomp with which you were marching through their prairies. If you take men there, and make a display without efficiency, you provoke their ridicule and supreme contempt.

XXXII.

" But, Mr. President, the course which has been pursued, since the days of William Penn to the present moment, has not been entirely successful in conciliating the Indians. Under the management of Washington, of the first Adams, of Madison, of Monroe, of the second Adams, of Jackson, and of Polk, we have, with few exceptions, been very successful in maintaining peace with them. The suggestions made by our fathers, in relation to their civilization and humanization, are exemplified and illustrated in the present condition of the southern tribes, who have received the greatest benefits of the light shed on them ; and they have responded to it by the cultivation of mind, by the development of resources, both physical and intellectual, which reflect lustre on their character. Cannot the Indian now be influenced in the same way, by the same means? Have we no landmarks to guide us? Have we not experience to teach us? Have we not humanity to prompt us to march on in the path which is already laid out before us? Sir, how different is the policy now pursued from what it once was? I must read, for the instruction of the Senate, an extract from the last annual report of the Commissioner of Indian Affairs, and I beseech your attention to it, because it contains more good sense and reflection than I could impart in the same number of words. It will be necessary in the examination of this subject, in relation both to the Indians and the Army, to see in what manner they harmonize with each other, and how far the one is necessary to the success of the other. The Commissioner of Indian Affairs, in his report to the Secretary of the Interior, describes a transaction to which I wish to call attention :

" ' As heretofore reported to you, an association of persons has undertaken to appropriate to their own use a portion of the land ceded by the Delawares, fronting on the Missouri river, and south of Fort Leavenworth ;

16*

have laid out a city thereon, and actually had a public sale of the lots of the same on the 9th and 10th of October last. These unlawful proceedings have not only taken place under the eyes of military officers stationed at the fort, but two of them are said to be members of the association, and have been active agents in this discreditable business. Encouraged by these proceedings, and prompted by those engaged in them, other persons have gone on other portions of the tract ceded by the Delawares in trust to the United States, and pretend to have made, and are now making, such 'claims' as they assert will vest in them the lawful right to enter the land at the minimum price under the preëmption law of July 12, 1854.'

XXXIII.

"This is a specimen of the aid and succor afforded by military commanders to the agents to maintain and preserve peace among the Indians. These are the gentlemen to whom the agents look for co-operation in the discharge of their duties, and to afford equal protection to the Indians against aggressions from the whites, as to the whites against aggressions from the Indians. Such a transaction, as is here disclosed, is an act of unmitigated infamy in the officers who have lent themselves to it. I hope the Executive, in the plenitude of his power, and in the exercise of a wise and just discretion, will erase their names from the records of the country, and redeem our annals from infamy so blackening as this. Think, sir, of an officer wearing an American sword, adorned with American epaulets, the emblem of office and the insignia of honor and manly pride, degrading himself by a violation of the faith of his Government, rendering him a disgrace to the uniform which he wears, and the earth upon which he treads!

XXXIV.

"It will be recollected that the Delaware Indians own one million eight hundred thousand acres of land. They ceded one million three hundred thousand acres to the Government of the United States for $10,000, reserving to themselves the land on which the city referred to has been laid out, on the banks of the Missouri. They confided five hundred thousand acres to the Government of the United States, as they could not themselves dispose of it, except to the Government; and, believing that it would be a source of wealth and independence to them, they have granted it to the Government, in trust, to be sold by it, the right of possession remaining in them until it should be disposed of. It appears, from the commissioner's report, that persons had gone and taken possession of this land. If they have not done so, they ought to be vindicated against the charge. I regard it as authentic and official, and until it is controverted, I have nothing to extenuate; nor do I set down aught in malice. Justice requires me to state the facts.

XXXV.

"Mr. President, I said to the Senate, on a former occasion, that eighteen tribes of Indians had been located by this Government within the limits of the present Territories of Nebraska and Kansas, and that most of them had been removed there from the east of the Mississippi. They were located there under the faith of solemn pledges, that while grass grew, or water ran, or the earth brought forth its fruits, they should remain on the lands assigned to them, unless they choose to abandon them; and that they should not be included within the boundaries of any State or Territory. Notwithstanding this, these Indians were embraced within the Nebraska and Kansas bill. They were taken in—yes, sir, as strangers are sometimes ' taken in.' What is now their condition, and what must it be in after time?"

XXXVI.

Here, Senator Houston having read an extract from the recent report of the Commissioner of Indian Affairs, in which he describes, with great fidelity and justice, the condition of the Indians in Kansas Territory, expressing his belief and hope that their complete civilization may be effected, then proceeded to say that it is the violation of treaties, and the bad faith of the white man, and his aggressive course, that cause the inquietude of the Red Men.

XXXVII.

"There is a remedy ; and that remedy must be applied, or the Indians exterminated, at an expense ten times beyond what would civilize in half a century, every Red man who walks upon the soil of America. I have seen tribes rise from a state of barbarism to a condition in which they are as civilized in their institutions, in their religion, and in their social refinement and habits, as citizens of the United States, and all this has been done within half a century. These things are as possible now as at any former time ; and a sum, very easily calculated, less than the amount estimated as necessary to raise these troops and subsist them for one year, would civilize every Indian on the continent, set him down on a piece of land, and give him ' a local habitation and a name.' Is it not worth an attempt ? Is it not worth accomplishment ? Sir, let me give you some experience in relation to Indians. The United States have regiments in Texas, and Texas is considered, by some, as a burden on the Treasury. Texas, it is said, exhausts the Army of the United States, and withdraws them from more eligible stations to protect her frontier. I will show you, sir, how that is. In 1842 and 1843 Texas had a war on hand which had been brought about by an exterminating policy proclaimed by a new Administration, and peace was not restored until 1843, when the head of the Government of Texas went about the work of their civilization. He went into the wilderness, on the prairies, and there met the Indians, who would not trust themselves within the timbered land, nor near any place where there was a possibility of ambuscade. A treaty was there made, which not only stayed the tomahawk and the scalping-knife, but preserved peace and safety on the frontier until 1849. We were for six years without massacre, without conflagration, without prisoners being taken. Not a Texan was killed in that time by the Indians. One man was killed in the Indian country, but whether by the Mexicans or Indians was a doubtful question ; at any rate he was not scalped.

XXXVIII.

"Now, sir, how was this done? By what means? By pursuing a policy which had been initiated in 1836, but was disrupted in 1838, which brought a war upon the entire borders of that young Republic. The old policy was re-established in 1843. Resistance was made to it, as there was to every attempt to consolidate a Government. There was an attempt on the part of some lawless men, to resist everything like order and organization, and throw the Government into anarchy and misrule ; but they failed. These Indians had been our enemies ; they had been exasperated by unprovoked aggressions upon them ; but the proper conciliatory disposition soon won their regard and affection. What was the expense of all this? I am almost afraid to state it, for I fear it will not be credited when we see the enormous estimates now made for the expense of treaties with the Indians. Sir, every dollar given to the Executive of Texas, to consummate these treaties, to feed the Indians, to make presents, was annually $10,000 ; and he rendered vouchers for the last cent. For this sum, peace was accomplished and maintained, the safety and protection of our frontiers insured, and the Indians became pacific and happy.

XXXIX.

" When Texas was annexed to the United States, these Indians, on account of faith having been maintained with them by the then Executive of Texas, refused to meet and confer with the commissioners sent to them by the President of the United States, until they had the sanction of the Government of Texas ; and the symbols of confidence were put in the hands of the commissioners before the Indians would treat with them. A treaty was then negotiated. What was the history of it? One of the commissioners—a noble and gallant gentleman, who afterwards fell at Chepultapec, in Mexico, at the head of his regiment—was too much indisposed to render any assistance. His co-commissioner assumed the whole business ; and what did he do ? He had the Indians' names signed with a mark on a sheet of paper, had it attested, and brought it on here. He made large promises to the Indians ; he assured them of an annuity of $14,000, to be paid annually, at a certain trading-house ; but when he wrote his treaty (for he did not write it until he came here, when he appended to it the sheet containing the signatures), it contained a provision that they should receive barely $14,000 as a full acquittance. It cost $60,000 to negotiate the treaty, as the records of the Treasury show. This is a sum equal to the price of six years' peace between the Indians and the Government of Texas. Perhaps, however, the people of Texas were better then than now. Since that time, they have been under the

Government of the United States. I simply state facts. I leave the inference to others.

XL.

" Sir, if the agent appointed by Mr. Polk, who has been restored by the present executive—it is a bright spot in his Administration, and I commend him for it—had never been removed, there would have been peace to this day on the borders of Texas ; but as soon as the Indian agent who was appointed to succeed him went there, he must forsooth establish a rancho : he must have a farm. The Indians who had been settled down there from 1843 to 1849, had been furnished by the Government of Texas with implements of husbandry, with seeds of every description, and they were cultivating their little farms. They were comfortable and independent. They were living in perfect peace. If you can get Indians located, and place their wives and children within your cognizance, you need never expect aggression from them. It is the Indian who has his wife in security, beyond your reach, who, like the felon wolf, goes to a distance to prey on some flock, far removed from his den ; or, like the eagle, who seeks his prey from the distance, and never from the flocks about his eyrie. The agent to whom I have referred, lost two oxen from his rancho where he kept his cattle. He went to the officer in command of Fort Belknap, got a force from him, and then marched to those Indians sixty miles distant, and told them they must pay for the oxen. They said, ' We know nothing about your oxen ; our people are here ; here are our women and children ; we have not killed them ; we have not stolen them ; we have enough to eat ; we are happy ; we have raised corn ; we have sold corn ; we have corn to sell ; we have sold it to your people, and they have paid us for it, and we are happy.' The agent and the military gentlemen scared off the Indians from the limits of Texas, and drove them across the Red River to the Wichita mountains, taking every horse and animal they had, to pay for the two oxen. This was done by an accredited agent of the Government, and by an officer who deserved but little credit. Are such things tolerable, and to be tolerated in the present age and condition of our government ?

XLI.

"What was the consequence ? Those Indians felt themselves agrieved.

They saw that a new *régime* had come; they had the era of peace and plenty, and now they were expelled by a different influence. They felt grateful for the benign effects of the first policy towards them, and that only exasperated them to a greater extent against the second; and they began to make incursions, ready to take vengeance on any white men they might meet in the neighborhood, and slay whoever they might find. They made their forays from the opposite side of the Red River, from the Wichita mountains, and came like an avalanche upon our unprotected citizens. There is one fact showing how your interference with the Indians within her limits has injured Texas. There is another fact in connection with the Indian policy of Texas which I shall mention. How was it with the Wichita Indians? Texas sought to conciliate them; they lived beyond her borders, and made incursions from the limits of the United States into Texas, while she was an independent Republic. She did everything in her power to bring about peace between them, and, through the friendly Indians, was pacifying them. One of their chiefs, with his wife and child and twelve men, came to Fort Belknap, some one hundred and fifty or two hundred miles west of the fort, at Hamilton's Valley. Property had been stolen by Indians. It was not known which of thirteen different tribes had taken it; for outlaws occasionally congregated from each, half a dozen of them stealing off from their tribes, without the influence of their chiefs operating upon them. They were outlaws, careless of the destiny of their tribes, and reckless of the crimes which they might commit, so long as they could gratify their cupidity and recompense their daring. These men had taken some property. Dragoons came on in the direction of Red River, and reached Fort Belknap. So soon as they arrived, the officer said to this chief: 'Sir, I retain you as a prisoner. It is true, you came under a white flag; but I am an officer; I have the power; I take you prisoner, and you must stay here a prisoner until the horses are brought back. Your men must stay, too, except one, whom I will send to your tribe with the intelligence of the fact.' The chief said; 'My tribe have not committed the robbery; it is a great distance from me; it is in another direction. I come from the rising sun; that is towards the setting sun; I was far from it; you are between me and it; I did not do it.' 'But,' said the officer, 'you are a prisoner.' The officer put him in the guard-house. Imprisonment is eternal infamy to an Indian. A prairie Indian would rather die a thousand deaths than submit to the disgrace of imprisonment. You may wound and mutilate him as you please, you may crush every limb in the body of a prairie Indian, and if he can make no other resistance, he will spit defiance at you when you come within his reach. This chief, meditating upon his deep disgrace, knowing that he was irreparably dishonored, unless he could wash out his stains with blood, resolved that night that he would either die a freeman, or rescue himself from dishonor. He rose in the night. He would not leave his wife and child in the hands of his enemy; so he took his knife, and stabbed his squaw and little one to the heart. Not a groan was heard, for he well knew where to apply the poignard. He went and shot down the sentinel, rushed upon the superior officers, was shot, and perished like a warrior, in an attempt to wipe a stain from his honor. His men fled and returned to their tribe, but it was to bring blood, carnage, and conflagration upon our settlements. They came not again as brothers to smoke the calumet of peace, but with brands in their hands to set fire to our houses. Contrast that with the previous years; contrast it with the harmony which had before existed, and you see the lamentable result of sending, as Indian agents and army officers to take charge of the Indians, men who know nothing about the Indian character.

XLII.

"Well, sir, how can Texas expect peace, how can she expect protection to her citizens? Not from your army. It has never given her protection; it is incompetent to give protection; and it is a reproach to the country. I will not say anything personally unkind of the officers who command, for they are gentlemen; but I say they know nothing about the Indians, and I shall prove it. Texas deserves protection, and she can have it if a rational effort be made to give it to her, but not by your troops. What sort of protection can she expect from hostile Indians when the commanding officer of that military department, a gallant gentleman, who has borne himself nobly in the heat of battle, skillful in design, bold and gallant in execution, and in all the martial arts replete, but unskilled amongst the Indians. He has issued an order that no Indian should go within twenty miles of a fortress on the frontier of Texas. The Indians think, 'Very well, you say the Indians shall not come within twenty miles of your forts, and we say your men shall not come within twenty miles of us, or we will shoot them.' That is a pretty good notion for an Indian; it is very natural. The boundary is fixed by the white man, and the Indian lives up to it. Well, sir, there is a remedy for all this, and it is very easy to apply it; but how are we circumstanced there? It is supposed by some that we are deriving great aid from the Army, and that the greatest portion of the disposable forces of the United States is in Texas, and protecting it? How can they protect us against the Indians when the cavalry have not horses which can trot faster than active oxen, and the infantry dare not go out in any hostile manner for fear of being shot and scalped! Can they pursue a party who pounce down on a settlement and take property, and reclaim that property? Have they ever done it? Did the old rangers of Texas ever fail to do it, when they were seated on their Texas ponies? They were men of intelligence and adroitness in regard to the Indian character, and Indian warfare. Do you think a man is fit for such service who has been educated at West Point Academy, furnished with rich stores of learning ; more educated in the science of war than any general who fought through the Revolution, and assisted in achieving our independence? Are you going to take such gentlemen, and suppose that by intuition they will understand the Indian character? Or do you suppose they can track a turkey, or a deer in the grass of Texas, or could they track an Indian, or would they know whether they were tracking a wagon or a carriage? [Laughter.] Not at all, sir. We wish, in the first place, to have men suited to the circumstance. Give us agents who are capable of following out their instructions, and who understand the Indian character. Give us an army, gentlemen, who understand not only the science of command, but have some notions of extending justice and protection to the Indian, against the aggression of the whites, while they protect the whites against aggressions from the Indians. Then, and not till then, will you have peace.

XLIII.

" How is this to be done? Withdraw your army. Have five hundred cavalry, if you will, but I would rather have two hundred and fifty Texas rangers (such as I could raise), than five hundred of the best cavalry now in service. I would have one thousand infantry, so placed as to guard the United States against Mexico, and five hundred for scouting purposes. I would have five trading-houses from the Rio Grande to the Red River for intercourse with the Indians. I would have a guard of twenty-five men out of an infantry regiment, at each trading house, who should be vigilant and always on the alert. Cultivate intercourse with the Indians.

Show them that you have comforts to exchange for their peltries ; bring them around you ; domesticate them ; familiarize them with civilization. Let them see that you are rational beings, and they will become rational in imitation of you ; but take no whisky there at all, not even for the officers, for fear their generosity should let it out. Do this, and you will have peace with the Indians. Whenever you convince an Indian that he is dependent on you for comforts, or for what he deems luxuries or elegances of life, you attach him to you. Interest, it is said, governs the world, and it will soon ripen into affection. Intercourse and kindness will win the fiercest animal on earth, except the hyena, and its spots and nature cannot be changed. The nature of an Indian can be changed. He changes with change of circumstances, and rises into the dignity of a civilized being. If you war against him, it takes a generation or two to regenerate his race, but it can be done. I would have fields around the trading houses. I would encourage the Indians to cultivate them. Let them see how much it adds to their comfort ; how it insures to their wives and children abundant subsistence, and then you win the Indian over to civilization ; you charm him, and he becomes a civilized man.

XLIV.

" Sir, while people are seeking to civilize and Christianize men on the banks of the Ganges, or the Jordan, or in Burrampootah, why should not the same philanthropic influence be extended through society, and be exerted in behalf of the American Indians ? Is not the soul of an American Indian, in the prairie, worth as much as the soul of a man on the Ganges, or in Jerusalem ? Surely it is. Then let the American Government step forward ; let it plant the standard of regeneration and civilization among the Indians, and it will command the coöperation of the citizens in their philanthropic efforts. I am willing to appeal to the venerable and distinguished Senator from Michigan, who knows what an Indian is, and what his disposition is, perhaps more thoroughly than I do myself. To him would I defer, but to no other man, for a certain and intimate knowledge of the Indian character.

XLV.

" There is another point in connection with the dealings of the Govern-

ment with the Texas Indians to which I will advert. There are Camanches of the woods, and the Camanches of the prairie. The Texas Indians
do not receive their annuities in Texas, but they are brought into Kansas,
a great distance from us, where they receive the munificence of the
Government in their annuities, on the east of the Red River and the
Arkansas. What is the consequence? They believe Texas is not their
friend, or that the Federal Government, from their crude notions of it,
would pay them in Texas, and would not make them travel over rivers,
and through trackless prairies, to receive their presents. They return to
Texas, not with feelings of respect for the benefits they receive, but with
contempt. This is bad policy. You should distribute your presents to
the Texas Indians within the limits of Texas. Her territory is broad
enough; her domain is fertile enough; her character is high enough to
justify you in doing so. She has done much for herself—more than this
Government has ever done for her. In order to treat with the Indians
properly, as I have said, you should take away your troops, except the
portion I have stated. The Indians, with the exception of the Osages,
Kiowas and Kaws are disposed to be friendly, I believe. As to the dis-
affection of the Sioux, I look on it only as an uprising to resist aggression. They were fired on by artillery and small arms, without provocation, and it is but natural that they should resist. Theirs is not a
confederation to assail the whites, but to protect themselves. I justify
them in doing it. I am sorry there is a necessity for it; but if I were
among them, and they proposed a confederacy to repel cruelty and
butchery, I would join them; and he would be a dastard who would not.
When gentlemen speak of a war upon the Indians, have they considered
the consequences? You may succeed in killing their women and
children, but it is a remarkable fact that you kill but very few of their
warriors. Those who march with martial display upon the Indians, find
them to-night at one point at dark; they may see the smoke of their fires;
and at dawn to-morrow they will be fifty or seventy miles away, with
their caravans and every child and woman, not even a dog being left
behind. What army that you could send of three thousand men, or any
other number, could affect anything by making war upon the Indians?
Why, sir, it would be like the redoubtable exploit of the celebrated king
of France, who, "with forty thousand men marched up a hill, and then
marched down again." [Laughter.] Yes, sir, that I predict would be
the history of such a campaign.

XLVI.

" To accomplish the object here contemplated, it is proposed to spend $5,000,000. As I have said before, that amount of money would civilize every Indian on the continent, if you sent men of intelligence and capacity among them to do it. I have been delighted with the reports which I have had the opportunity of glancing at, accompanying the annual report of the Commissioner of Indian Affairs. One from a gentleman who now occupies a seat in the other House [Mr. WHITFIELD] gratified me exceedingly. I have had the pleasure of seeing him but once since my arrival. I knew him, when a youth, in Tennessee, and he has more than met my expectations, though then they were not indifferent. He has proved himself to be a man of fine perceptions, of excellent judgment, and of good heart. He has capacity to treat with and to reclaim the Indians; and, I doubt not, that he and other gentlemen who could be associated with him, could go to the Indians, with five hundred troops, if you please—not march through the Indian country, but send word to the chiefs ; let them know they had a force, and there is not a chief, who has had any relations with the United States, but would come forward willingly, make treaties, and maintain them in good faith. But you must establish trading houses ; you must protect them, and then you may command the Indians absolutely, and you will have no murders upon your roads. Sir, would it not be much wiser to send a few wagons with presents than to send an army ? Would not the object be effected much sooner by sending commissioners with presents ? The Executive and Senate are the treaty-making power, and all that is necessary for Congress to do, is to make an appropriation for the purpose. Would it not be much easier to take presents to the Indians, and would not the object of attaining and preserving peace be much sooner effected in this way than by an army ? While you were clothing and equipping your army, and marching it there, the Indians might kill half the people on the frontier. Your army would have to march thousands of miles to reach them ; but commissioners could go quietly along, with four or five hundred troops, or as many as might be necessary ; I would leave that to their discretion ; I would select men of capacity for fighting as well as for treating. Send such men, and there will be no trouble in bringing about peace. My life upon it, $5,000,000 would suffice to civilize every Indian who has ever been in treaty with the United States, and settle him in a quiet, comfortable home.

XLVII.

"Some time since, the present agent in Texas was ordered to lay off a section of country in that State for the use of the Indians. He did so. He said to the fierce Camanches, 'Come here, my brothers, and settle down.' They have done so. The Indians to whom I before alluded, who were driven off by the former agent, after robbing them of their horses, upon the assurances given at the return of the present worthy and intelligent agent, faithful to his trust, came back in perfect confidence, and set themselves to building their houses to shelter their women, old men, and children, while the warriors went out to kill game. There they are. The southern Camanches went within the border, and said, 'Let us settle;' but they were immediately told, through the influence of the army, I suppose, that they must not settle there. I saw, not long since, a letter from a most intelligent gentleman, who said that the officer at Fort Belknap, with three companies of rangers, and two of regulars, was daily expecting to make a descent on the poor Indians who had been settled there by the agent, under the pledges of the Government, which promised them that they should have a country where they should throw away the arts of the wild and the Red man, and become domestic, agricultural, and civilized in their pursuits. They have acquiesced in that policy of the Government, but are in constant dread lest the military gentleman in command of the fort, in order to gain laurels and acquire glory, and do honor to his profession, may make a descent with the regulars and volunteers, or rangers, upon the poor Indians. If intelligence of such a descent should arrive, I should not be surprised. I shall be distressed, to be sure; but it will only be one of a thousand distresses which I have felt at the wrongs inflicted on the Indians.

XLVIII.

"Now, sir, is it politic to increase the regular force of the United States? To govern a country well, where intelligence predominates over selfishness and interest, I think the smaller the army is the better. I have had some experience in that. It is very well to take care of arms and ordinance stores, and army stores, which would be useful in time of war. It is necessary, I think, to have an army for that purpose. You may have as great a stock of science as you please; but it does not follow that you are bound to make an officer of every gentleman you educate at West Point. I do not think it would be wise policy to extend the army to suit the establishment of the Military Academy, but rather the Military Academy to the interests and exigencies of the country. That is my opinion of the army. The nominal number of the army is fourteen thousand. There is not a vacancy, I presume, for an officer in the whole service. According to the data I have before me, and the items I have given, I suppose there are about four thousand five hundred men in the service. To make the actual number of fourteen thousand complete, you would have to make the nominal force three times fourteen thousand. Let the head of the department show that they can keep this establishment perfect before they would go to ingrafting new limbs on it, in its present imperfect condition. Let the trunk be sound before you graft it. I know that the officers will never be less than the establishment; it shows that it is too large, and ought rather to be reduced. Whenever we see that the present establishment is kept in order, and the requisite number of men to make it complete always in the service, it will commend itself to consideration; and if a greater amount of force, or a larger establishment, be necessary, it would be acceded to. I do not, however, now see any necessity for it. If you increase it, it will never get less. We know that, even when the army is increased in time of war, there is difficulty in reducing it to a peace establishment afterwards. It has always been the case, and always will be, that a man, by holding an office temporarily, acquires a claim to it which is enforced by relatives and friends; and the army thereby will become an eye-sore to the people, and a carbuncle upon the body politic.

XLIX.

"Sir, in the course of my remarks I have said some things which might seem to bear upon the officers of the army as a class. My partialities for military men, and for gentlemen of the army, are of a character not to be doubted. I know their high-toned feeling, their honorable bearing, and their chivalry; and when I commented upon some of them, I only spoke of such as brought themselves within the purview of my remarks by impropriety of conduct, deserving the reprobation of every man who appreciates honorable feelings, integrity and truthfulness. As a class, however, I admire and respect them. I have experienced their hospitalities. Once I enjoyed their association with pleasure; and my recollections of early habits, formed in their companionship, always mark a verdant spot in memory's waste. It is only the guilty and the culpable that I condemn.

Sir, I believe the honorable chairman of the Committee on Military Affairs has withdrawn that portion of the amendment relating to the appointment of three commissioners to treat with the Indians. But, Mr. President, if we wish to do good to the Indians, we have it in our power; if we wish to destroy them, we can starve them out. If we intend to save them, we can do so by appealing to their best feelings. There is one pathway to an Indian's heart. If you show him that comforts and benefits are to result to his wife and children, you may command him absolutely, and he yields implicitly. He has no opposing thought to their interest. I have always seen that if you could impress an Indian with the conviction that comfort and security would inure to his squaw and papooses, from the adoption of a particular policy, he would submit to it. My colleague [Mr. Rusk] knows that this is the way to the heart of an Indian. The proudest warrior is humiliated at the thought of his wife and little ones being in the least uncomfortable. Whenever an Indian intends to conciliate the whites, he brings his family and settles as near as he can to a fort or agency, and says, ' Here are the hostages I give you for my fidelity to you; if I do wrong, I know they will suffer; they are dearer to me than my life.' The Indians can be brought around trading-houses.

L.

" I have lost all hope of the stations in Texas doing any good. I would not have more than twenty-five men at a trading-house to give protection, in the event of any sudden ebullition among the Indians of a violent character. It would be entirely accidental if such a necessity happened around the trading-houses, as to require protection to be given to the caravans emigrating to California and Oregon. I would encourage the Indians in the arts of peace. You need no armies; you need no Indian allies to butcher them. All you have to do is to maintain your faith in carrying out the treaties which have been made, and not directly or indirectly encourage men to violate every principle of honor and humanity, and deride even faith itself."

LI.

Such was the noblest defence of the Red men of America, ever pronounced in the Senate of the United States. It was listened to with interest, but it produced little effect upon the action of the Senate. The poor Red man has had few friends on this continent ; while the African race have, for a quarter of a century, been the exciting topic of noisy sympathy, and inflammatory appeals. And yet, who will pretend to compare the wrongs of the Africans with the outrages that have been perpetrated upon the Aborigines ? The former were brought hither from a land of barbarism and Pagan darkness, to be elevated in the scale of social life more rapidly than four millions of men have ever been elevated, in the history of the world. They may be called adventurers, having no prescriptive right to the soil. But the Indian was the original possessor of the soil. He received this broad continent from the hands of his Creator. He has been driven from it by invasion ; and what the white man's rifle, and the white man's fire-water failed to accomplish in his extermination, has been made up by treachery and fraud.

Houston has always been a friend of the Red man ; and in this respect, there has been no variation in his conduct. This country will one day wake up to the atrocities and inhumanity we have inflicted upon the Aborigines. Houston's long efforts in their behalf will then stamp him as the philanthropist of the age. Then, too, will the following eloquent words of Charles Sprague be dragged forth from the library, and printed in letters of gold.

LII.

"Not many generations ago, where you now sit, circled with all that exalts and embellishes civilized life, the rank thistle nodded in the wind, and the wild fox dug his hole unscared. Here lived and loved another race of beings. Beneath the same sun that rolls over your heads, the Indian hunter pursued the panting deer ; gazing on the same moon that smiles for you, the Indian lover wooed his dusky mate. Here the wigwam blaze beamed on the tender and helpless, the council fire glared on the wise and daring. Now they dipped their noble limbs in your sedgy lakes, and now they paddled the light canoe along your rocky shores. Here they warred ; the echoing whoop, the bloody grapple, the defying death-song, all were here ; and when the tiger strife was over, here curled the smoke of peace. Here, too, they worshiped ; and from many a dark bosom went up a pure prayer to the Great Spirit. He had not written His laws for them on tables of stone, but He had traced them on the tables of their hearts. The poor child of Nature knew not the God of revelation, but the God of the universe he acknowledged in everything around. He beheld Him in the star that sunk in beauty behind his lonely dwelling, in the sacred orb that flamed on him from His mid-day throne, in the flower that snapped in the morning breeze, in the lofty pine that defied a thousand whirlwinds ; in the timid warbler that never left its native grove, in the fearless eagle, whose untiring pinion was wet in the clouds ; in the worm that crawled at his feet, and in his own matchless form, glowing with a spark of that light, to whose mysterious source he bent, in humble, though blind adoration.

LIII.

" And all this has passed away. Across the ocean came a pilgrim bark, bearing the seeds of life and death. The former were sown for you, the latter sprang up in the path of the simple native. Two hundred years have changed the character of a great continent, and blotted for ever from its face, a whole, peculiar people. Art has usurped the bowers of nature, and the anointed children of education have been too powerful for the tribes of the ignorant. Here and there a stricken few remain, but how unlike their bold, untamed, untamable progenitors ! The Indian of falcon glance, and lion bearing, the theme of the touching ballad, the hero of the pathetic tale, is gone! and his degraded offspring crawl upon the soil where he walked in majesty, to remind us how miserable is man, when the foot of the conqueror is on his neck.

17

LIV.

"As a race they have withered from the land. Their arrows are broken, their springs are dried up, their cabins are in the dust. Their council-fire has long since gone out on the shore, and their war-cry is fast dying out to the untrodden West. Slowly and sadly they climb the distant mountains, and read their doom in the setting sun. They are shrinking before the mighty tide which is pressing them away ; they must soon hear the roar of the last wave, which will settle over them for ever. Ages hence the inquisitive white man, as he stands by some growing city, will ponder on the structure of their disturbed remains, and wonder to what manner of person they belonged. They will live only in the songs and chronicles of their exterminators. Let these be faithful to their rude virtues as men, and pay due tribute to their unhappy fate as a people."

SECTION TWENTY-TWO.

HOUSTON AT HOME.

I.

ONE of the greatest evils which this country has suffered for the last twenty years, has been the " Caucus System." The Caucus has governed our political world. It has been our king—our tyrant. Beginning with each local district and ward, where there were but few voters, it has extended up to the municipalities, counties, cities, and States. From the States, it has extended itself over the whole length and breadth of the Confederation. Hence we have witnessed the strange and disgraceful spectacle of the nomination of men to office, for districts, wards, towns, cities, counties, States, and even for the Presidential office, by the mere force of political and party machinery, under the lowest and most degrading forms.

II.

In old times—say forty or fifty years ago—things were done differently. The Legislators of States, who were going out of office, nominated State officers ; and a retiring Congress nominated the next President. This system was far better than the one which took its place. Both have been impositions and usurpations upon the intelligence and the rights of the American people. They have resulted in giving us several Presidents whom the people would never have chosen, if they could have had an opportunity of voting for anybody else ; and we have suffered the natural results of that kind of policy.

III.

By this system, we were saddled with the nomination of several Presidents, who had no fair claim to the high position to which they were elevated. Such men as Henry Clay, Daniel Webster, and Lewis Cass, were overlooked ; and such men as Gen. Harrison—a very good man—and Gen. Taylor—another good man—but both entirely incompetent to the duties of the Presidential office, were raised to positions of influence and power, without the ability to administer the affairs of the Nation.

IV.

The most lamentable instance in our history, in illustration of this state of things, was the nomination of Frank Pierce. It is perfectly certain that not one hundred people in the United States had the slightest suspicion that this Concord politician would ever be nominated for the Presidency. The evils of this " Caucus System" were fully developed by his nomination ; and the country has grown so sick of the consequences, that hereafter we shall most likely take better care of our national affairs.

We now feel, as Americans, that we can no longer afford to risk the fortunes of the country, upon the hazards of this faro-bank of party and caucus nomination. We think the time has come when, if a Presidential Chief is to be chosen to preside over the affairs of the Nation, the People of the Country should have something to say in the choice. King Caucus is dead—the tyrant has been dragged out and executed. Hereafter, the *American People* will determine who shall be their President.

V.

Sam Houston has always acted upon this system. He has never bowed his neck, nor his judgment, to party intrigues, nor to corrupt Caucuses. He has despised and abhorred both. The records of the fact may be found in his whole life. His earliest achievements were bent upon driving foreign invaders from our soil. His later efforts were expended upon the construction of a new and independent Anglo-Saxon Republic in the forests, and on the prairies of Texas. His last efforts have been to preserve, unimpaired, the union of these States ; and, therefore, he is the choice of millions of the American people, for the highest office in their gift.

VI.

He has been a Democrat all his life ; having been trained, from the beginning, in the school of Jackson.

He fought through THE SECOND WAR with England, where he won a brilliant fame. He never was nominated for an office to which he was not elected. He is the only American, whose name is known, who has, in dealing with the Red men of the forests, gained their affection and confidence, while he commanded the respect of white men. He has penetrated the forests, and lived in the wildernesses of America, where he has learned all the mysteries of frontier life.

He has bled in the cause of two Republics.

VII.

He has been the Founder, as well as the chieftain of a noble

Republic, and when that Republic had established its independence, he brought it as an offering, and laid it upon the Federal
altar.

The whole force of our Republic was expended upon the capture of Santa Anna ; and the two best Generals of the American Army were nominated for the Presidency of the United
States, because they defeated the Mexican Dictator. Houston
not only defeated him, but captured him ; and by paralyzing his
power, at the time, gave life and vigor to a new commonwealth.

Houston has been the champion of that great movement
which promises, at last, to redeem the American Nation from
the vices and the curses of intoxication.

Fired by the spirit of nationality, and inspired by its
"Councils," he has stood forth among the brightest, the greatest,
and the best impersonations of the Spirit of American
Patriotism.

VIII.

Mrs. Houston's maiden name was Margaret Moffatt Lea, of
Marion, Alabama. Their oldest boy, Sam, is about eleven years
of age. The four daughters are named Nancy Elizabeth,
Margaret Lea, Mary William, and Antionette. The youngest
child is a boy, and he has been named Andrew Jackson Houston. General Houston's residence is at Independence, Texas.
He was immersed in November, 1854, by Rev. Rufus C. Burleson ; and he is a member of "the Independence Church."

IX.

General Houston lives in a log house, and we are informed by
a gentleman who visited him recently, that he still retains the
chairs which he owned while President of the Republic. These

chairs have turned posts, and they are bottomed with cow-hides tanned with the hair on.   Everything about his home, indicates frugality ; for he has devoted more time and attention to the salvation and prosperity of his country, than to the acquisition of wealth.   Holding the position twice, as President of the Republic of Texas, had he been less honest than he is, he could have amassed boundless wealth ; for he could have gathered into his hands extensive domains of land, which, at the time, fell into the possession of others, who had rendered few or no services to the State.   Had he been disposed to profit by the station he held, he could now have been the owner of hundreds of thousands of dollars of Texas liabilities, which will soon enrich those who hold them.   But instead of this, we are assured on reliable authority, that he has never speculated to the extent of a single dollar in soldiers' lands, or Texas stocks—and yet, in the opinion of men, he might have done it without any imputation of dishonor.   But Houston has always been governed by a higher code of honor than most men are guided by.

X.

In his private relations, no one who regarded the truth, has ever dared to arraign his honesty, or his punctuality.   Hence, after more than forty years in public life, he is at this time a man of moderate fortune : not rich, nor has he ever cared for more than a competency for himself and a young family, to whom he wishes to leave only a spotless reputation.

And now, when he has finally retired from the Senate, to his distant home on the far-off frontier—full of honors, and surrounded by the halo of victory—we learn that he has added a new lustre to his private character, by uniting himself with the Christian Church, as a humble communicant in the great body of worshipping believers, who have confided all they have to hope for here and hereafter, to the Saviour of the world.

XI.

Such a record as this, ought not to invade the privacy of that sanctuary where man holds communication with God. But there are millions of our countrymen who will join with us, in the honest congratulation that such a man as this, who never was awed in the presence of human power, should sit in penitent reverence, at the feet of Him who was baptized by the Prophet of the Desert, before he went forth to redeem mankind.

XII.

Thus we find ourselves at the close of our narrative. Would that some better pen had performed the task ! But we could not forbear to make this offering, however unworthy it may be, to history, to heroism, to virtue, and to truth.

If then it be an honor to human nature to repent, and abandon errors of opinion, and frailties of conduct, why may not the biographer rejoice to weave the woof of such a history as Houston's, and throw it before the world, that all the wrong a great man may have, perhaps, inflicted by the splendor of his talents—and above all a man who stooped to waste his time as Charles James Fox did, in garnishing vice by his genius, and ornamenting it by its elevation—may be at last atoned for, by the reformation of the admired individual transgressor? "Greater is he that ruleth his own spirit, than he that taketh a city." Gen. Houston has for many years been the father of a family ; and no man better illustrates the virtues that belong to that relation. A soldier in many wars, and a hero in the achievement of the liberties of two Republics—a file leader in the great movement which is to give America back to the Americans—an enemy of all sections and factions, and a champion of the country in which he was born—superior to party—greater than all *isms*—A NATIONAL MAN, who has fought, and bled, and lived for the great North American Republic—such a man presents one of the most captivating subjects of all history, for the pen of the biographer.

Americans who have a country to live for, are looking to Gen. Houston, for the future.

This Volume could hardly be brought to a better termination, than by a republication, from the vigorous pen of Edmund Burke of New Hampshire, of the following :—

ADDRESS

To the People of the State of New Hampshire, and of the United States.

THE General Committee of the Democracy of New Hampshire, having convened at Concord, on the 11th day of October, 1854, for the purpose of taking into consideration the present condition of the Democratic Party of this State and of the Union, after due deliberation, came to the conclusion to recommend and nominate Gen. SAM HOUSTON, of Texas, as the people's candidate for the office of President of the United States, to be supported in the election which is to take place in 1856.   And in taking a step so important, they have deemed it their duty to submit their reasons therefor, to the people of the United States.

Two years ago, the great Democratic party of the Union was a powerful and triumphant party.   Planted upon the rock of the Constitution and its compromises, and the great measures of conciliation and amity embodied in the acts of Congress, of 1850, touching the subject of Slavery and the admission of new territory into the Union, it achieved the most signal and transcendent victories which ever crowned the efforts of any party since the formation of the Republic. Its triumph was complete. Its opponents were overwhelmed and confounded, by the omnipotence of that expression of the popular voice which elevated the present administration to power, and inaugurated a new era in the history of Democracy and of the Republic. The factions that had arrayed themselves against the peace and stability of the Union, were abashed and terrified at the magnitude of the disaster which fell upon them. The secret of the great Revolution in the popular sentiment of the country, is to be sought only in the fact, that the Democratic party had pledged itself to the sacred maintenance of the Constitution and its compromises, and thus, to the preservation of the Union. It was the Union Sentiment of the country, which triumphed in that election.

The completeness of this transcendent and unprecedented victory, gave reasonable ground of hope to the patriotic portion of the people, that the Democratic party would be consolidated upon the great and noble principles upon which it had so signally triumphed, and its ascendency thereby secured, at least, for the present generation. Such were the confident and cheering anticipations of the great body of the victorious party. The Democracy can hardly realize that those brilliant anticipations, so well-founded and reasonable, should all be dissipated in the lapse of two short years, from the occurrence of the great event in which they originated. Such, however, is the melancholy and disheartening fact. Almost from the moment of the inauguration of the present administration in office, its course has been attended with defeat and disaster. Since its policy and measures have been developed, it has hardly succeeded in a single State in which elections have been held. In Maine,

New Hampshire, Vermont, Rhode Island, Connecticut, New York and Iowa, to which may be added Pennsylvania and Ohio, it has been defeated ; in some of the States, it has been overwhelmed. And in North Carolina, a State in which its policy might be supposed to be acceptable, it has succeeded with a greatly diminished vote.

We point to these pregnant facts in the recent experience of the Democratic party under the leadership of the present incumbent of the Presidency, without designing to enter into an explanation of their causes. It is enough that the Democratic party has suffered defeats, signal and unprecedented, in the States we have mentioned, indicating on the part of the present administration, a loss of the confidence of the people. But the future of the Democratic party would not be so overcast with clouds, as it now is, if the results of the elections in the States above mentioned, did not indicate more than simple defeat. In our judgment, they point unerringly to a disorganization and dissolution of the Democratic party, as at present organized, unless some means can be devised by which the process of demoralization, so fearfully begun, and so rapidly progressing, can be averted.

This Committee have gravely and maturely considered the exigent perils which now environ the Democratic party, and we have deliberately come to the conclusion that there is no way by which it can be saved from defeat and overthrow, except by the immediate nomination by the people, for the office of President of the United States, of some citizen of the Republic, distinguished alike for his abilities, experience in public affairs, and unquestionable statesmanship. Such a man would serve as a rallying point for the disjointed fragments of the party, arrest the progress of demoralization, and reorganize its dissevered elements into a compact and consolidated organization.

With a view of bringing about results so desirable, the democratic republicans of New Hampshire, nominate and recommend for the office of President of the United States, Gen. Sam Houston, of Texas, to be supported by the people, independent of nominations which may be made by Conventions, State or National. We nominate him as the people's candidate, and we invite our democratic brethren in other States, also to nominate him, in which event his election will be sure.

We believe that in the present crisis of political affairs, it is expedient for the people to take the matter of the nomination of the chief magistrate of the Republic—the officer who, for the time being, represents the majesty and sovereignty of the people —into their own hands. The day when nominations by National Conventions will be respected, is past. They, like their predecessors, Congressional caucuses, have become obsolete. The intelligent and reflecting people of the United States cannot shut their eyes to the momentous and humiliating fact, that, as National Conventions are at present organized and conducted, no distinguished citizen of the Republic, who has gained the confidence of the people, by commanding ability displayed in a long life of eminent and valuable public service, can aspire to the Presidency. National Conventions rule all such men off the line of promotion to that exalted office. None but men of inferior capacities, unknown to the people, and never thought of, except by intriguing demagogues, who, in elevating such men to the highest honors of the Republic, secure thereby their own advancement in inferior spheres, can now hope for a nomination by National Conventions. Instead of being fair exponents of the popular sentiment, National Conventions now stifle and suppress the will and voice of the people. Who can doubt that Gen. Cass was the choice of more than three-fourths of the democracy of the Union, as their candidate and standard-bearer at the last Presidential canvass? Yet, he was excluded from the nomination by the late Baltimore Convention ; the event to which the present embarrassment of the Democratic party may, in a great measure, be attributed.

The only way in which these immense evils can be corrected, and the people restored to their sovereign and constitutional right to choose the Chief Magistrate of the Republic, of which they have been denied by the machinery of National Conventions, is, to take the business of making Presidents into their own hands—to make the nominations themselves, inasmuch as they have to make the elections. In such a manner was Gen. Jackson, the honored and revered of the people, and one of the most illustrious of Presidents, nominated and elected. He was nominated in opposition to the nomination of the old Congressional caucus of his day. That caucus was instituted in the early days of the Republic. It did good service in the struggle with the federalists, in the days of John Adams. By a Congressional caucus, Mr. Jefferson was nominated for the Presidency ; as were also his successors, Mr. Madison and Mr. Monroe. It was the *regular nomination* of the democracy of that day. Its last candidate was William H. Crawford, in 1824. *Gen. Jackson was nominated and run as the people's democratic candidate against the nomination of Mr. Crawford.* And although he failed of an election in the House of Representatives, by trickery, he succeeded at the next election before the people. His success was the downfall of the old Congressional caucuses, which, like the National Conventions of the present day, had become the instrument of intriguing demagogues for their own aggrandizement.

As Gen. Jackson was nominated by the people, we nominate Gen. Houston. We nominate him to be supported by the people, independent of National Conventions. And we invoke the people of all sections and States of the Union, to unite with us in the election of this distinguished and eminent man to the Chief Magistracy of the Republic.

Is it asked, who is Gen. Houston? If so, the history of the Republic affords ample answer. His deeds and achievements have illustrated its most brilliant pages. He was born in the State of Virginia—like Gen. Jackson, he emigrated to Tennessee. He was the companion, the friend and confidant of that illustrious man. Under the command of Gen. Jackson, he distinguished himself by his bravery and courage at the celebrated Indian battle of the Horse Shoe. He was among the few friends whom the dying Hero of the Hermitage invited to his bed-side in the last moments of his ebbing life. Gen. Jackson knew him, stood by him, confided in him, and endorsed him as a true and honest man, and Gen. Jackson never endorsed anything that was untrue, false or spurious. No man living possesses more of the noble virtues of Gen. Jackson than Gen. Houston. And his career has been equally illustrious and brilliant. The most remarkable and wonderful Battle of San Jacinto will ever rank in history with that of New Orleans. Moreover his administration of the affairs of Texas, while it was an independent republic, and he its chief magistrate, was most able and consummate. It was through his rare ability and tact, so far as Texas was concerned, that that State was annexed to the American Union. It was Gen. Houston who conquered Texas and brought her into the Union, thereby adding to the Republic a country as large, as beautiful, and as congenial in climate, as the Empire of France, and laying the foundation for the expansion of the Republic southward to the river Rio Grande, and westward to the Pacific Ocean, thus elevating her to the first rank among the nations of the earth. These are the achievements of Gen. Sam Houston, of Texas. No public man now living in the United States, belonging to the Democratic party, has performed such signal service for his country, or shed such lustre upon its historic pages.

Throughout his long career, Gen. Houston has been an

inflexible democrat. He is a disciple of the school of Jefferson and Jackson. He has filled many of the highest public offices, in all which, he has acquitted himself with remarkable ability and with unsuspected integrity. In all positions, the most responsible, as well as the most trying and perilous, he has been eminently successful. He has ever proved himself equal to any emergency in which he has been placed. As General, Statesman, Orator and Legislator, he has displayed talents and ability of the first order. He is a man of honor. He keeps faith with the humblest as well as the highest. He has never broken his word with the humblest Indian with whom he has had to deal, nor with sovereign States. He believes in the sacredness of treaties, of compacts, and of compromises, whether in the form of conventions, constitutions, or solemn acts of Congress. He preserves his faith with the North, as he would require the North to preserve its faith with the South. Under his administration, the rights of all sections of the Union would be protected and preserved. He is a Union man, and never would permit this glorious confederacy of sovereign States to be dissevered by the aggressions of fanaticism on one side, nor by unjustifiable rebellion on the other. He would secure justice to the States and to the people. Such is the history and character of " Old Sam Houston," the Hero of San Jacinto, the friend of Gen. Jackson, who was the great and beloved President of the people, as Gen. Houston will be if he shall be elected.

Can he be elected? We have no doubt of it. He can be elected, if the people say that he shall be. Let the people put him forward, and the politicians will be paralyzed. The great mass of the Democratic party will support him. They are tired of the feeble and incompetent contingent candidates imposed upon them by National Conventions, as they and the whole country are tired of mere military chieftains. Both have had their day. The people now want a man of talents, of character, of experience—a well-tried statesman.   Such are the wants of the Democracy—such the demands of the people generally.   At present, the Democratic party have no commanding leader, and no well-defined system of political measures, to rally them to party allegiance.   A man and a policy are now the great desiderata of the Democratic masses.   Gen. Houston would command the support of the great body of the Democratic voters of the country.   He would also receive the support of a numerous portion of the people who have hitherto acted with the Whig party.   The utter prostration and defeat of that party, the permanent ascendency of the system of Democratic measures propounded to the country by General Jackson, the abolitionization of the Whig party, and its consequent destruction as a national party, have drawn a large number of the people formerly acting with the Whigs from the pale of the Whig organization.   They are now, in fact, without the limits of any party. In national sentiment, they sympathize with the Democracy. All this class of voters would give their support to Gen. Houston.

The true interests of the people of the South, and especially those who are sincerely desirous of preserving and perpetuating the union of this glorious confederacy of sovereign and independent States, all point to Gen. Houston as the man, above all others, for the crisis now impending over the South and the country.   They cannot fail to note the formidable and fearful combination now forming in the North, under the banner of abolitionism, which has for its basis and incentive to action, unrelenting hostility to the institutions of the South.   That combination will grow and expand in potency and virulence, until even the most sanguine will admit its danger, and tremble at the consequences which may flow from it.   If, under such circumstances, a man from the South, not acceptable at the North for his conservative sentiments, shall be run for the Presidency, it will only augment the dangers and the perils which now menace the peace of the country and the stability of the Union. If a candidate from the North shall be nominated, who is in the least suspected of subserviency to the South, the danger will be still more increased. Gen. Houston is the only man who can meet and prostrate this portentous coalition of factions in the North to which we have alluded. The course which he took with respect to the Nebraska Bill, has placed him in a position which will command the confidence of the patriotic men of the North, and should commend him to the confidence of the South. While he has, with a courage and true intrepidity which command our admiration, taken his stand in favor of the inviolable sanctity of compacts between the North and the South, no man can say that he is hostile to the institutions or the interests of either section of the Union. In the present crisis, we are confident that the people of the South, will, on reflection, see in Gen. Houston the very man for the present emergency—the only man who can save the South and Union from the dangers which now impend over them.

We, therefore, unfurl the banner of the veteran Hero and Statesman, fearlessly to the breeze, confident of ultimate victory. We, as a part of the people, independent of any organization of politicians, nominate GEN. SAM HOUSTON, AS THE PEOPLE'S CANDIDATE FOR THE OFFICE OF PRESIDENT OF THE UNITED STATES, and we invoke our brethren, the Democracy of this State, and of the United States, and the people generally, to rally promptly around his banner, assuring them a glorious triumph in 1856.

And, in conclusion, for the purpose of ensuring efficient co-operation among the friends of Gen. Houston, we recommend the immediate formation, by the people, of San Jacinto Clubs in every State, district and town in the Republic.

On motion, voted, That the proceedings of this meeting be

signed by the officers thereof, and published in the *State Capital Reporter*, and other Democratic papers.

On motion, voted, That when this Committee adjourn, it be to meet at the call of the President, at such time and place as he may designate.

Voted to adjourn.

WILLIAM PRESCOTT, *President.*

WILLIAM TENNEY, ⎫
WILLIAM W. EASTMAN, ⎬ *Secretaries.*

FINIS.

THE MORNING STARS OF THE NEW WORLD.

BY H. F. PARKER.

1 elegant 12mo. volume, over 400 pages, six Illustrations.   Price $1 25.

CONTENTS :—Columbus—Vespucius—De Soto—Raleigh—Hudson—Smith—Standish—Arabella Stuart—Elliott and Penn.

"An unpretending work, yet a valuable one. The authoress must have entered upon her task with hearty enthusiasm, as, while adhering strictly to the simplest truth, she has thrown around her portraits a new charm, and given to them a refreshing novelty of aspect. A gallery of striking portraits worthy of preservation and a galaxy of stars whose morning light must not be obscured in the noon-tide brilliancy of a successful present. In just such a form as this should they lie on our book-tables, reminders of the past, shorn of the technicalities of the history, and presented in strong relief. The name of the authoress is one almost unknown ; but she deserves the thanks of the public for her well written book in which she has given a convenient medium of communication with days of long ago—days that never should be forgotton even by the busy, bustling world that cannot stop to go back even to the days of their own forefathers. The book proves itself a very entertaining one for the young, who declare themselves unable to leave its fascinating pages."— *Worcester Palladium.*

" A more appropriate name could not have been given to a book which contains all that is interesting in the lives of the master spirits to whom the world may be said to owe, firstly the discovery of this great continent ; and secondly, the establishment upon it, of European colonies. In no other single work, of whose existence we are aware, are there to be found so many sketches of the discoverers and first settlers of the principal parts of the new world, which are at once so concise and comprehensive, as those given in the ' Morning Stars.' They are truly *multum in parvo.*"—*Philadelphia News.*

" The authoress has fashioned her materials in a very winning garb, and with a spirit and feeling rarely kindled in preparing succint biographies, imparts her glowing appreciation of their subject to the reader. We hope this volume, while in itself it will be valuable to the young, will lead them to more extended historical reading, and especially of that which pertains to our colonial life, and to our own country. It is well that they should be reminded of the conflicts and sacrifices which purchased their present luxurious immunities. They cannot begin better than with this charming volume, which they will not leave unfinished."—*New Bedford Mercury.*

" This book is alike novel, and fortunate in its title and its character. It contains very satisfactory sketches of ten of the great spirits the history of whose lives blends itself most intimately with the earliest history of our country. It was a beautiful thought ; and it is carried out in a manner that can hardly fail to secure to the work many delighted readers."—*Albany Argus.*

" The book has all the charm of romance, and the value of genuine history. It is written with spirit and vigor, and at the same time with precision and taste. The grouping together of such men brings the reader into the best of company."—*Utica Herald.* 3

THE LIFE AND SAYINGS OF MRS. PARTINGTON,

AND OTHERS OF THE FAMILY.

BY B. P. SHILLABER.

1 elegant 12mo., 43 Illustrations.   Price $1 25.

"'Hang the books!' said an appreciative examiner, to whom we handed a copy for inspection, 'I can't afford to buy them, but I can't do without this;' and laughing until the tears ran, he drew forth the purchase-money. It is just so, reader; you can't do without this book. It is so full of genial humor and pure human nature that your wife and children must have it, to be able to realize how much enjoyment may be shut up within the lids of a book. It is full of human kindness, rich in humor, alive with wit, mingled here and there with those faint touches of melancholy which oft-times touch Mirth's borders."—*Clinton Courant.*

"She has caused many a lip to relax from incontinent primness into the broadest kind of a grin—has given to many a mind the material for an odd but not useless revery—has scooped out many a cove on the dry shores of newspaper reading, and invited the mariner reader to tarry and refresh himself. 'Ruth Partington' is a Christian and a patriot. Such a book will go everywhere—be welcomed like a returned exile—do good, and cease not."—*Buffalo Express.*

"If it is true that one grows fat who laughs, then he who reads this book will fat up, even though he may be one of Pharaoh's 'lean kine.' That it does one good to laugh, nobody doubts. We have shook and shook while running through this charming volume, until it has seemed as though we had increased in weight some fifty gounds, more or less."—*Massachusetts Life Boat.*

"A regular Yankee institution is Mrs. Partington, and well deserves the compliment of a book devoted to her sayings and doings. She is here brought before the public, which is so greatly indebted to her unique vocabulary for exhaustless stores of fun, in a style worthy of her distinguished character."—*N. Y. Tribune.*

"There is a world of goodness in her blessed heart, as there is a universe of quiet fun in the book before us. 'A gem of purest ray serene' glitters on almost every page. Everybody should buy the book; everybody, at least, who loves genial, quiet wit, which never wounds, but always heals where it strikes."—*Independent Democrat.*

"It is crammed full of her choicest sayings, and rings from title page to 'finis' with her unconscious wit. It is just the book for one to read at odd moments—to take on the cars or home of an evening—or to devour in one's office of a rainy day. It is an excellent antidote for the blues."—*Oneida Herald.*

"Housewives who occasionally get belated about their dinner, should have it lying round. It will prevent a deal of grumbling from their 'lords,' by keeping them so well employed as to make them forget their dinner."—*New Hampshire Telegraph.*

"Her 'sayings' have gone the world over, and given her an immortality that will glitter and sparkle among the records of genius wherever wit and humor shall be appreciated."
—*Worcester Palladium.*

A BOOK OF RARE BEAUTY AND GREAT INTEREST.

FOURTH EDITION NOW READY.

MRS. OAKES SMITH'S NEW ROMANCE.

BERTHA AND LILY;

OR, THE PARSONAGE OF BEECH GLEN.

1 elegant 12mo. vol.   Price $1.

The following brief extracts are but the key-notes of lengthy reviews. No recent book has received more marked attention from the press:

" It compels the reader to linger over its pages."—*N. Y. Tribune.*

" Sparkling thoughts and humane and benevolent feelings."—*Albany Argus.*

" More powerfully written than any recent work of fiction."—*N. Y. Day Book.*

" Another story of exquisite beauty—graceful and fascinating."—*Phila. News.*

" Altogether it is a remarkable book."—*N. Y. Christian Enquirer.*

" No romance more deserves a wide-spread popularity."—*Providence Post.*

" Striking truths boldly represented."—*Rural New Yorker.*

" Springing from a heart overflowing with love and sympathy."—*Pittsburg Visitor.*

" Strange scenes, powerful dialogue, and exquisite imagery."—*Transcript.*

" We know of one woman who says it is a brave book."—*Boston Commonwealth.*

" Elegant with mountain and valley flowers and water lilies."—*N. Y. Dispatch.*

" Womanly genius under its happiest and purest inspirations."—*Albany Atlas.*

" A ' romance,' but full of life. It has power ; it has truth."—*Boston Bee.*

" Sure to captivate the reader."—*N. Y. Atlas.*

" The ladies will find it a graceful and fascinating production."—*Phila. City Item.*

" Just what might be expected from a brilliant woman."—*Albany Express.*

" A female delicacy of taste and perception."—*Ladies' Repository.*

" A moral perspective of rare beauty and significance."—*Harpers' Magazine.*

" So intensely interesting, we read it at one sitting."—*Cleveland Farmer.*

" A ' prose poem,' replete with melody and imagery."—*Boston Chronicle.*

" Well vindicated her reputation as a woman of genius."—*N. Y. Herald.*

" True to nature and every day life."—*Albany Spectator.*

" Cannot fail to inspire the reader with noble purposes."—*Christian Freeman.*

" Will be eagerly sought for and read."—*Water Cure Journal.*

" The style is glowing and impassioned."—*Rochester American.*

" Its pages leave a very attractive impression."—*Salem Gazette.*

" Will prove a valuable accession to the home circle."—*Ladies' Enterprise.*

" Will be read, and find many enthusiastic readers."—*Bangor Mercury.*

" A beautiful creation."—*Boston Transcript.*

" Comes before the reader with freshness, earnestness and power."—*Eclectic.*

" The book before us is bravely written."—*Providence Una.*

" The very best fiction we have read for years."—*Glen's Fall Republican.*

" Characters in it worthy of lasting fame."—*Hartford Republican.*

" All her works bear the impress of genius."—*Olive Branch.*

" It is a beautiful story."—*Sandusky Democrat.*

7

THE MOST NATURAL NOVEL WE EVER PERUSED.

THE NEWSBOY.
BY MRS. E. OAKES SMITH.

1 large 12mo. vol., 530 pages. Price $1 25.

Reader, the following extracts from lengthy notices—from some of the most respectable and impartial papers—are but a few of those received. The Press universally unite in calling THE NEWSBOY one of the great books of the day. Buy, read, and believe.

" ' The Newsboy ' is a good book. Its moral is wholesome. Its lesson is good."—*New York Daily Times.*

"It has all the merits of the Lamplighter, and is, from the first page to the last, intensely interesting,"—*Philadelphia Saturday Mail.*

" The tone of the narrative in its moral bearings is pure and excellent."—*N. Y. Tribune.*

" None but a woman with womanly instincts could spread such delicate pictures on a canvas."—*Albany Express.*

" It has pathos, and reality of hope and fear, joy and sorrow, rarely met with in the world of romance."—*N. Y. Democrat.*

" It is so full of brilliant and original illustrations, as actually to dazzle and confound the judgment."—*Philadelphia American Courier.*

" We would commend it (' The Newsboy ') for the practical, earnest Christian spirit in which its lessons are inculcated."—*N. Y. Home Journal.*

"Bob is bound on his way to immortality with the living creations of Fielding, and Scott, and Dickens, and Cooper, and Irving."—*U. S. Journal.*

" It is a book to read more than once ; to think over ; to dream over ; to lay to your heart."—*Chicago Tribune.*

" It is, *par excellence*, the most natural novel we have ever perused."—*Bost. Eve. Gaz.*

" We are involuntarily reminded of the touching word-painting of Dickens."—*Troy Budget.*

" The midnight lamp burned to its socket before we could lay it down."—*True American.*

"It embraces a multitude of thrilling pictures, which stir up the fountains of our hearts."—*Highland Eagle.*

" It is a wonderful production, replete with wit and pathos, humor and sentiment."—*Philadelphia Daily News.*

" It has a plot full of stirring incidents, extraordinary adventure, and exquisite conceptions of character."—*New York Evening Post.*

" The author holds a ready and graceful pen, and unites with a poet's fancy a keen perception of human nature."—*Worcester Palladium.*

" The book bears the impress of true genius, and is not unworthy the pen of a Dickens."—*Hampshire (Mass.) Gazette.*

" This book is an excellent one for the parlor, study, or quiet fireside."—*Chicago Daily Times.*

" It is a book that arouses and rivets the attention."—*N. Y. Evening Mirror.*

JACK DOWNING'S NEW BOOK!

'WAY DOWN EAST;

OR, PORTRAITURES OF YANKEE LIFE.

BY SEBA SMITH, ESQ.

Illustrated, 12mo. Price $1.

" We greet the Major, after a long interval, with profound pleasure and respect. Well do we remember how, years ago, we used to pore over his lucubrations on the events of the time—how he enlightened us by his home-views of the Legislature's doings, of the Gineral's intentions, and of the plans of ambitious Uncle Joshua. Here was the ' spot of his origin,' and around us were the materials from which he drew his stores of instructive wit. Therefore we, of all the reading public, do the most heartily greet his reappearance. We find him a little more artistic than of old, more advanced in grammar and orthography, but withal displaying the same intimate knowledge of Down Eastdom, and retaining the same knack of genuine Yankee humor. In fact, taking all things together, no other writer begins to equal him in the delineation of the live Yankee, in the points where that individual differs from all the ' rest of mankind.' This is his great merit as an author, and one which the progress of manners will still further heighten—for it is only in some portions of our own State that the real Yankee can now be found.

" The present book has sixteen chapters devoted to home-stories. They are racy and humorous to a high degree."—*Portland Daily Advertiser.*

" It is now generally conceded that Seba Smith is the ablest, and at the same time the most amusing delineator of Yankee life who has hitherto attempted that humorous style of writing—not excepting even Judge Haliburton himself. This is no rash expression, for there is not a passage in 'Sam Slick' so graphic, funny and and comical, but we find equalled if not surpassed in the sensible and philosophic, although ludicrous epistles, of ' Major Jack Downing '—epistles of which we defy the most stupid to glance at a paragraph without reading the whole."—*Philadelphia News.*

" This is a book of real Yankee life, giving the particulars of character and incidents in New England, from the Pilgrim fathers and their generations, Connecticut Blue Laws, and the civic and religious rules, customs, &c., from the Nutmeg State away down East, as far as Mr. Jones ever thought of going. It is a very laughable affair, and every family in all Yankeedom will enjoy its perusal."—*Hingham (Mass.) Journal.*

" There are few readers who do not desire to keep up an acquaintance with the original Major Jack Downing, whose peculiar humor, while it is irresistible in its effects, is never made subservient to immorality. But these stories are an improvement on those originally given by the author, as they are illustrative of Yankee life and character in the good old times of the Pilgrim Fathers."—*Christian Advocate and Journal.*

" The stories are the most humorous in the whole range of Yankee literature, full of genuine wit, rare appreciation of fun, and giving an insight into human motive which shows the close observation and keen relish of life, of a good-humored philosopher."—*Saturday Evening Mail.*

" A charmingly interesting book, this, for all who hail from Down East, or who like to read good stories of home life among the Yankees."—*Salem Register.*

EXTRAORDINARY PUBLICATION!

MY COURTSHIP AND ITS CONSEQUENCES.
BY HENRY WIKOFF.

A true account of the Author's Adventures in England, Switzerland, and Italy, with Miss J. C. Gamble, of Portland Place, London. 1 elegant 12mo. Price, in cloth, $1 25.

The extraordinary sensation produced in literary circles by Mr. Wikoff's charming romance of real life, is exhausting edition after edition of his wonderful book. From lengthy reviews, among several hundred received, we extract the following brief notices of the press:

"We prefer commending the book as beyond question the most amusing of the season, and we commend it without hesitation, because the moral is an excellent one."—*Albion*.

"With unparalleled candor he has here unfolded the particulars of the intrigue, taking the whole world into his confidence—'bearing his heart on his sleeve for daws to peck at'—and, in the dearth of public amusements, presenting a piquant nine days' wonder for the recreation of society."—*N. Y. Tribune*.

"The work is very amusing, and it is written in such a vein that one cannot refrain from frequent bursts of laughter, even when the Chevalier is in positions which might claim one's sympathy."—*Boston Evening Gazette*.

"A positive autobiography, by a man of acknowledged fashion, and an associate of nobles and princes, telling truly how he courted and was coquetted by an heiress in high life, is likely to be as popular a singularity in the way of literature as could well be thought of."—*Home Journal*.

"The ladies are sure to devour it. It is better and more exciting than any modern romance, as it is a detail of facts, and every page proves conclusively that the plain, unvarnished tale of truth is often stranger than fiction."—*Baltimore Dispatch*.

"The book, therefore, has all the attractions of a tilt of knight-errants—with this addition, that one of the combatants is a woman—a species of heart-endowed Amazon."—*Newark Daily Mercury*.

"If you read the first chapter of the volume, you are in for 'finis,' and can no more stop without the consent of your will than the train of cars can stop without the consent of the engine."—*Worcester Palladium*.

"Seriously, there is not so original, piquant and singular a book in American literature: its author is a sort of cross between Fielding, Chesterfield, and Rochefoucault."—*Boston Chronicle*.

"With the exception of Rosseau's Confessions, we do not remember ever to have heard of any such self-anatomization of love and the lover."—*N. Y. Express*.

"The book has cost us a couple of nights' sleep; and we have no doubt it has cost its author and principal subject a good many more."—*N. Y. Evening Mirror*.

"The work possesses all the charm and fascination of a continuous romance."—*N. Y. Journal of Commerce*.

12